THE OTHER WAY ROUND

How did it feel in war-time London to be a German refugee? For fifteen-year-old Anna and her family the anxieties were special and horrifying as the Nazis overran Europe. What hope was there for them if Hitler, who had put a price on their papa's head, invaded England? How could they survive, not only the bombs but the financial hardships of every day, when neither Mama nor Papa could get a job? How could Max, who looked, sounded and felt, English, persuade the Air Force to accept him in spite of his background? And all the time, the only thing that Anna really wanted was to go to art school . . .

In this book, Judith Kerr describes how the family introduced in her first novel, *When Hitler Stole Pink Rabbit*, lived through the war.

Judith Kerr was born in Berlin and left Germany with her family in 1933 to escape from the Nazis. They arrived in England in 1936, having spent the intervening years in Switzerland and France. Later, Judith won a scholarship to the Central School of Arts and Crafts.

'Miss Kerr has written a most sympathetic book that is powerfully evocative.' *Daily Telegraph*

THE
OTHER WAY ROUND

Judith Kerr

British Primary
Stationstraat 6
3080 TERVUREN

Fontana Lions

First published 1975 by William Collins Sons & Co. Ltd
First published in Fontana Lions 1977
8 Grafton Street, London W1X 3LA
Fourth impression March 1986

Fontana Lions is an imprint of
Fontana Paperbacks, a division of
the Collins Publishing Group

Made and printed in Great Britain by
William Collins Sons & Co. Ltd, Glasgow

FOR MY BROTHER MICHAEL

Part One

CHAPTER 1

Anna was standing in her room at the top of the Bartholomews' London house. She had finally remembered to stitch up the hem of her skirt which had been hanging down and she was wearing new lisle stockings – not black ones from Woolworth's but the more expensive beige kind from Marks and Spencer's. Her sweater, which she had knitted herself, almost matched her skirt, and her pretty shoes, inherited from one of the Bartholomews' daughters, were newly polished. She tilted the mirror on the dressing-table to catch her reflection, hoping to be impressed.

It was disappointing, as usual. The room outdid her. It was clear that she did not belong in it. Against the quilted, silky bedspread, the elegant wallpaper, the beautiful, gleaming furniture, she looked neat but dull. A small person dressed in brown. Like a servant, she thought, or an orphan. The room needed someone careless, richer, more smiling.

She sat on the chintzy stool and stared at her face with growing irritation. Dark hair, green eyes, an over-serious expression. Why couldn't she at least have been blonde? Everybody knew that blonde hair was better. All the film stars were blonde, from Shirley Temple to Marlene Dietrich. Her eyebrows were wrong, too. They should have been thin arcs, as though drawn with a pencil. Instead they were thick and almost straight. And as for her legs . . . Anna did not like even to think of her legs, for they were shortish, and to have short legs seemed to her not so much of a misfortune as a lapse of taste.

She leaned forward and her reflection came to meet her. At least I look intelligent, she thought. She frowned and pursed her lips, trying to increase the impression. Clever, they had called it at the Metcalfe Boarding School for Girls. That clever little refugee girl. She had not realized at first that it was derogatory. Nobody much had liked her at Miss Metcalfe's. At least I've finished with all that, she thought.

She picked up her handbag – cracked brown leather, an old one of Mama's brought from Berlin – extracted a powder compact and began carefully to powder her nose. No lipstick, yet. You didn't wear lipstick at fifteen unless you were fast.

I need never have gone to Miss Metcalfe's, she thought, if only we'd had a home. It was living in a hotel that had caused all the trouble – that, and having no money. Because when Mama and Papa could no longer pay for her hotel room (even though the hotel was so cheap) she had become like a parcel, to be tossed about, handed from one person to another, without knowing who would be holding her next. The only reason she had gone to Miss Metcalfe's was that Miss Metcalfe had offered to take her for nothing. The reason she was now living at the Bartholomews' (though the Bartholomews were, of course, old friends and much nicer than Miss Metcalfe) was that here, too, it did not cost anything.

She sighed. Which hair ribbon? she wondered. For once she had two to choose from – brown or green? She decided on green, slipped it over her head and then back over her hair, and looked at herself. It's the best I can do, she thought.

A clock somewhere struck ten – time she left. Mama and Papa were expecting her. She picked up her coat and checked her handbag. Keys, torch, identity card, purse. Her purse felt curiously light and she opened it. It was empty. The fourpence for her fare must have fallen out into the bag. She turned the bag upside down. Keys, torch, identity card, powder compact, two pencils, a bus ticket, the paper wrapping off a chocolate biscuit and some crumbs. There was no money. But it must be there, she thought. She'd had it. She was sure she'd had it the previous night. Feverishly, she searched through the pockets of her coat. It wasn't there either. Oh damn! she thought. Just when I thought I was all right. Oh damn and damn and damn!

She swept the contents back into the bag, took her coat and went out of the room. What am I going to do? she thought, they'll be waiting for me and I haven't got my fare.

The landing was dark – the maids must have forgotten to draw back the blackout curtains. Could she borrow from the maids? No, she thought, I can't. Hoping that, somehow, a miracle would happen, she started down the thickly-carpeted stairs.

In the hall, as she passed what had been the school-room but was now a kind of sitting-room, a friendly American voice called out, 'Is that you, Anna? Come in a minute – I haven't seen you for days.'

Mrs Bartholomew.

Could she ask her?

She opened the door and found Mrs Bartholomew drinking coffee in her dressing-gown. She was sitting at the old school-room table and in front of her on the ink-stained surface were a tray and an untidy pile of old children's books.

'You're up early on a Sunday,' said Mrs Bartholomew. 'Are you off to see your parents?'

Anna thought of answering, 'Yes, but I'm afraid I haven't . . .' or 'Could you possibly lend me . . . ?' Instead, she stood just inside the door and said, 'Yes.'

'I bet they'll be glad to see you.' Mrs Bartholomew waved what appeared to be Hans Andersen. 'I've been sitting here missing the girls. Judy used to love this book – three, four years ago. Jinny too. It was such fun, wasn't it, when you all did lessons together!'

Anna reluctantly dragged her mind away from her problem.

'Yes,' she said. It had been fun.

'This war really is crazy,' said Mrs Bartholomew. 'Here we all sent our children out of London, thinking that Hitler was going to bomb it out of existence, and a half-year later still nothing at all has happened. Personally, I'm tired of it. I want them back here with me. Jinny says there's a chance the whole school may move back into town – wouldn't that be nice?'

'Yes,' said Anna.

'They'd enjoy having you live in the house with them.' Mrs Bartholomew seemed suddenly to notice how Anna was hovering half-in and half-out of the room.

'Well, come in, dear!' she cried. 'Have some coffee and tell me – how is everything? How's the great Polytechnic art course?'

'I really should go,' said Anna, but Mrs Bartholomew insisted, and she found herself sitting at the school-room table with a cup in her hand. Through the window she

7

could see grey clouds and branches waving in the wind. It looked cold. Why couldn't she have asked for her fare money when she had the chance?

'So what have you been doing? Tell me,' said Mrs Bartholomew.

What had she been doing?

'Well, of course it's only a junior art course.' It was difficult to bring her mind to bear on it. 'We do bits of everything. Last week we all drew each other. I liked doing that.'

The teacher had looked at Anna's drawing and had told her that she had real talent. She warmed at the memory.

'But of course it's not very practical – financially, I mean,' she added. The teacher was probably just being nice.

'Now listen!' cried Mrs Bartholomew. 'You don't have to worry about finance at your age. Not while you're in this house. I know it's difficult for your parents being in a strange country and everything, but we love having you and you can stay just as long as you like. So you just concentrate on your education. I'm sure you'll do very, very well, and you must write and tell the girls all about it because they'd love to hear.'

'Yes,' said Anna. 'Thank you.'

Mrs Bartholomew looked at her. 'Are you all right?' she asked.

'Yes,' said Anna. 'Yes, of course. But I think I should go.'

Mrs Bartholomew walked with her into the hall and watched her put on her coat.

'Wait a minute!' she cried, diving into a cupboard, to emerge a moment later with something thick and grey. 'You'd better wear Jinny's scarf.'

She made Anna wind it round her neck and then kissed her on the cheek.

'There!' she said. 'Are you sure you've got everything you need? Nothing you want?'

Now, surely, was the moment to ask. It would be so simple, and she knew Mrs Bartholomew wouldn't mind. But standing there in Judy's shoes and Jinny's scarf and looking at Mrs Bartholomew's kind face she found it suddenly impossible. She shook her head and smiled. Mrs Bartholomew smiled back and closed the door.

Damn! thought Anna as she started to trudge up

Holland Park Avenue. Now she would have to walk all the way to Bloomsbury because she didn't have fourpence for the tube.

It was a cold, bright day, and at first she tried to think of it as an adventure.

'I really like exercise,' she said experimentally to Miss Metcalfe in her mind, 'as long as it isn't lacrosse.' But, as usual, she could not extract a satisfactory reply, so she abandoned the conversation.

A few people were still in bed as it was Sunday and you could see their blackout curtains drawn above the shuttered shops. Only the paper shop at Notting Hill Gate was open, with Sunday papers displayed on racks outside and printed posters saying 'Latest War News' but, as usual, nothing had happened. The pawnbroker next to the tube station still had the sign which had so much puzzled Anna when she had first come to London and couldn't speak English properly. It said 'Turn Your Old Gold Into Cash', but a little piece had fallen off the G in Gold, turning it into Cold. Anna remembered how every day when she had passed it on her way to do lessons with Jinny and Judy she had wondered what it meant and whether, if she went into the shop and sneezed, they would give her some money.

Of course nowadays no one talking to Anna would guess that she hadn't spoken English from birth, and she had lost the American accent she had originally picked up from the Bartholomews. She hadn't been meant just to learn English from them – they had also been meant to learn some of her native German and the French she had acquired in Paris after escaping from Hitler. But it hadn't worked out like that. She and Jinny and Judy had become friends and spoken English, and Mrs Bartholomew hadn't minded.

There was a sharp wind blowing across Kensington Gardens. It rattled the signs pointing to air-raid shelters which no one had ever used and the few crocuses still growing between newly-dug trenches looked frozen. Anna pushed her hands deep into the pockets of her old grey coat. Really, she thought, it was ridiculous for her to be walking like this. She was cold, and she would be late, and Mama would wonder where she'd got to. It was ridiculous being so short of money that the loss of fourpence threw everything out of gear. And how could anyone be so stupidly shy as not to be able to borrow fourpence when they needed it? And how had she managed to lose the money, anyway – she was sure she'd had it the previous day, a silver threepenny bit and two halfpennies, she could see them now. I'm sick of it, she thought, I'm sick of being so ineffectual – and Miss Metcalfe's tall figure rose unbidden before her, cocked a sarcastic eyebrow and said, 'Poor Anna!'

Oxford Street was deserted, the windows of the big stores covered in criss-crossings of brown paper to stop them splintering in case of air raids, but Lyons Corner House was open and filled with soldiers queuing for cups of tea. At Oxford Circus the sun came out and Anna felt more cheerful. After all, the reason for her predicament was not only that she was shy. Papa would understand why she couldn't borrow money from Mrs Bartholomew, not even such a small sum. Her feet were tired, but she was two thirds of the way home and perhaps she was really doing something rather splendid.

'Once,' said a grown-up Anna negligently to an immensely aged Miss Metcalfe, 'once I walked all the way from Holland Park to Bloomsbury rather than borrow fourpence,' and the aged Miss Metcalfe was suitably impressed.

At Tottenham Court Road a newsvendor had spread an array of Sunday papers along the pavement. She read the headlines ('Tea Ration Soon?' 'Bring Back The Evacuees!' and 'English Dog Lovers Exposed') before she noticed the date. It was the fourth of March 1940, exactly seven years since she had left Berlin to become a refugee. Somehow this seemed significant. Here she was, penniless but coping triumphantly, on the anniversary of the day her wanderings had begun. Nothing could get her down. Perhaps one day when she was rich and famous everyone would look back . . .

'Of course I remember Anna,' said the aged Miss Metcalfe to the interviewer from Pathe Newsreel. 'She was so bold and resourceful – we all admired her tremendously.'

She trudged up High Holborn. As she turned down Southampton Row, not very far now from the hotel, she noticed a faint clinking in the hem of her coat. Surely it couldn't be . . . ? Suspiciously, she felt around in her pocket. Yes, there was a hole. With a sinking feeling of anticlimax she inserted two fingers and, by lifting up the hem of her coat with the other hand, managed to extract two half-pennies and a threepenny piece which were lying in a little heap at the bottom of the lining. For a moment she stood quite still, looking at it. Then she thought, 'Typical!' so vehemently that she found she had said it out loud, to the astonishment of a passing couple. But what could be more typical than her performance that morning? All that embarrassment with Mrs Bartholomew, all that worrying about whether or not she had done the right thing, all that walking and her aching legs, and in the end it had just been a huge waste of time. No one else behaved like this. She was tired of it. She would have to change. Everything would have to change.

With the money clutched in her hand she strode across to the other side of the road where a woman was selling daffodils outside a tea-shop.

'How much?' she asked.

They were threepence a bunch.

'I'll have one,' she said.

It was a ridiculous piece of extravagance – and the daffodils weren't worth it, either, she thought, seeing them droop over her hand – but at least it was something. She would give them to Mama and Papa. She would say, 'It's seven years today since we left Germany and I've brought you some flowers.' And perhaps the flowers would bring them luck, perhaps Papa would be asked to write some-thing or someone would send him some money and perhaps everything would become quite different, and it would all be just because she'd saved her fare money and bought some daffodils. And even if nothing happened at all, at least Mama and Papa would be pleased and it would cheer them up.

As she pushed open the swing-doors of the Hotel Con-tinental the old porter who had been drowsing behind his desk greeted her in German.

'Your mother has been in quite a state,' he said, 'won-dering where you'd got to.'

Anna surveyed the lounge. Scattered among the tables and sitting in shabby leatherette chairs were the usual German, Czech and Polish refugees who had made the hotel their home while hoping for something better – but not Mama.

11

'I'll go up to her room,' she said, but before she could start a voice called, 'Anna!' and Mama burst in from the direction of the public telephone. Her face was pink with excitement and her blue eyes tense.

'Where have you been?' she cried in German. 'I've just been talking to Mrs Bartholomew. We thought something had happened! And Max is here – he can only stay a little while and he wanted specially to see you.'

'Max?' said Anna. 'I didn't know he was in London.'

'One of his Cambridge friends gave him a lift.' Mama's face relaxed as always when she spoke of her remarkable son. 'He came here first and then he's meeting some other friends and then they're all going back together. English friends, of course,' she added for her own pleasure and for the edification of any Germans, Czechs or Poles who might be listening.

As they hurried upstairs Mama noticed the daffodils in Anna's hand. 'What are those?' she asked.

'I bought them,' said Anna.

'Bought them?' cried Mama, but was interrupted in her astonishment by a middle-aged Pole who emerged from a door marked WC.

'The wanderer has returned,' said the Pole in satisfied tones as he observed Anna. 'I told you, Madame, that she had probably just been delayed,' and he disappeared into his room on the other side of the corridor.

Anna blushed. 'I'm not as late as all that,' she said, but Mama hurried her on.

Papa's room was on the top floor and as they went in Anna almost fell over Max who was sitting on the end of the bed just inside the door. He said, 'Hi, sister!' in English like someone in a film and gave her a brotherly kiss. Then he added in German, 'I was just leaving. I'm glad I didn't miss you.'

Anna said, 'It took me ages to get here,' and squeezed round the table which held Papa's typewriter to embrace Papa. 'Bonjour, Papa,' she said, because Papa loved to speak French. He was looking tired but the expression in the intelligent, ironically smiling eyes was as usual. Papa always looked, thought Anna, as though he would be interested in whatever happened even though nowadays he clearly did not expect it to be anything good.

She held out the daffodils. 'I got these,' she said. 'It's

seven years today since we left Germany and I thought they might bring us all luck.'

They were drooping more than ever but Papa took them from her and said, 'They smell of spring.' He filled his toothglass with water and Anna helped him put the flowers in. They immediately fell over the edge of the glass until their heads rested on the table.

'I'm afraid they've already overstrained themselves,' said Papa and everyone laughed. Well, at least they had cheered him up. 'Anyway,' said Papa, 'the four of us are together. After seven years of emigration perhaps one shouldn't ask for more luck than that.'

'Oh yes one should !' said Mama.

Max grinned. 'Seven years is probably as much as anyone actually needs.' He turned to Papa. 'What do you think is going to happen about the war? Do you think anything is going to happen at all?'

'When Hitler is ready,' said Papa. 'The problem is whether the British will be ready too.'

It was the usual conversation and, as usual, Anna's mind edged away from it. She sat on the bed next to Max and rested her feet. She liked being in Papa's room. No matter where they had lived, in Switzerland, Paris or London, Papa's room had always looked the same. There had always been a table with the typewriter, now getting rather rickety, his books, the section of the wall where he pinned photographs, post cards, anything that interested him, all close together so that even the loudest wallpaper was defeated by their joint size; the portraits of his parents looking remote in Victorian settings, a Meerschaum pipe which he never smoked but liked the shape of, and one or two home-made contraptions which he fondly believed to be practical. At present he was going through a phase of cardboard boxes and had devised a mousetrap out of an upside-down lid propped up by a pencil with a piece of cheese at the base. As the mouse ate the cheese the lid would drop down over it and Papa would then somehow extract the mouse and give it its freedom in Russell Square. So far he had had little success.

'How is your mouse?' asked Anna.

'Still at liberty,' said Papa. 'I saw it last night. It has a very English face.'

Max shifted restlessly on the bed beside her.

'No one is worrying about the war in Cambridge,' he was saying to Mama. 'I went to see the Recruiting Board the other day and they told me very firmly not to volunteer but to get my degree first.'

'Because of your scholarship!' cried Mama proudly.

'No, Mama,' said Max. 'It's the same for all my friends. Everyone has been told to leave it for a couple of years. Perhaps by then Papa might be naturalized.' After four years of public school and nearly two terms at Cambridge Max looked, sounded and felt English. It was maddening for him not to be legally English as well.

'If they make an exception for him,' said Mama.

Anna looked at Papa and tried to imagine him as an Englishman. It was very difficult. Just the same she cried, 'Well, they should! He's not just anyone – he's a famous writer!'

Papa glanced round the shabby room.

'Not very famous in England,' he said.

There was a pause and then Max got up to go. He embraced Mama and Papa and made a face at Anna. 'Walk to the tube with me,' he said. 'I've hardly seen you.'

They went down the many stairs in silence and as usual the residents of the lounge glanced at Max admiringly as he and Anna walked through. He had always been handsome with his fair hair and blue eyes – not like me, thought Anna. It was nice being with him, but she wished she could have sat a little longer before setting out again.

As soon as they emerged from the hotel Max said in English, 'Well, how are things?'

'All right,' said Anna. Max was walking fast and her feet were aching. 'Papa is depressed because he offered himself to the BBC for broadcasting propaganda to Germany, and they won't have him.'

'Why on earth not?'

'It seems he's too famous. The Germans all know that he's violently anti-Nazi, so they won't take any notice of anything he says. At least that's the theory.'

Max shook his head. 'I thought he looked old and tired.' He waited for her to catch him up before he asked, 'And what about you?'

'Me? I don't know.' Suddenly Anna didn't seem to be able to think of anything but her feet. 'I suppose I'm all right,' she said vaguely.

Max looked worried. 'But you like your art course?' he asked. 'You enjoy that?'

The feet receded slightly from Anna's consciousness.

'Yes,' she said. 'But it's all so hopeless, isn't it, when no one has any money? I mean, you read about artists leaving their homes to live in a garret, but if your family is living in a garret already . . . ! I thought perhaps I should get a job.'

'You're not sixteen yet,' said Max and added almost angrily, 'I seem to have had all the luck.'

'Don't be silly,' said Anna. 'A major scholarship to Cambridge isn't luck.'

They had arrived at Russell Square tube station and one of the lifts was about to close its gates, ready to descend.

'Well –' said Anna, but Max hesitated.

'Listen,' he cried, 'why don't you come up to Cambridge for a weekend?' And as Anna was about to demur, 'I can manage the money. You could meet some of my friends and I could show you round a bit – it would be fun!' The lift gates creaked and he made a dash for it. 'I'll write you the details,' he cried as he and the lift sank from sight.

Anna walked slowly back to the hotel. Mama and Papa were waiting for her at one of the tables in the lounge and a faded German lady had joined them.

'. . . the opera in Berlin,' the German lady was saying to Papa. 'You were in the third row of the stalls. I remember my husband pointing you out. I was so excited, and you wrote a marvellous piece about it next morning in the paper.'

Papa was smiling politely.

'*Lohengrin*, I think,' said the German lady. 'Unless it was *The Magic Flute* or perhaps *Aïda*. Anyway, it was wonderful. Everything was wonderful in those days.'

Then Papa saw Anna. 'Excuse me,' he said. He bowed to the German lady and he and Mama and Anna went into the dining-room for lunch.

'Who was that?' asked Anna.

'The wife of a German publisher,' said Papa. 'She got out but the Nazis killed her husband.'

Mama said, 'God knows what she lives on.'

It was the usual Sunday lunch, served by a Swiss girl who was trying to learn English but was more likely to pick up a bit of Polish in this place, thought Anna. There were prunes for pudding and there was some difficulty afterwards about paying for Anna's meal. The Swiss waitress said she would put it on the bill, but Mama said no, it was not an extra item since she herself had missed dinner on the previous Tuesday when she wasn't feeling well. The waitress said she wasn't sure if it was all right to transfer meals from one person to another. Mama got excited and Papa looked unhappy and said, 'Please don't make a scene.' In the end the manageress had to be consulted and decided that it was all right this time but must not be regarded as a precedent. By this time a lot of the good had gone out of the day.

'Shall we sit down here or shall we go upstairs?' said Mama when they were back in the lounge – but the German lady was looming and Anna didn't want to talk about the opera in Berlin, so they went upstairs. Papa perched on the chair, and Anna and Mama sat on the bed.

'I mustn't forget to give you your fare money for next week,' said Mama, opening her handbag.

Anna looked at her.

'Mama,' she said, 'I think I ought to get a job.'

CHAPTER 2

Anna and Mama were sitting in the waiting-room of the Relief Organization for German Jewish Refugees.

'If only they'll help us with the fees for this secretarial course,' said Mama for at least the sixth time, 'you'll always be able to earn your living.'

Anna nodded.

All round the room other German refugees were sitting on hard chairs like Mama and herself, waiting to be interviewed. Some were talking in nervous, high-pitched voices. Some were reading newspapers – Anna counted one English, one French, two Swiss and one Yiddish. An elderly couple were eating buns out of a paper bag and a thin man was hunched up in a corner by himself, staring into space. Every so often the receptionist came in and called out a name and the owner of the name followed her out.

'You'll have something to build on,' said Mama, 'which I've never had, and you'll always be independent.'

She had at first been taken aback by Anna's suggestion of getting a job but then had thrown herself into the search for some suitable training with her usual energy. She had been adamant that Anna must have training of some sort, but it was hard to decide what. A secretarial course was the obvious choice, but Anna's complete inability to learn shorthand had been one of her many failures at Miss Metcalfe's. 'It's not so much that it's difficult but it's so boring!' she had cried, and Miss Metcalfe had smiled pityingly as usual and had pointed out that arrogance never helped anyone.

Mama had quite understood about the shorthand and by dint of asking everyone she knew for advice had discovered a secretarial school where they taught a different system. It was not written down but tapped out on a little machine like a typewriter and had the further advantages of being quickly learned and easily adapted to other languages. The only trouble was that the full course cost twenty-five pounds.

'Mr and Mrs Zuckerman!' The receptionist had come

in again, catching the elderly couple in the middle of their buns. They hastily stuffed the half-eaten remains back into the paper bag and followed her out.

'I think we're bound to get some help,' said Mama. 'We've never asked for anything before.' She had not wanted to ask the Refugee Organization even this time, and it was only the fear that Anna, like herself, might have to get a job without any qualifications that had persuaded her. Mama spent five and a half days a week in a basement office typing and filing letters, and she hated it.

'Mr Rubinstein! Mr and Mrs Berg!'

A woman opposite Mama shifted uneasily. 'What a long time they keep you waiting!' she cried. 'I don't think I can bear to sit here much longer, I really don't!'

Her husband frowned. 'Now then, Bertha,' he said. 'It's better than queueing at the frontier.' He turned to Anna and Mama. 'My wife's a bit nervous. We had a bad time in Germany. We only just managed to get out before the war started.'

'Oh, it was terrible!' wailed the woman. 'The Nazis were shouting and threatening us all the time. There was one poor old man and he thought he'd got all his papers right, but they punched him and kicked him and wouldn't let him go. And then they shouted at us, "You can go now, but we'll still get you in the end!"'

'Bertha . . .' said her husband.

'That's what they said,' cried the woman. 'They said, "We're going to get you wherever you go because we're going to conquer the world!"'

The man patted her arm and smiled at Mama in embarrassment.

'When did you leave Germany?' he asked.

'In March 1933,' said Mama. Among refugees, the earlier you had left the more important you were. To have left in 1933 was like having arrived in America on the Mayflower, and Mama could never resist telling people the exact month.

'Really,' said the man, but his wife was unimpressed. She looked at Anna with her frightened eyes.

'You don't know what it's like,' she said.

Anna closed her mind automatically. She never thought about what it was like in Germany.

'Miss Goldstein!'

The next person to be called was a woman in a worn fur coat, clutching a briefcase. Then came a bespectacled man whom Mama recognized as a minor violinist and then suddenly it was Anna's and Mama's turn. The receptionist said, 'You want the students' section,' and led them to a room where a grey-haired lady was waiting behind a desk. She was reading through the application form which Anna had filled in before making the appointment and looked like a headmistress, but nicer than Miss Metcalfe.

'How do you do,' she said, waving them into two chairs. Then she turned to Anna and said, 'So you want to be a secretary.'

'Yes,' said Anna.

The grey-haired lady glanced at her form. 'You did extremely well in your School Certificate examinations,' she said. 'Didn't you want to stay on at school?'

'No,' said Anna.

'And why was that?'

'I didn't like it,' said Anna. 'And almost no one stayed on after School Certificate.' She hesitated. 'They didn't teach us very much.'

The lady consulted the form again. 'The Lilian Metcalfe School for Girls,' she said. 'I know it. Snob rather than academic. What a pity.' And having thus disposed of it, she applied herself to solving the problems of Anna's secretarial course. Had Anna tried it? How long would it take? And what sort of job did Anna have in mind? Buoyed up by the demolition of Miss Metcalfe, Anna answered fully and less shyly than usual, and after a surprisingly short time the lady said, 'Well, that all seems very satisfactory.'

For a moment Anna thought it was all over, but the lady said a little reluctantly to Mama, 'Forgive me, but there are so many people needing help that I have to ask you a few questions as well. How long have you been in this country?'

'Since 1935,' said Mama, 'but we left Germany in March 1933 . . .'

Anna had heard it all explained so many times that she almost knew it by heart. Six months in Switzerland . . . two years in France . . . the Depression . . . the film script on the strength of which they had come to England . . .

No, the film had never been made . . . No, it didn't seem to matter then that Papa didn't speak English because the script had been translated, but now of course . . . A writer without a language . . .

'Forgive me,' said the lady again, 'I do realize that your husband is a very distinguished man, but while you're in this difficulty, is there not anything more practical he could do, even for a little while?'

Papa, thought Anna, who couldn't bang a nail in straight, who couldn't boil an egg, who could do nothing but put words together, beautifully.

'My husband,' said Mama, 'is not a practical man. He is also a good deal older than I am.' She had flushed a little and the lady said very quickly, 'Of course, of course, do excuse me.'

It was funny, thought Anna, that she should be so much more impressed by Papa's age which no one meeting him would particularly notice, than by his impracticality, which stuck out a mile. Once in Paris Papa had spent nearly all the money they had on a sewing machine which didn't work. Anna remembered going with him to try and return it to the second-hand dealer who had landed him with it. They had had no money in Paris either, but somehow it hadn't mattered. She had felt as though she belonged there, not like a refugee.

Mama was telling the lady about her job.

'For a while I worked as social secretary,' she said. 'To Lady Parker – you may have heard of her. But then her husband died and she moved to the country. So now I'm helping sort out the papers belonging to his estate.'

The lady looked embarrassed. 'And – er – how much . . . ?'

Mama told her how much she earned.

'I have no qualifications, you see,' she said. 'I studied music as a girl. But it helps to pay the bills at the Hotel Continental.'

Perhaps, thought Anna, she had felt different in Paris because Mama hadn't had to work, or because they had lived in a flat instead of a hotel – or perhaps it was simply that England didn't suit her. She didn't really know a lot of English people, of course, only the ones at Miss Metcalfe's. But certainly a lot of things had gone wrong for her soon after her arrival. For one thing she had grown much fatter, bulging in unexpected places, so that all her clothes suddenly looked hideous on her. Mama had said it was puppy fat and that she would lose it again, and in fact much of it had already melted away, but Anna still suspected England of being somehow to blame. After all, she had never been fat before.

The other girls at boarding school had been fat too — Anna remembered great red thighs in the changing room and heavy figures lumbering over the frozen grass of the lacrosse field. But at least they hadn't been shy. Her shyness was the worst thing that had happened to Anna in England. It had come upon her soon after the puppy fat, quite unexpectedly, for she had always been easy with people. It had paralysed her, so that when the English girls had made fun of her for being bad at lacrosse and for speaking with a funny accent, she hadn't been able to answer. She had never had this trouble with Judy and Jinny, who were Americans.

'Well, Anna,' said the grey-haired lady as though she had been listening to Anna's thoughts. 'I hope you'll enjoy the secretarial course more than your time at Miss Metcalfe's.'

Anna came back to earth. Was it all settled then?

'I'll speak to my committee tomorrow,' said the lady, 'but I'm quite sure that there will be no difficulty.' And as Anna stammered her thanks she said, 'Nonsense! I think you'll be a very good investment.'

The sun had come out and it was quite warm while Anna and Mama walked back to the hotel.

'How much do you think I'll be able to earn?' asked Anna.

'I don't know,' said Mama, 'but with your languages you should get at least three pounds.'

'Every week!' said Anna. It seemed an enormous sum.

Papa congratulated her, a little sadly.

'I must say, I'd never seen you as a secretary,' he said and Anna quickly pushed aside the thought that she hadn't either.

'Papa,' she cried, 'they said I was a good investment!'

'There I agree with them,' said Papa. He was wearing his best suit, or the one he considered least worn at present, ready to go out. 'A meeting of the International Writers' Club,' he explained. 'Would you like to come? It's not much of a celebration, but there is to be a tea.'

'I'd love to,' said Anna. The Writers' Club was not very exciting, but now that her future was settled she felt restless. She walked quickly to the bus stop with Papa, trying not to think of the fact that soon her days would be filled with shorthand instead of drawing.

'The meeting is for the German section,' said Papa who was its president. 'But the tea –' he smiled at himself for explaining the treat – 'will be genuine English.'

When they arrived at the club's premises near Hyde Park Corner most of the other writers were already assembled – a collection of the usual intelligent refugee faces and the usual frayed refugee collars and cuffs. Several of them came to greet Papa at the door, were introduced to Anna and said how like him she was. This often happened and always cheered her up. Nobody, she thought, who looked so like Papa could be completely hopeless.

'Is she going to follow in your footsteps?' asked a small man with pebble lenses.

'I used to think so,' said Papa, 'but now I think she is more interested in drawing. At the moment –' he raised a hand regretfully – 'she is planning to become a secretary.'

The man with the pebble lenses raised both hands in regretful echo. 'What can one do?' he said. 'One has to live.'

He and Papa went to sit on a small platform while Anna found a seat among the other writers. The theme of the meeting was 'Germany' and a number of writers got up to speak. What a lot of them there were, thought Anna. No wonder there was no work for them.

The first one spoke about the rise of the Nazis and how it could have been avoided. Everyone except Anna was very interested in this and it provoked a whole succession of smaller speeches and arguments. 'If only . . .' cried the writers. If only the Weimar Republic . . . the Social Democrats . . . the French in the Rhineland . . .

At last it came to an end and a sad man in a pullover rose to read out extracts from a diary smuggled out through Switzerland which had been kept by a Jewish writer still at liberty in Germany. Anna knew how such people lived, of course, but it was still horrifying to hear the details – the penury, the petty persecutions, the constant threat of the concentration camp. When he had finished the other writers sat in silence and gazed gratefully at the moulded ceiling, the large windows overlooking Hyde Park. At least they had got out in time.

There followed a completely uninteresting dissertation on the regional differences between Frankfurt and Munich, and then Papa stood up.

'Berlin,' he said, and began to read.

When, at the age of eight or nine, Anna had first realized that Papa was a famous writer, she had begged him to let her see something he had written and he had finally given her a short piece that he thought she might understand. She could still remember her embarrassment after reading it. Why, she had thought in shame, why couldn't Papa write like everyone else? She herself was going through a phase at school of writing long, convoluted sentences full of grandiose phrases. She had imagined that Papa's writing would be the same, only even grander. But instead Papa's sentences had been quite short. He used ordinary words that everyone knew, but put them together in unexpected ways, so that you were startled by them. It was true that once you got over your surprise you saw exactly what he meant, but even so . . . Why, Anna thought, oh why couldn't he write like other people?

'A little too soon, I think,' Papa had said afterwards and for years she had been shy of trying again.

Now Papa was reading something he must have typed quite recently on the rickety typewriter in his room. It was about Berlin. She recognized the streets, the woods nearby, there was even a bit about their house. That's just what it was like, thought Anna.

Then Papa had written about the people – neighbours, shopkeepers, the man who looked after the garden (Anna had almost forgotten him), the owl-eyed secretary who typed Papa's work. This bit was rather funny and the writers in the audience all laughed. But where were all these people now? asked Papa. Did the owl-eyed secretary raise her hand in the Hitler salute? Had the grocer joined the Storm Troopers – or had he been dragged off to a concentration camp? What had become of them after the Nazis had stolen their country? (Here Papa used a very rude word which made the writers gasp and then titter in relief.) We do not know, said Papa. Hitler has swallowed them up. And yet, if one went back perhaps it would all look just as it had looked before. The streets, the woods nearby, the house . . . He ended with the words with which he had begun. 'Once I lived in Berlin.'

There was a moment's silence and then the writers rose up as one writer and clapped and clapped. As Papa came down from the platform a small crowd formed round him, congratulating him and shaking his hand. Anna kept back but he found her near the door and asked, 'Did you like it?' She nodded, but before she could say any more they were swept into the room beyond where tea had been prepared. It was a lavish spread and while some writers made an effort not to appear too keen, others could not resist flinging themselves upon it. The tea had been provided by the main English section of the club and a sprinkling of English writers appeared along with it. While Anna ate an eclair and tried to tell Papa how much she had liked the piece about Berlin, one of them came up to talk to them.

'I heard the applause,' he said to Papa. 'What were you speaking about?'

Papa, as usual, did not understand, so Anna translated for him.

'Ach so!' said Papa and adjusted his face to speak English. 'I talk-ed,' he said, mispronouncing the mute *ed* at the end of the word as usual, 'about Germany.'

The Englishman was taken aback by the Shakespearian accent but recovered quickly.

'It must have been most exciting,' he said. 'I wish so much that I could have understood it.'

When Anna got back to the Bartholomews', much later, she found a letter from Max inviting her to Cambridge for the weekend. Everything is happening at once, she thought. She forgot her shyness in telling Mrs Bartholomew all about the invitation, about Papa's reading at the club and about her new career.

'And when I've finished the course,' she ended triumphantly, 'I'll be able to earn three pounds a week!'

Like Papa, Mrs Bartholomew looked a little regretful.

'That's very good news,' she said after a moment. 'But you know, don't you, that you can live in this house as long as you like, so that if ever you should change your mind . . .'

Then she went off to find a coat of Jinny's for Anna to wear during her weekend with Max.

CHAPTER 3

All the way to Cambridge in the train Anna wondered what it would be like. What would they do? What would Max's friends be like? Would she be expected to talk to them and if so, what on earth would she say? The weather had turned cold again and soon after the train had left London it began to drizzle. Anna sat staring out at the soggy fields and the cattle sheltering under dripping trees and almost wished she hadn't come. Supposing nobody liked her? And indeed, why should they like her? Nobody else did much, she thought morosely – at least not people of her own age. The girls at Miss Metcalfe's had not thought much of her. They had never elected her as a prefect, or as dormitory captain, or even as dining-room table monitor. For a brief time there had been talk of making her guinea-pig orderly, but even that had come to nothing. And Max's friends were boys. How did one talk to boys?

'Not a very nice day,' said a voice, echoing her thoughts. It belonged to a tweedy woman in the seat opposite. Anna agreed that it wasn't and the woman smiled. She was wearing a hat and expensive, sensible shoes like the mothers at Miss Metcalfe's on Parents' Day.

'Going up to Cambridge for the weekend?' said the woman. Anna said, 'Yes,' and the woman went at once into a description of the social delights of what she called the 'varsity'. Her three brothers had been there years ago, and two of her cousins, and they had all invited her for weekends – a gel could have such fun. Theatre parties! cried the tweedy woman, and May balls, and picnics at Grantchester, and everywhere you went so many, many delightful young men!

Anna's heart sank farther at this account but she comforted herself with the thought that there could hardly be May balls in March and that Max would surely have warned her if he had planned any grand goings-on.

'And where do you come from, my dear?' asked the tweedy woman, having exhausted her reminiscences.

Normally when people asked her where she came from

Anna said, 'London,' but this time for some inexplicable reason she found herself saying, 'Berlin,' and immediately regretted it.

The woman had stopped in her tracks.

'Berlin?' she cried. 'But you're English!'

'No,' said Anna, feeling like Mama at the Refugee Relief Organization. 'My father is an anti-Nazi German writer. We left Germany in 1933.'

The tweedy woman tried to work it out. 'Anti-Nazi,' she said. 'That means you're against Hitler.'

Anna nodded.

'I should never have thought it,' said the tweedy woman. 'You haven't got a trace of an accent. I could have sworn that you were just a nice, ordinary English gel.'

This was a compliment and Anna smiled dutifully, but the woman was suddenly struck by another thought.

'What about the war?' she cried. 'You're in enemy country!'

Damn, thought Anna, why did I ever start this?

She tried to explain as patiently as she could. 'We're against Germany,' she said. 'We want the English to win.'

'Against your own country?' said the woman.

'We don't feel that it is our country any more,' began Anna, but the tweedy woman had become offended with the whole conversation.

'I could have sworn you were English,' she said reproachfully and buried herself in a copy of *Country Life*.

Anna stared out at the grey landscape rolling past the spattered window. It was ridiculous, but she felt put out. Why couldn't she just have said she came from London as usual? Max would never have made such a mistake. This whole expedition is going to be disaster, she thought.

When the train finally drew into the station at Cambridge her worst suspicions seemed to be confirmed. She stood on the platform with an icy wind blowing straight down it, and Max was nowhere to be seen. But then he appeared from behind a corner, breathless and with his gown flying behind him.

'Sorry,' he said. 'I had a lecture.' He looked at the scarlet coat which Mrs Bartholomew had lent her. 'That's very dashing,' he said. 'Judy's or Jinny's?'

'Jinny's,' said Anna and felt better.

He picked up her case and hustled her out of the station.

'I hope you've brought a thick woollen nightie as well,' he said. 'Your lodgings are somewhat cool.'

They turned out to have no heating at all – a vast, icy cave of a room – but it was not far from his own and the landlady promised to put a hot-water bottle in her bed at night. While Anna was tidying herself she tried to imagine the tweedy woman spending a night there and decided that her Cambridge weekends must have been very different. Max paid for the room – bed and breakfast cost ten shillings – and then they set off to walk through the town.

By now the rain had stopped, but there were still patches of water everywhere. The sky above the rooftops was wet and grey with shambling clouds which thinned occasionally to shimmer in half-hearted sunlight. They crossed the market-place, picking their way between shoppers and dripping tarpaulins, and then they were suddenly engulfed by a crowd of undergraduates. The High Street was filled with them. They were splashing through the puddles on their bicycles and pushing along the pavement in noisy groups. There were black gowns everywhere, and long striped scarves, and everyone seemed to be talking, or shouting greetings to friends across the road. Several of them waved to Max, who seemed to be very much at home among them, and Anna thought what fun it must be to belong here.

Every so often, between greetings, he pointed out a landmark through the turmoil – a building, an ancient bit of wall, a cloistered passage where, centuries ago, someone had walked, a seat where someone else had written a poem. The stone of which they were made was the same colour as the sky and looked as though it had been there for ever.

In the doorway of a tea-shop Max was accosted by two gowned figures.

'Discovered at last!' cried one. 'And with a strange woman!'

'A strange scarlet woman,' said the other, pointing to Anna's coat.

'Don't be an idiot,' said Max. 'This is my sister Anna. And these are George and Bill who are having lunch with us.'

Anna remembered hearing about George who had been to school with Max. He was a good foot taller than herself, so that she would have to throw back her head to see what he looked like. Bill's face was more within range and looked pleasant and ordinary. They pushed their way through the crowded shop to a table in the corner. As they sat down George's face sank into view and turned out to be cheerful, with an engaging look of permanent astonishment.

'Are you really his sister?' he asked. 'I mean, if you had to be somebody's sister, surely you could have found someone better than old Max here.'

'With his lecherous ways –'

'And his boots so stout –'

'And his eyes which swivel round about –'

'And the horrible way his ears stick out!' George finished triumphantly.

Anna stared at them in confusion. Had they just made that up? Or was it some kind of English verse that everyone except her knew?

George was leaning towards her.

'Surely, Anna – I trust I may call you Anna – surely you could have found someone more suitable?'

She would have to say something. 'I think –' she began, but what did she think? At last she brought out, 'I think Max is very nice.' She was blushing as usual.

'Loyal,' said George.

'And comely,' said Bill. 'Wouldn't you say comely, George?'

'Definitely comely,' said George.

They were off again and she found that all that was required of her was to laugh, which was easy. They ate baked beans on toast followed by doughnuts and cups of strong tea. Bill tried to wheedle an extra spoonful of sugar out of the waitress, but she refused.

'Don't you know that there's a war on?' she said, and Bill pretended to be amazed and cried, 'No one told me – how ghastly!' and made so much noise that she gave him some sugar just to stop him.

'You young gentlemen are so insinuating,' she said, snatching the sugar bowl away and, as an afterthought, 'I don't know what the Government would say.'

The idea of the Government worrying about Bill's extra teaspoonful of sugar was so remarkable that George, Bill and Max all needed another doughnut to get over it.

Anna watched them admiringly. How witty they were,

she thought, and how handsome, and how English – and how strange to see Max virtually indistinguishable from the other two.

'Actually it's funny,' said George. 'That business of "Don't you know that there's a war on?" It doesn't really seem as though there were, does it?'

'No,' said Max. 'I don't know what I thought it would be like if there was a war, but you'd imagine something more – well, urgent.'

Bill nodded. 'When you think about the last one. All those people being killed.'

There was a pause.

Anna took a deep breath and decided to contribute to the conversation. 'When I was small,' she said, 'I was always very glad that I was a girl.'

They stared at her. Max frowned slightly. She'd made a mess of it as usual.

'Because of wars,' she explained. 'Because girls couldn't be sent into the trenches.'

'Oh yes, I see,' said George. They seemed to expect something more, so she gabbled on.

'But later my mother told me that there'd never be another war. Only by then I'd got used to the idea – of being glad that I was a girl, I mean. So I suppose it was really a good thing. Because,' she added with a degree of idiocy that astonished even herself, 'I *am* a girl.'

There was silence until, mercifully, Bill laughed.

'And a jolly good thing too!' he said.

Never again, thought Anna. Never again will I say anything to anybody, ever.

But George nodded just as though she had said something sensible. 'My mother was the same. She was always telling us that there'd never be another war. She was quite upset when this one happened.' His normal look of astonishment had intensified and some sugar from the doughnut had become stuck round his mouth, so that he looked suddenly very young. 'But I suppose if someone carries on like Hitler in the end there's nothing you can do but fight him.'

'Fight him to the death!' Bill narrowed his eyes. 'My God, Carruthers, there's a machine gun nest on that hill!'

George raised his chin. 'I'll go alone, sir.' His voice trembled with emotion. 'But if I don't come back . . .'

'Yes, yes, Carruthers?'

'Tell them it was – for England.' George stared bravely into the distance. Then he said in his ordinary voice, 'Well, I mean, it's so silly, isn't it?'

They finished their doughnuts thinking how silly it was. Then Bill said, 'I must fly.'

'Literally?' asked Max.

'Literally,' said Bill. He belonged to the University Air Squadron and they practised every Saturday afternoon.

George struggled to extract his long legs from under the table. 'Flicks tonight?' he said.

'Sure.' Bill waved in a way that might or might not include herself, thought Anna. 'See you then.' And he loped off into the street.

They waited while George wrapped a scarf round his long neck. 'Actually,' he said, 'I suppose it must feel even funnier to you – the war, I mean.' He looked at Max reflectively. 'I always forget that you weren't born here. It never occurs to anyone, you see,' he explained to Anna. 'I'm sure Bill thinks he's British to the backbone.'

'Sometimes I almost forget myself,' said Max so lightly that only Anna guessed how much it meant to him.

They walked back to the digs which Max and George shared. The landlady had lit a fire in their little sitting-room and Max at once sat down by it with a pile of books and papers to write an essay on some aspect of Roman Law. George disappeared with the intention of taking a bath and could be heard in the next room discussing with the landlady the chances of the water becoming hot enough in time for him to profit from it before he had to go out again.

'Max,' said Anna, 'I'm sorry – I know I'm not good with people.'

Max looked up from his work. 'Nonsense,' he said. 'You're all right.'

'But I say such stupid things. I don't mean to but I do – because I'm nervous I suppose.'

'Well, so is everyone else. You should have seen George and Bill before you came. They don't know many girls. I'm the only one who does.'

Anna looked at him admiringly. 'The trouble is,' she said, 'I'm not like you.' In a burst of confidence she added,

'Sometimes I wonder if I really belong in this country.'

'Of course you do!' Max looked shocked. 'You belong just as much as I do. The only difference is that you went to a lousy school and it put you off.'

'Do you really think so?'

'I know it,' said Max.

'Well,' said Anna, 'don't you ever feel that we're unlucky?'

'Unlucky? You mean about being refugees?'

'No, I mean for the countries we live in.' He looked puzzled, so she added, 'Well, look what's happened to Germany. And in France we'd hardly been there a year before they had a Depression. And as for England – you remember how solid it all seemed when we came, and now there's a war, and rationing . . .'

'But that's not our fault!' cried Max.

Anna shook her head glumly. 'Sometimes,' she said, 'I feel like the Wandering Jew.'

'You don't look like the Wandering Jew. He had long whiskers. Anyway, as far as I remember he wasn't considered to bring bad luck.'

'No,' said Anna. 'But I don't suppose anyone was very pleased to see him.'

Max stared at her for a moment and then burst out laughing. 'You're potty,' he said affectionately. 'Absolutely potty. And now I must do some work.'

He went back to his books and Anna watched him. The room was quiet except for the crackling of the fire. How marvellous to live like this, she thought. For a moment she tried to imagine herself at University. Not, of course, that they'd ever give her a scholarship like Max. But anyway, what would she do? Study law like Max, or English like George, or engineering like Bill? No – the only thing she really liked was drawing, and that was no use.

'By the way,' said Max telepathically, 'what's all this you wrote to me about a secretarial course?'

She said, 'I'm starting next week.'

He considered it, looking already, she thought, like a lawyer weighing up a tricky question in Court. Finally he said, 'Well, I suppose it's the right thing to do at the moment. But not for good. Not for you. Not in the long run.' Then a thought occurred to him. He leafed im-

31

patiently through one of his books, found what he wanted and started again to write.

Anna walked back to her digs, brushed her hair and changed into the only other dress she had. It was her old school dress made of grey corduroy and when she had worn it at Miss Metcalfe's on Sundays she had thought it hideous. But Mama had found an old lace collar at the bottom of one of the trunks they had brought away from Berlin and with that, now that Anna had lost most of her puppy fat, it looked quite elegant. She returned to find Max putting away his papers and George surveying the high tea which the landlady had spread out in front of the fire. George's bath had not been a success. Fearing that if he delayed too long he would not be able to have one at all, he had plunged in when the water was barely luke-warm and had sat in it, getting progressively colder, unable to face climbing out into the even colder air of the bathroom. However, at least it had now been dealt with and the problem of washing himself would not arise for another week, he told Anna with satisfaction. 'Which prompts me to remark,' he added, 'that you look remarkably clean and wholesome. Is that the latest fashion?'

She explained that it was what she had worn at school on Sundays.

'Really?' said George. 'How extraordinary. My sister always wears a sort of a brown sack.'

From this they got to talking about George's sister's school where they had to curtsey to the headmistress every time they met her and which sounded not much better than Miss Metcalfe's, and then about schools in general. Perhaps Max was right, thought Anna. Perhaps George was just as nervous of her as she was of him, and with this thought she began to relax a little. She was in the middle of telling him about a remarkable ceremony at Miss Metcalfe's when a guinea-pig monitor had been stripped of her rank, when it was time to leave for the cinema.

They picked their way through the icy blackout to see a thriller in the company of Bill and a girl with frizzy hair whom Max, to Anna's surprise, appeared to admire. Her name was Hope and she looked at least three years older than Max, but when he whispered, 'Don't you think she's

32

attractive?' Anna did not like to say 'no'. The film was very bad and the audience, which consisted largely of under-graduates, took a noisy interest in it. There were boos for the villain and ironical cheers for the heroine who was trying to ward him off, and cries of 'Come on, Clarence!' whenever the lumbering hero appeared in pursuit. In the end the villain threatened to throw the heroine to a poorly-looking crocodile which, the audience pointed out, was clearly in need of feeding, and when she was rescued in the nick of time the remaining dialogue was drowned in cries of 'Shame!' and 'RSPCA!' Anna thought it all wonderfully funny and glowed through the rest of the evening which they spent eating more doughnuts in a café. At last George and Max said good night to her at the door of her lodgings and she felt her way through the darkened house to her room and her freezing bed where she clutched her hot-water bottle, thought in wonder about this extra-ordinary world her brother was part of, and fell asleep.

'Well, how do you like Cambridge?' asked Max the next afternoon. They were waiting for her train at the station and she did not in the least want to leave. They had spent part of the day punting on the river – the weather had been warmer – with Max and Hope arguing fitfully in a punt propelled by George while Anna was in another with Bill. George and Bill had tried to ram each other and in the end Bill had fallen in and had invited them back to sherry in his rooms while he changed his clothes. He lived in a college three hundred years old, and under the mellow-ing influence of the sherry George and Bill had both urged her to come back to Cambridge soon.

She looked earnestly at Max on the darkening platform. 'I think it's marvellous,' she said. 'Absolutely marvellous.'

Max nodded. 'I'm glad you've seen it.' She could see the happiness in his face in spite of the darkness. Suddenly he grinned. 'And there's another thing,' he said. 'Don't tell Mama, but I think I'm going to get a First.'

Then the train roared in, astonishingly filled with soldiers and sailors. She had to squeeze past a pile of kit-bags to get on, and by the time she had managed to pull the window down the train had started. She shouted, 'Thank you, Max! Thanks for a marvellous weekend!' But there was a lot of noise and she was not sure whether he heard her. One of the sailors offered her part of his kit-bag and she sat on it all the way back to London. It was a long, weary journey – much slower than on the previous day. The light from the blue-painted bulb in the corridor was too dim to read by and every time the train stopped more soldiers got on, even though there hardly seemed room for them. Liverpool Street too was filled with troops and as Anna picked her way among them in the patchy half-light of the station she wondered where they could all be going. Then a newspaper poster caught her eye. It said, 'Hitler Invades Norway And Denmark!'

CHAPTER 4

At first when Anna had learned the news of Hitler's attack on Scandinavia she had been very frightened. In her mind she had heard again the voice of the woman at the Relief Organization talking about the Nazis. 'They said, "We'll get you wherever you go because we're going to conquer the world!"' But then nothing had happened and life seemed to go on much as usual. Some troops were sent to Norway – the Danes had given in without a fight – and there had been a battle at sea, but it was hard to tell who was winning. And after all, Scandinavia was a long way off.

She started her secretarial course and Judy and Jinny came home for the holidays. Papa was asked by the Ministry of Information to compose the text of some leaflets to be dropped over Germany – the first work he had had for months – and Max and George went on a walking tour and sent her a postcard from a Youth Hostel.

Her one overwhelming desire now was to learn short-hand as quickly as possible, so as to get a job and earn some money. Each day she went to the secretarial school in Tottenham Court Road and practised taking down dictation on the little machine provided. It was quite fun. Instead of pressing down the keys singly as on a typewriter you pressed them down like chords on a piano, and each time the machine printed a syllable in ordinary letters on a paper tape. It reproduced the sound of the syllable rather than the spelling so that 'general situation' for instance became 'jen-ral sit-you-ai-shn', but it was still quite easy to read, unlike the shorthand squiggles which had defeated her in the past.

Judy and Jinny were impressed with her new grown-up status, and she did not mind leaving them every morning to lounge about in the spring sunshine while she went off to practise her shorthand. There were one or two other refugees like herself at the school and the Belgian principal Madame Laroche said that with their knowledge of languages they were all bound to get good jobs. Anna, she said, was one of her best students, and she often sent for her to demonstrate the system to potential clients.

The week before Whitsun was warm and sunny and by Friday Anna was looking forward to the long weekend, as the secretarial school was closing at lunch time and Monday was a holiday as well. She was going to spend the afternoon with Mama and Papa, and Mama's cousin Otto was coming to see them. For once she was bored with practising and she was glad when, half-way through the morning, Madame Laroche sent for her to demonstrate her shorthand to a middle-aged couple and their mousy daughter. They did not seem very promising customers, as the father kept saying how stupid it was to waste money on new-fangled methods and the daughter just looked frightened.

'Ah, and here is one of our students,' cried Madame Laroche as Anna came in – or at least that was what Anna thought she had probably said. Madame Laroche talked with an impenetrably thick Belgian accent and was very hard to understand. She motioned Anna to a chair and took a book from a shelf. Anna looked round for the English assistant who normally dictated to her, but there was no sign of her.

'I will dictate to you myself,' said Madame Laroche excitedly, or words to that effect. Clearly the father had stung her into determination to prove the excellence of her system at all costs. She opened the book and said, 'Der doo glass terweens.'

'What?' said Anna, startled.

'Der doo glass terweens.'

'I'm sorry,' said Anna, beginning to blush, 'I didn't quite understand . . .'

'Der doo glass terweens, der do glass terweens!' cried Madame Laroche impatiently and she tapped her finger on Anna's machine and shouted something that sounded like 'Write!'

There was nothing for it but to take it down.

Anna typed 'der doo glass ter-weens' carefully on the paper tape and hoped that the next bit might be easier to understand – but it wasn't. It was just as incomprehensible as the beginning and so was the next bit and so was the bit after that. Every so often Anna recognized a real word, but then the dictation dropped back again into gibberish. She sat there, red-faced and miserable, and took it all down. She wished it would stop, but she knew that when it did she would have to read it back, which would be worse.

It stopped.

And just as Anna was wondering how she could possibly survive the next few minutes she was struck by an idea. Perhaps the dictation really had no meaning. Perhaps Madame Laroche had dictated gibberish to her on purpose, to demonstrate that the system could record even sounds that did not make sense. She suddenly felt much happier and began quite confidently to read back what she had taken down.

'Der doo glass terweens,' she read, carefully pronouncing it just as Madame Laroche had done, and went on from there.

But something was wrong. Why was the father puffing and choking with suppressed laughter? Why were the mother and even the mousy daughter tittering? Why had Madame Laroche's face gone pink with anger and why was she shouting at Anna and piling the book, the machine, the paper into her arms and pushing her out of the room? The door slammed behind her and Anna stood in the corridor, dumbfounded.

'What happened?' asked one of the English teachers, emerging from another room. She must have heard the noise.

Anna shook her head. 'I don't know,' she said.

The teacher took the book which was still open from the top of the machine. 'Is this what she dictated to you?' she asked. 'The Douglas twins?'

'No,' said Anna. What Madame Laroche had dictated to her started with 'der doo glass terweens'. You could not possibly mistake 'the Douglas twins' for 'der doo glass terweens'.

But you could, with Madame Laroche!

'Oh!' she cried. 'They must have all thought . . .' She looked at the teacher. 'What shall I do? They must have all thought I was making fun of her accent! D'you think I'd better explain?'

They could hear Madame Laroche shouting excitedly in her office.

'Not just now,' said the teacher.

'But I've got to do something!'

There was the sound of chairs being pushed back in the office, overlaid by a burst of masculine laughter and an incomprehensible but clearly unfriendly remark from Madame Laroche.

'Come along,' said the teacher firmly and propelled Anna along the corridor and into one of the classrooms. 'Now you just get on with your work and put this little misunderstanding right out of your mind. I'm sure that by Tuesday it will all have been forgotten.'

Anna sat down at an empty desk and began, automatically, to take down the dictation slowly read out by a senior student. But how could she forget all about it? she thought. It had been so unfair. Madame Laroche had no right to shout at her when she had always worked so well. No one in the school could understand her Belgian accent – she must know that. And as for thinking that Anna was making fun of her . . . I'll go and tell her! thought Anna. I'll tell her she can't treat me like this! Then she thought, suppose she doesn't believe me? Could one be expelled from secretarial school?

By the end of the morning she was in such a state of confusion that she could not make up her mind either to go home or to face Madame Laroche. She went to the cloakroom where she stared at her reflection in the mirror and alternated between framing grand phrases with which to justify herself and taking the teacher's advice and forgetting the whole thing. Eventually a cleaner came to lock up and she had to go.

When she emerged into the corridor she found that everyone else had left. Probably Madame Laroche had gone home too, she thought, half-relieved – but now the whole weekend would be spoiled with worrying. Oh, damn! she thought – and then, as she passed Madame Laroche's office, she heard someone talking inside. Quickly, without giving herself time to think, she knocked and went in. She had expected to see one of the teachers, but Madame Laroche was alone. The voice came not from her but out of her radio.

'Madame Laroche,' said Anna, 'I just wanted to explain . . .' She had meant to sound fierce but found to her annoyance that she merely sounded apologetic. 'About this morning . . .' she started again.

Madame Laroche looked at her blankly and then waved

38

to her to go away.

'But I want to tell you!' cried Anna. 'It wasn't at all as you thought!'

The radio had suddenly stopped and her voice sounded absurdly high in the silence.

Madame Laroche got up and came towards her and Anna saw to her horror that there were tears in her eyes.

'Mon enfant,' said Madame Laroche quite clearly in French, 'the Germans have invaded Belgium and Holland.'

Anna stared at her.

'What will my people do?' asked Madame Laroche as though Anna would be able to tell her. Then she said again, 'What will they do?'

Anna wanted to say something sympathetic but could think of nothing. 'I'm sorry,' she stammered. Guiltily, she realized that she was still fretting about the misunderstanding over the Douglas twins. But as Madame Laroche seemed to have forgotten all about it, it must be all right.

'Mon Dieu!' cried Madame Laroche. 'Don't you understand what it means? How would you like to have the Germans here, in England?' And as Anna remained helplessly silent she shouted, 'Well, don't just stand there! Go home, for heaven's sake! Go home to your parents!'

Anna went out of the office, through the building and out into the sunshine. The street looked just as usual. Even so, she began to run, dodging the other pedestrians on the pavement. When she was out of breath she walked as fast as she could, then she ran again until she reached the Hotel Continental. There she found Mama and Papa in the lounge with Cousin Otto and surrounded by excited Germans, Czechs and Poles. Cousin Otto's eyes were shining above his large Jewish nose and his hair hung untidily into his face. Everyone was talking and even the porter behind the desk was giving his views to anyone who would listen.

'They'll be smashed to pieces!' Cousin Otto was saying triumphantly. 'It's just what the English have been waiting for. They'll go in there and smash the Germans to smithereens. The French will help, of course,' he added as an afterthought. Cousin Otto had an infinite admiration for England. To be English to him was to be perfect, and he was quite upset when Papa disagreed with him.

'I don't trust Chamberlain,' said Papa. 'I don't believe

the English are ready for battle.'

'Aha!' cried Cousin Otto. 'But you don't understand them. Just because a man like Chamberlain *appears* not to be doing anything doesn't mean that he's not organizing it all secretly. That is the British understatement. No drama or fuss – and he's fooled the Germans completely.'

'He seems also to have fooled the British Government,' said Papa. 'I understand they are trying to get rid of him at this very moment.'

'Such a time to choose!' wailed an old Czech lady, astonishingly dressed in a tweed coat and flowery hat as though ready to flee from the Germans at a moment's notice.

Cousin Otto looked troubled. 'Parliamentary procedure,' he said, comforting himself with the Englishness of the phrase.

It was touching, thought Anna, that he should be so pro-English for he had, so far, not fared too well in his adopted country. In spite of two Physics degrees he had only succeeded in finding work in a shoe factory.

'What I want to know,' cried the old lady, poking Cousin Otto in the chest with a bony finger, 'is, who is minding the shop?'

'Perhaps we should go upstairs,' said Mama.

The Hotel Continental did not provide lunch on weekdays and they usually filled in the gap between breakfast and dinner with a snack in Papa's room.

Cousin Otto accepted gratefully. 'I'm dying for a cup of tea,' he confessed as Mama went scurrying in and out with the kettle, cups and some buns she had stored in her room next door. He sat on Papa's bed, drinking tea with milk like the English, and asked Anna if she had any messages for her brother, as he was leaving for Cambridge himself that afternoon in the hope of getting a job.

'What sort of a job?' Mama wanted to know.

Cousin Otto began to touch every bit of wood within reach. 'Touch wood!' he cried. 'In my own line. There is a professor of physics there – I was a student of his in Berlin – and he has asked me to come and see him.'

'Oh, Otto, it would be wonderful,' said Mama.

'Touch wood! Touch wood!' said Cousin Otto and touched the bits of wood all over again. It was difficult to remember, with his old-maidish eyes, that he was barely thirty.

'Well, just give Max lots of love and ask him to write,' said Mama.

'And wish him luck for his exams,' said Anna.

'Oh, I forgot,' cried Mama. 'The exams must be quite soon. Tell him not to write – he'll be too busy.'

Papa said, 'Would you give Max a message for me?'

'Certainly,' said Cousin Otto.

'Would you tell him –' Papa hesitated. Then he said, 'I think that now the Germans have attacked, Max may want to volunteer for one of the fighting forces. And of course he must do whatever he thinks right. But would you ask him, please, to discuss it with the University authorities first, before he makes up his mind?'

'But he's only eighteen!' cried Mama.

'It's not too young,' said Cousin Otto. He nodded at Papa. 'I promise I'll tell him. And when I get back to London I'll ring you up and tell you how he is.'

'That would be most kind,' said Papa.

Cousin Otto stayed a little longer, chatting and drinking tea, and then it was time for him to catch his train. Soon afterwards Anna went back to the Bartholomews'. She had arranged to spend Saturday with Judy and Jinny. She had hardly seen them since their return from school and they had such a good time playing tennis and sunning themselves in the garden that they decided to spend Sunday the same way.

Most of the Sunday papers carried pictures of Winston Churchill, who had become Prime Minister instead of Chamberlain, and there were several eye-witness accounts of the German invasion of Holland. Huge numbers of Nazi parachutists had been dropped from aeroplanes, disguised as Dutch and British soldiers. To add to the confusion, Germans who had been living in Holland for years and whom no one suspected of being Nazis, had immediately rushed to their aid. The Dutch were fighting back and the French and the British were on their way to help them, but clearly the Germans had a strong foothold. There was a map of Holland with thick arrows breaking into it from Germany and an article headed 'If Germany Captures Dutch And Belgian Coasts', but, said Jinny, the

Sunday papers always exaggerated and it was no use minding them.

Monday was hotter and sunnier than ever and when Anna arrived at the Hotel Continental to spend the day with Mama and Papa it seemed a pity to waste such lovely weather indoors.

'Couldn't we go to the Zoo?' she asked on a sudden inspiration.

'Why not?' said Papa. He was feeling cheerful because Winston Churchill had been made Prime Minister – the only man who understood the situation, he said.

Mama was worried about how much it would cost, but then she too found the sunshine irresistible and they decided to be extravagant and go.

It was an extraordinary day. Anna had not been to the Zoo for years and she walked round in a daze, looking. The sand-coloured and orange tigers with their black stripes which seemed to have been poured over them, peacocks with unbelievable embroidered tails, monkeys with elegant beige fur and tragic eyes – it was as though she had never seen any of them before. And giraffes! she thought. How could anyone have invented giraffes!

She looked and looked, and all the time some other part of her mind was being careful not to think of the map in the Sunday papers and of the Nazi horror seeping out of Germany into other parts of Europe which had, until now, been safe.

They stayed until late afternoon and by then Anna's mind was so full of all she had seen that it no longer needed any effort to forget about the war. It was as though those long hours in the sun had changed something, as though everything were suddenly more hopeful. Mama and Papa, too, were more light-hearted. Papa had discovered a creature in the Small Cat House which looked, he said, exactly like Goebbels, and all the way home in the bus he imagined it making speeches in German to the other small cats and inspecting them for signs of Jewishness. He kept Mama and Anna laughing and they arrived back at the Hotel Continental tired and relaxed, as though they had been away on a holiday.

The lounge was dark after the sunlit street and it took Anna a moment to focus on the porter who looked up from his desk as they came in.

'Someone rang you from Cambridge,' he said, and she wondered why Max should telephone rather than write.

Papa lingered for a moment, glancing at a newspaper that someone had left lying on a table, and the porter observed him. 'Nothing in there,' he said. 'But it's bad – I've heard the radio.'

'What's happened?' said Papa.

The porter shrugged. He was a little discouraged man with a few hairs carefully arranged in stripes across his bald head. 'The usual,' he said. 'It's all up in Holland. The Nazis are everywhere and the Dutch royal family have escaped to England.'

'So quickly!' said Papa, and the feeling of having been away on holiday slipped away as though it had never been.

Just then the telephone rang. The porter answered it and said to Anna, 'For you – from Cambridge.'

She rushed to the telephone cabin and picked up the receiver.

'Max?' she said – but it was not Max, it was George.

'Look, something awkward has happened,' he said. 'I don't quite know how to put it, but Max – he's been arrested.'

'Arrested?' What had he done? Anna thought of undergraduate pranks, getting drunk, knocking off policemen's helmets, but surely Max would never . . . Stupidly, she asked, 'You mean by the police?'

'Yes,' said George and added, 'as an enemy alien.'

'But they don't arrest people for being enemy aliens!' cried Anna. 'And anyway he isn't one. We lost our German nationality years ago. He's just waiting to become naturalized British.'

'I know, I know,' said George. 'We told them all that, but it made no difference. They said they were interning all male enemy aliens in Cambridge and his name was on the list.'

'Interning?'

'Yes,' said George. 'In some kind of camp.'

Anna suddenly felt quite empty, as though it were pointless even to go on talking.

'Are you still there?' said George anxiously and continued, 'Listen, everyone here has made an awful fuss. Me, his tutor, the College – everyone. Bill got so wild at the police station that they threw him out. But we can't move

43

them. It's a Government order. Bit of a panic, if you ask me, after what's been happening in Holland.'

'Yes,' said Anna because it seemed to be expected of her.

'Max was hoping – I don't know how much use it would be – that perhaps your parents could do something. Exams start in two weeks and he thought perhaps if they knew someone who could explain to the police . . . He's only taken his law books with him, almost no clothes.'

'Yes,' said Anna again.

'Anyway, I promised to let you know at once.' George sounded suddenly depressed, as if it had in some way been his fault. 'It's all a mess,' he said. 'I'll ring again if I hear anything.'

Anna roused herself. 'Of course,' she said. 'Thank you very much, George. And thank you for all you did. I'll tell my parents at once.'

That would be almost the worst part of it.

CHAPTER 5

Explaining to Mama and Papa about Max was just as bad as Anna had feared. Papa said almost nothing, as though Max's internment were only part of a huge catastrophe that he could see rolling towards them, towards England, perhaps towards the whole world, and that he was helpless to avert. Mama shouted and got excited and would not be calmed. Why hadn't Max explained to the police about Papa? she asked again and again. Why hadn't the College done anything? Why hadn't his friends? When Anna told her that indeed they all had, she simply shook her head disbelievingly and cried, 'If only I'd been there! I would never have let them take Max away!'

The nine o'clock news brought an announcement that all male enemy aliens in southern and eastern coastal areas had been arrested and were to be sent to internment camps. ('If only Max had come to spend Whitsun in London!' cried Mama.) Anna had not realized that Cambridge was in a coastal area – it must be just on the edge. Presumably these were the parts of England most vulnerable to attack. The announcer went on to say that the government understood the hardship to innocent people that might result from its action, but that it was hoped to alleviate this in due course. This was cold comfort and the rest of the news was no more encouraging. At the end there was an interview with the Dutch royal family, who had escaped from the Nazis by the skin of their teeth, and a quote from Churchill's first speech as Prime Minister. 'I can offer you nothing,' he told the House of Commons, 'except blood and toil and tears and sweat.'

The next day the Dutch army collapsed.

Anna heard the news at the Bartholomews' that evening.

'That's lousy!' said Jinny. 'I'm sure now they'll get all worried again about air raids and they won't let our school come back to London!'

Judy agreed. 'I don't think I could bear to go back to that place in the middle of nowhere.'

45

'Well, you may not . . .' began Mr Bartholomew and suddenly looked at Anna and stopped.

'Pa!' cried Judy. 'You mean we might go back to the States?'

'Oh, how do we know what's going to happen?' said Mrs Bartholomew. 'Your father's business is here and obviously we'd only leave if things became really serious, so let's not even talk about it.' She turned to Anna and asked, 'Did you hear from your mother today? Has she had any more news of Max?'

Anna shook her head. 'We don't even know where he is,' she said. 'Mama rang the police in Cambridge, but they're not allowed to tell us.' The call had cost over two shillings and Mama had been full of hopes that she might be able to speak to Max, but the police would only say that Max was no longer in their charge and that he would, in any case, not be allowed to receive or send any messages.

'I'm so very sorry,' said Mrs Bartholomew.

'His exams are quite soon,' said Anna. She kept thinking of the law books Max had packed instead of clothes.

'I believe they've even interned some of the professors,' said Mr Bartholomew, and added, 'Everything's in chaos.'

The weather continued very hot and made everyone irritable. When Anna went round to the Hotel Continental on Wednesday after her secretarial course she found Papa depressed and Mama in a terrible state of nerves. They had been trying to contact anyone who might be able to help about Max, or at least advise them what action to take, but their acquaintances were few and no one seemed to know.

'There must be something we can do!' cried Mama and listed, yet again, her various forlorn hopes. If one wrote to the College, to the University, if George asked again at the police station . . . Her tense, unhappy voice went on and on and only stopped at the ringing of the porter's telephone. Then she sat with her hands clenched in her lap, willing him to tell her that it was for her, that it was news of Max. But the only call that came was from Otto's mother, to say that Otto, too, had been interned, and so had the professor of physics who had invited him to Cambridge.

'You see, it's the same for everyone – a national emergency,' said Papa, but Mama would not listen.

She had had a wretched day at her office. Instead of sorting Lord Parker's innumerable bills and receipts, she had tried to telephone people she hardly knew about Max, all to no avail. In the end her boss had objected and she had had a row with him.

'As though it mattered about Lord Parker,' she cried. 'He's dead, anyway. The only thing that matters is doing something about Max!'

Papa tried to reason with her, but she shouted, 'No! I didn't care about anything else, but now it's too much!' She stared accusingly at an innocent Polish lady who happened to be sitting at the next table. 'Wasn't it enough,' she said, 'for us to have lost everything in Germany? Wasn't it enough to have to rebuild our lives again and again?'

'Of course – ' began Papa, but Mama swept him aside.

'We've been fighting Hitler for years,' she shouted. 'All the time when the English were still saying what a fine gentleman he was. And now that the penny's finally dropped,' she finished in tears, 'the only thing they can do is to intern Max!'

Papa offered her his handkerchief and she blew her nose. Anna watched her helplessly. The Polish lady got up to greet a man who had just come in and they began to talk in Polish. Anna caught the word Rotterdam and then some other Poles joined them and they all became excited.

At last one of them turned to Papa and said haltingly in English, 'The Germans have bombed Rotterdam.'

'It is thought,' said another, 'that ten thousand people were killed.'

Anna tried to imagine it. She had never seen a dead person. How could one imagine ten thousand dead?

'Poor people,' said Papa.

Did he mean the dead or the ones who were still alive?

The Polish lady sat down on a spare chair and said, 'It is just like Warsaw,' and another Pole who had seen Warsaw after the Germans had bombed it tried to describe what it was like.

'Everything is gone,' he said. 'House is gone. Street is gone. You cannot find . . .' He spread his hands in a vain attempt to show all the things you could not find. 'Only dead people,' he said.

The Polish lady nodded. 'I hide in a cellar,' she remembered. 'But then come the Nazis to seek for Jews . . .'

It was very warm in the lounge and Anna suddenly found it difficult to breathe.

'I feel a bit sick,' she said, and was surprised by the smallness of her voice.

Mama at once came over to her and Papa and one of the Poles struggled to open a window. A rush of cool air came in from the yard at the back of the hotel and after a moment she felt better.

'There,' said Papa. 'You've got your colour back.'

'You're worn out with the heat,' said Mama.

One of the Poles got her a glass of water, and then Mama urged her to go home to the Bartholomews', to go to bed, get some rest. She nodded and went.

'I'll ring you if we hear anything about Max,' Mama cried after her as she started down the street.

It was awful of her, but when she reached the corner of Russell Square, out of reach of Mama's voice, of everyone's voice, she felt a sense of relief.

By Friday Brussels had fallen and the Germans had broken through into France. A French general issued the order, 'Conquer or Die!' but it made no difference – the German army swept on across France as it had swept across Holland. Madame Laroche was too upset to come to the secretarial school and some of the students, especially the refugees, spent their time listening to the radio and running out to buy newspapers – but not Anna.

Curiously enough she was no longer worried about the German advance. She simply did not think about it. She thought a lot about Max, wherever he had been taken, desperately willing him to be all right, and every morning at the Bartholomews' she rushed to the letter box, hoping that at last he might have been able to write. But she did not think about what was happening in the war. There was nothing she could do about it. She did not read the papers and she did not listen when the news was on. She went to her secretarial school each day and worked at her shorthand. If she became good enough at it she would get a job and earn some money. That was why the Refugee Organization had paid her fees and that was what she was going to do. And the more she thought about her shorthand the less time she would have to think about anything else.

When she returned to the house one afternoon, Mrs Bartholomew was waiting for her. Anna had stayed on at the school after hours to do some typing and she was late.

'My dear,' said Mrs Bartholomew, 'I must talk to you.'

Mei dea-r, thought Anna, automatically moving her fingers into position on an imaginary keyboard, Ei mus-t tor-k tou you. Lately she had developed this habit of mentally taking down in shorthand everything she heard. It had improved her speed and saved her from having to make sense of what she did not want to hear.

Mrs Bartholomew led her into the drawing-room.

'We have been advised by the American Embassy to return at once to the States,' she said.

Wea hav bean ad-veis-d bei the A-me-ri-can Em-be-sea tou re-turn at wuns tou the Stai-ts, went Anna's fingers, but then something in Mrs Bartholomew's voice broke through her detachment.

'I'm very sorry,' cried Mrs Bartholomew, 'but we shall have to give up this house.'

Anna looked at her face, and her fingers stopped moving in her lap.

'What will you do?' asked Mrs Bartholomew.

It was nice of her, thought Anna, to be so upset about it. 'I'll be all right,' she said. 'I'll go and stay with my parents.'

'But will they be able to manage?' asked Mrs Bartholomew.

'Oh yes,' said Anna airily. 'And anyway, I'll probably get a job quite soon.'

'Oh dear,' said Mrs Bartholomew, 'I hate doing this.' Then she picked up the telephone to explain to Mama.

Mama always shouted when she was excited and Anna realized that of course she must have been hoping that the call would bring her news of Max. All the same, she wished that her sole reaction to Mrs Bartholomew's news had not been so loud and accusing.

'Does that mean,' cried Mama, and her distorted voice came right out of the telephone to where Anna was sitting across the room, 'that Anna won't be able to stay in your house any more?'

Anna knew as well as Mama that there was no money to pay for her to stay at the Hotel Continental, but what was the use of shouting at Mrs Bartholomew about it? There was nothing she could do. Mama should at least have wished her a safe journey, thought Anna, and her fingers tapped out in her lap, shea should at lea-st have wi-shd her a sai-f jur-nea.

The Bartholomews began to pack up their possessions and a growing pile of garments was put aside for Anna because Jinny and Judy would not need them in America. She carried them to the Hotel Continental with her own, a few at a time, on the tube, so as to save a taxi for the move. Mama had counted all their money – she had added what was left of Papa's earnings from the leaflets to the few pounds she had managed, somehow, to save from her meagre weekly wage, and she had worked out that there would be enough to pay Anna's bills at the hotel for three weeks. After that they would have to see. It was really no use looking farther ahead. In the meantime they did not spend a halfpenny that was not absolutely necessary and Anna hoped that the Bartholomews would not mind her staying at the house until the last moment.

'Well, of course we don't mind,' Mrs Bartholomew re-assured her. 'We'd love you to be here just as long as you can.'

All the same, as the preparations progressed and more and more familiar objects disappeared into packing cases, it began to feel rather strange. Judy and Jinny still played tennis and sat in the sun and chatted, but they were excited at the prospect of going to America and sometimes it was as though they had already gone. When the day for their departure arrived it was difficult to know what to say. They stood outside the house in Campden Hill Square and looked at each other.

'Promise you'll write,' said Jinny.

'And don't let any bombs drop on you,' said Judy.

Mr Bartholomew said, 'We'll be seeing you . . .' and then looked confused and said, 'Good luck!'

Mrs Bartholomew hugged Anna and murmured, 'Take care of yourself,' and then climbed quickly into the taxi, dabbing at her face with her handkerchief. Then the taxi drove off and Anna waved until it turned the corner. When it had completely disappeared she began to walk, slowly, towards the tube station.

The square was green and leafy and the chestnut tree at the bottom was covered with blossom. She remembered how, her first spring in England, Jinny had shown it to her and pointed out the 'candles'. 'Candles?' Anna had said. 'Candles are only on Christmas trees,' and everyone had laughed. She could hear the plop of tennis balls from the courts where they had played only a few days before. When she reached the shop in Holland Park Avenue where they had always gone for sweets she stopped for a moment and looked in through the window. She was tempted to buy a chocolate bar as a sort of memento. But she would probably only eat it and then it would be a waste of money, so she didn't. A poster outside the tube station said 'Germans Reach Calais'.

It was May 26th, exactly a fortnight since Whitsun – the day Max should have started his exams.

CHAPTER 6

At the Hotel Continental Anna was allowed a small room close to Mama's and Papa's on the top floor.

When they had first come to England and still had some money they had lived lower down where the rooms were larger and more expensive, but Anna liked this better. From her window she could see right across the rooftops with only the sky above, or down into the scrappy yard, four storeys below, where cats fought among the dust and the weeds. A church clock nearby chimed out the quarters and sparrows hopped and fluttered on the sooty tiles. She was so busy settling into her new surroundings that she almost did not notice Dunkirk.

In a way it was quite easy to miss, even if one read the papers, which Anna didn't, because no one said much about it until it was over. Dunkirk was a place in France on the Normandy coast, and at the end of May the re-treating British army was trapped there by the Germans. Only the papers, trying to keep everyone cheerful, never quite said so in so many words. However, by fighting off the Germans and with the help of the Navy and the Air Force, nearly all the soldiers managed to escape back to England, and by the beginning of June the papers sud-denly came out in triumphant headlines. 'Bloody Mar-vellous!' said one, surprising Anna into reading it. She discovered that apart from the Navy thousands of ordinary people had crossed the Channel in tiny boats, again and again, to help take the soldiers off the beaches in the midst of battle. It was disappointing that what had sounded like a great victory was only an ingenious escape from defeat. But weren't the English amazing, she thought. She could not imagine the Germans doing a thing like that.

The Hotel Continental had become very crowded. In addition to the German, Czech and Polish refugees, there were now Dutchmen, Belgians, Norwegians and French. You never knew what language you were going to hear in the narrow corridors and on the stairs. The Swiss waitress who had come to London to learn English complained constantly, and after supper the lounge was like the tower of Babel.

The streets, too, were in turmoil. Every day there were long crocodiles of children with gas masks slung over their shoulders, each with a label attached somewhere to its person, trudging in the wake of grown-ups who were taking them to the railway stations, to be sent out of London, to the safety of the country.

Everyone was talking about the invasion of England, for now that Hitler was only the other side of the Channel he would surely want to cross it. To confuse the Germans when they came, names were being removed from street corners and Underground stations, and even buses lost their destination plates, so that the only way to find out where they were going was to ask the conductor.

One morning on her way to the secretarial school Anna discovered a rusty car with no wheels and two broken bedsteads dumped in the middle of the grass of Russell Square. First she thought it was some kind of joke, but then the porter at the Hotel Continental explained to her that it was to stop German parachutists from landing.

'Could they really land in Russell Square? There doesn't seem room,' said Anna, startled.

'There's no knowing what they can do,' said the porter.

Parachutists were an inexhaustible source of speculation. There were endless stories of people who claimed actually to have seen some, disguised as British soldiers, as farm workers or most often as nuns, in which case, according to the stories, they always gave themselves away by their carelessness in wearing army boots under their habits.

Anna tried, as always, not to think about them, but sometimes in bed at night her guard slipped and then she saw them dropping down silently among the trees of Russell Square. They were never in disguise but in full uniform covered with black leather and swastikas which were clearly visible even though it was dark. They called whispered commands to each other, and then they set off down Bedford Terrace towards the Hotel Continental to look for Jews ...

One morning after she had been kept awake a long time by her imaginings she came down late to find a stranger sitting at the breakfast table with Mama and Papa. She looked more closely and discovered that it was George.

Mama was in a state of confusion between happiness and distress, and as soon as she saw Anna she jumped from her chair.

'Letters from Max!' she cried.

George waved an envelope. 'I got one this morning, so I brought it round,' he said. 'But I see you've got your own. They must all have been posted at the same time.'

'Max is all right,' said Papa.

She began quickly to read.

There were four letters, all addressed to Mama and Papa. Max had written them at intervals of a week or so and their tone changed gradually from indignant surprise at being interned to a kind of despairing resignation. He had had a bad time, being pushed from one temporary camp to another, often without the simplest necessities. Now he had reached his permanent destination which was better organized, but he was not allowed to say where it was. ('On the Isle of Man!' said George impatiently. 'Everyone knows that's where they've been put – why can't they be allowed to say so?') The camp was full of students and professors from Cambridge – so many that it might even be possible to continue with some of his studies. 'So it's not too bad,' wrote Max. But he clearly hated it. He hated being imprisoned and he hated being treated as an enemy, and most of all he hated being forced back into some kind of German identity which he had long discarded. If there was anything Mama and Papa could do ...

'We must!' cried Mama. 'We must think of something!'

'I'll do anything to help, of course,' said George and got up to leave.

Papa got up too. 'Are you going backwards to Cambridge now?' he asked politely. His French was perfect, but he could never get his English right.

George did not smile.

'I'm no longer at Cambridge,' he said. 'I got tired of fiddling with bits of Chaucer while Rome burns, as it were.' Then he said almost apologetically, 'I've joined the Army.' He caught Anna's eye and added, 'Ridiculous, isn't it? English Youth Fights Nazi Hordes. D'you think I'll be terribly, terribly brave?'

A few days later it was Anna's birthday.

'What would you like to do?' asked Mama.

Anna thought. She had already spent two full weeks at the Hotel Continental and did not see how they could afford to do anything, but Mama was looking at her expectantly, so she said, 'Could we go to a film?' There was a cinema in Tottenham Court Road where you could get in at half-price before one o'clock. She added quickly, in case it was too expensive, 'Or we could have a knickerbocker glory at Lyons.'

Mama worked it out. The film would cost one shilling and threepence and the knickerbocker glory would be a shilling. She was looking in her purse, but suddenly she threw it down and cried, 'I don't care! You're going to be sixteen and you're going to have a proper birthday even if we are broke. We'll do both.'

'Are you sure?' said Anna.

'Yes,' said Mama quite fiercely. 'It's your birthday and it's going to be a nice day for you.' Then she said, 'God knows what will have happened to us all by next year.'

Papa said he did not want to come. He must have arranged it with Mama beforehand, thought Anna, for even in a fit of extravagance they could hardly have afforded cinema tickets and knickerbocker glories for three. So Anna and Mama went to see a film called *Mr Deeds Goes To Town*.

It was about a young millionaire who wanted to give away his money to the poor. ('I wish he'd give us some!' whispered Mama.) But some other mean millionaires wanted to stop him and tried to have him declared insane. In the end he was saved by a girl journalist who loved him, and all ended happily.

The leading part was played by a young actor called Gary Cooper, and both Anna and Mama thought it very good. Afterwards they went to Lyons and ate their knickerbocker glories very slowly, to make them last. They were a recent importation from America and consisted of layers of strawberry and vanilla ice-cream, interspersed with other layers of cream, strawberries and nuts, all served in a tall glass with a special long spoon. Anna had only eaten one once before, and knowing how much it cost, was a little nervous in case it wasn't quite as good as she remembered – but as soon as she tasted the first mouthful she was reassured.

While they ate they talked – about the film, about Anna's shorthand course and the money she would earn when she had finished. 'Then we'll be able to go to the cinema every day,' said Mama, 'and buy knickerbocker glories for breakfast.'

'And for lunch and for tea,' said Anna. When she got to the bottom of her glass she scraped it out so assiduously with her spoon that the waitress asked if she would like another. This made both her and Mama laugh, and they strolled back contentedly to the Hotel Continental.

On the way they met Papa, who had been sunning himself on a bench in Russell Square.

'How was the film?' he asked.

'Marvellous,' said Anna.

'And the other thing – the knickerbocker splendour or whatever it was?'

'Marvellous too,' said Anna, and Papa seemed very pleased.

It was a pity that the news of the fall of Paris had to come through that evening. Everyone had been expecting it, of course, but Anna had been hoping against hope that the French would manage to hold out until the next day. If it didn't happen on her birthday it wouldn't be quite so bad. As it was, it seemed somehow as though it were her fault. She thought of the French family who had befriended them when she and Max and Mama and Papa had first gone to live in Paris after leaving Germany, of her teacher who had taught her to speak French, of the Arc de Triomphe and the Champs Elysées, which she had passed every day on her way to school, of the chestnut trees and the people drinking in cafés and the Prisunic and the métro. Now the Nazis had taken possession of it all and France, like Germany, had become a black hole on the map, a place you could no longer think about.

She sat next to Papa in the lounge and tried not to cry because after all it was worse for the French. There was a middle-aged couple from Rouen staying in the hotel and they both wept when they heard the news. Afterwards the husband said to Papa, 'It is the end,' and Papa could find no answer.

A little later he got up and went to the telephone, and when he came back he told Mama, 'I've spoken to Sam and he'll see me tomorrow. And Louise said, could you and Anna come as well.'

'Are you ill, Papa?' asked Anna.

Professor Sam Rosenberg was a doctor and though his wife Louise had been at school in Germany with Mama, and Anna could not remember a time when they had not known them, they did not usually see them without some reason.

'No, I'm not ill,' said Papa. 'It's just something I want to talk to him about.'

The Rosenbergs lived in a vast flat in Harley Street with a porter and a lift and a brass plate on the door. When Anna rang the bell a maid let them in, deposited Papa in the waiting-room and led Anna and Mama along a passage filled with packing-cases to Aunt Louise's boudoir.

This too was in a state of upheaval. There were dust covers over some of the pretty velvet chairs, an open packing case stood in a corner and a gilt mirror had been taken down and was leaning against the wall, half-smothered in wadding. In the midst of it all Aunt Louise was sitting in her silk dress and pearls and with her hair beautifully curled, looking distraught.

'My dear it's all so awful!' she cried in German as soon as they came in. 'We have to pack up everything – Sam has taken a house in the country, he says it will be safer there.'

'Where in the country?' asked Mama, embracing her.

'Buckinghamshire, I think – or perhaps it's Berkshire – anyway, it's miles from anywhere, and he's going to close up this flat completely except for the consulting-room and drive up to see his most important patients only.' She drew a deep breath, looked at Anna and said, 'How are you?'

'All right, thank you,' said Anna indistinctly.

Aunt Louise with her delicate features and beautiful clothes always made her feel uncomfortable. Also it was Aunt Louise who, admittedly with the best intentions in the world, had persuaded Miss Metcalfe to take Anna into her school.

Aunt Louise smiled. 'Still at the awkward age,' she cried gaily to Mama. 'Never mind, they all grow out of it. And how are those charming American friends of yours?'

Mama explained that the Bartholomews had gone back

57

to America and that Anna was now living at the Hotel Continental.

'Oh dear, how difficult for you!' cried Aunt Louise, but it was not clear whether she meant the financial aspect or simply the fact that Mama had someone in the awkward age living with her.

'It's all such a rush,' she wailed. 'Sam says we've got to be out of London in two days, or he won't be responsible, with the French collapsing the way they have. And you can't get anyone to move the furniture – so many people have had the same idea. Do you know, I rang up eleven different firms before I found one which could do it?'

Mama made a sympathetic noise in her throat.

'And I'm sure they're going to break all the china, they're such galumphing great louts,' said Aunt Louise. Then, quite unexpectedly, she flung her arms round Mama's shoulders to cry disarmingly, 'And I know it's dreadful of me to fuss about it when people like you are staying behind in London and God only knows what's to happen to us all – but you know, my dear, that I was always a fool, ever since you were at the top of the class in Berlin and I at the bottom!'

'Nonsense,' said Mama. 'You were never a fool, and even at school you were always the prettiest, most elegant . . .'

'Oh yes I am,' said Aunt Louise. 'Sam has told me so many a time and he knows.'

As though settling the matter once and for all, she rang a bell by her side and the maid appeared almost at once with a silver tea-pot on a tray and little sandwiches and cakes. Aunt Louise poured out delicately. 'I looked out a few things for you while I was packing,' she said. 'I thought they might be useful.' Then she cried, 'Oh, she's forgotten the lemon again, I can't bear tea without lemon, she knows that perfectly well! Anna dear, could you possibly . . . ?'

Anna set off obediently in search of a lemon. The flat was large and rambling, with the dust-sheets everywhere making it more confusing, and she got lost several times before she found the kitchen. There she discovered half a lemon in the huge refrigerator and by the time she had ransacked all the drawers for a knife and cut the lemon into slices, which she was sure were much too thick, she feared Aunt Louise must have lost all interest in her tea.

She decided to try a different way back and after going down a passage and through a little ante-room found herself in the Professor's study. The blinds had been drawn against the sun, so that you could only guess at the medical books which lined the walls. Her feet sank into the deep carpet and it was almost spookily silent.

Suddenly she heard Papa's voice.

'How long does it take to act?' he asked, and Professor Rosenberg's voice answered, 'Only a few seconds. I've got the same for myself and Louise.'

Then she rounded a bookcase and discovered Papa and the Professor on the other side. Papa was putting something into his pocket and the Professor was saying, 'Let's hope none of us will ever need it.' Then he saw Anna and said, 'Hullo – you're growing up. You'll be as tall as me soon!' This was a joke, for the Professor was short and round.

Anna smiled half-heartedly. She felt uneasy in this room, in the half-darkness, at finding Papa and the Professor so close together and talking about – what?

The Professor looked at her with his sad black eyes which were like a monkey's and said to Papa, 'If things get bad in London send the girl to us. All right?' he added to Anna.

'All right,' said Anna out of politeness, but she thought that even if things did get bad she would rather stay with Mama and Papa. Then she took the lemon to Aunt Louise and they all had some tea.

When it was time to leave Aunt Louise handed Mama a parcel of clothes which she had packed up for her. (At the rate people were leaving London, thought Anna, she and Mama would soon have a vast wardrobe.) She hugged Mama several times and even the Professor embraced Papa and came down to the bus stop with them.

Back at the Hotel Continental Mama opened her parcel and found that it contained three dresses and an envelope. In the envelope was a note which said, 'To help you through the next difficult weeks,' and twenty pounds.

'Oh God!' cried Mama. 'It's like a miracle! Anna, this will pay your hotel bills until you get a job!'

Anna thought Papa might say that they shouldn't accept the money or at least treat it as a loan, but he didn't. He just stood by the window as though he hadn't heard. It was very strange. He was staring out at the evening sky and fingering, fingering something in his pocket.

She felt suddenly very frightened.

'What is it?' she cried, although she really knew. 'Papa! What did the Professor give you in his study?'

Papa tore his gaze away from the sky and looked at Mama, who stared back at him. At last he said slowly, 'Something I had asked him to give me – for use in an emergency.'

And Mama threw her arms round Anna as though never to let her go.

'Only in an emergency!' she cried. 'Darling, darling, I promise you – only in an emergency!'

CHAPTER 7

Three days later the French signed an armistice with the Germans and the only people left to fight Hitler were the English.

London was curiously empty. All the children had gone, and so had many of the old people. There were air-raid warnings almost every day. The first few times everyone rushed for shelter as soon as the sirens started. At the secretarial school they filed into the cellar of the building which was damp and smelled of mice. At the Hotel Continental they went into the basement which was also the kitchen and stood about awkwardly among the pots and pans. But nothing happened, no bombs fell, and after a while people began to ignore the warnings and just go on with whatever they had been doing.

Once Anna heard what sounded like a heavy piece of furniture being knocked over a long way off, and next day everyone said that a bomb had been dropped in Croydon, and once Anna and Papa saw two planes in a dog-fight right above the hotel. It was in the evening – the sky was pink and the planes were very high up so that you could hardly hear their engines or the rattle of their guns. They circled and dived and you could see little orange flashes and puffs of smoke as they fired at each other. But it didn't seem real. It looked like some beautiful, exciting display, and Papa and Anna craned out of the window, admiring it, until an air-raid warden shouted at them that there was shrapnel dropping all over Bedford Terrace and to get inside.

Every day, you wondered if the invasion would come. There were notices in the newspapers telling people what to do when it did. They were to stay in their homes – they must not panic and try to escape.

'Like in France,' said the Frenchman from Rouen. 'The people fled from the cities and blocked the roads, so that our armies could not get through. And then the Germans flew over them in their Stukas and machine-gunned them.'

'Terrible,' said Mama.

The Frenchman nodded. 'The people were mad,' he said. 'They were so frightened. Do you know, after Holland we put our German residents into camps because we did not know – some of them might be collaborators. But of course most of them were Jews, enemies of Hitler. And when the Nazis were coming, these people cried and pleaded to be set free so that at least they could hide. But the guards were too frightened. They just locked the Jews into the camps and handed the keys over to the Nazis, to do with them what they would.'

Then he saw Mama's face.

His wife said, 'Madame's son has been interned,' and he added quickly, 'Of course such a thing could never happen in England.'

After this Mama was more desperate than ever about Max. All the appeals which had been made on his behalf by friends, teachers, even important professors at Cambridge, had come to nothing. They simply were not answered. Gradually people grew to feel that it was hopeless and gave up. Anyway, they all had their own worries.

The only one still trying was the headmaster of Max's old school. He wanted Max to come back there to teach. 'It's not much for a boy of his ability,' he told Mama, 'but it's better than being stuck in a camp,' and he continued to bombard the authorities with demands for his release. But so far he had had no more luck than anyone else.

In the meantime, letters from Max arrived at irregular intervals, informative, matter of fact and sometimes funny, but always with the same underlying note of despair.

Cousin Otto had arrived at the camp and they were sharing a room. He was very upset at having been interned and Max was trying to cheer him up. Food was a bit short sometimes. Could Mama send some chocolate? One of the internees had committed suicide – a middle-aged Jew who had been in a German concentration camp before escaping to England. 'He just couldn't face being in a camp again – any camp. It was nobody's fault, but we are all very depressed . . .' Cousin Otto was very low. The only thing that cheered him up was reading P. G. Wodehouse. 'He reads late into the night as he can't sleep, and I don't get to sleep either because he will laugh out loud at the funny bits. I daren't say anything for fear of making him depressed again . . .' The authorities were sending shiploads of internees to the Commonwealth and quite a lot had chosen to go, rather than face indefinite intern- ment in England. 'But not me. I still think I belong in this country, even though they don't seem to agree with me at the moment. I know you're trying all you can to get me out, Mama, but if there is anything more you can do . . .'

The weather continued hot and dry.

'Best summer we've had for years,' said the porter of the Hotel Continental. 'No wonder Hitler wants to come here for his holidays.'

There were battles now every day in the sky above England, and each night on the nine o'clock news the BBC announced the results as though they were cricket scores. So many German planes shot down, so many British planes lost, eighteen for twelve, thirteen for eleven. The Germans always lost more planes than the British, but then they could afford to. They had so many more to start with.

Each night the porter switched on the old-fashioned radio in the lounge and the assembled refugees from countries already overrun by the Nazis stopped talking in their various languages and listened. If they could under- stand nothing else they could understand the figures, and they knew that they meant the difference between survival and the end of their world.

In August the fighting in the sky came to a head. No one knew how many British planes there were left, but everyone guessed that they must be nearly exhausted. The American press announced that according to reliable sources the invasion of England would take place within three days. It became more difficult to ignore the air-raid warnings, for you wondered each time whether the sirens had been set off yet again by a stray dog-fight in the vicinity of London or whether this time it was something quite different.

In bed at night Anna's wide-awake dreams grew worse. She no longer saw the Nazis dropping from the sky above Russell Square. Now they had already landed and England was occupied by them. She was alone, for when the Nazis had come battering on the doors of the Hotel Continental Mama and Papa had swallowed what the Professor had given Papa that day in the half-darkness of his study, and now they were dead. She was stumbling through a vast grey landscape all by herself, searching for Max. But there were Nazis everywhere and she dared speak to no one. The landscape was huge and hostile and unfamiliar, and she knew that she would never find him . . .

In the daytime she applied herself more assiduously than ever to her shorthand, and she was glad when one of the Germans in the hotel asked her to do some typing for him, so that even her spare time would be accounted for. He was writing a book on the nature of humour and wanted one chapter typed out so that he could submit it to a publisher who, he was convinced, would wish at once to have it translated into English. It was a good moment, said the German, to publish a book about humour, for everyone was clearly much in need of it, and once he had explained exactly what it was everyone would be able to have it.

Anna thought the German was probably being over-optimistic, for the sample chapter struck her as very dull. Most of it was taken up with denunciations of various other authors who had thought they knew what the nature of humour was, but who had been quite wrong. She could not imagine people queueing up to read it. But she was going to be paid a full pound for the job and the manager-ess said she could use the office typewriter, so each day, as soon as she got back from secretarial school, she settled down to work in a corner of the lounge.

One evening she had just begun to type after supper when Mama cried in English, 'Anna, we have a visitor.'

She looked up and saw a thin man with untidy grey hair and a nice smile. It was Mr Chetwin, Max's head-master.

'I'm afraid I have no news of Max,' he said at once. 'But I happened to be in town and I thought I'd just drop in to tell you that I haven't given up hope.'

They all sat down together at one of the tables, and Mr Chetwin began to tell Mama and Papa to what government departments he had already written about Max and to what others he was still going to write, even though no one so far had replied. From this he got on to talking about Max himself.

'One of the best boys I ever had,' he said, 'though he

would eat peppermints in prep – I remember having to beat him for that. But a brilliant footballer. He made the school team his first term, you know . . .'

Then he remembered Max's various successes at school – the scholarship after only two terms, so that there were no more fees to be paid, the major scholarship to Cambridge later – and Mama remembered all sorts of smaller successes that Mr Chetwin had forgotten, and Papa thanked him for all his kindness, and at the end of the conversation, even though nothing at all had changed, Anna noticed that Mama and Papa looked much happier than before.

By this time people were crowding into the lounge for the nine o'clock news and an elderly Pole excused himself and sat down at their table. He eyed Mr Chetwin respectfully.

'You are English?' he asked. Englishmen were rare in the Hotel Continental.

Mr Chetwin nodded, and the Pole said, 'I am Pole. But I wish very, very much that England shall win this war.'

There was a murmur of assent from other Poles and Czechs nearby and Mr Chetwin looked pleased and said, 'Very good of you.' Then all conversation was drowned by the deafening tones of Big Ben, for the porter had put the radio on too loud as usual.

A familiar voice said, 'This is the BBC Home Service. Here is the news, and this is Bruce Belfrage reading it.'

The voice did not sound quite as usual and Anna thought, what's the matter with him? It had a breathlessness, a barely discernible wish to hurry, which had never been there before. She was listening so hard to the intonation of each word that she hardly took in the sense. Air battles over most of England . . . Heavy concentrations of bombers . . . An official communiqué from the Air Ministry . . . And then it came. The voice developed something like a tiny crack which completely robbed it of its detachment, stopped for a fraction of a second and then said slowly and clearly, 'One hundred and eighty-two enemy aircraft shot down.'

There was a gasp from the people in the lounge, followed by murmured questions and answers as those who did not understand much English asked what the news-reader had said, and the others checked with each other that they had heard aright. And then the elderly Pole was leaping up from his chair and shaking Mr Chetwin by the hand.

'It is success!' he cried. 'You English show Hitler he not can win all the time! Your aeroplanes show him!' and the other Poles and Czechs crowded round, patting Mr Chetwin on the back, pumping his hand and congratulating him.

His grey hair became untidier than ever and he looked bemused but glad. 'Very kind of you,' he kept saying, 'though it wasn't me, you know.'

But they insisted on treating him as though he personally had been out there and shot down a whole lot of German bombers, and when at last he left to catch his train, one of them called after him triumphantly, 'Now Hitler must think from something else!'

The trouble was, thought Anna a few days later, what would he think of? The fine weather had broken at last, heavy cloud had put an end to all air activity, and no one knew what would happen next.

Anna had finally got to the end of the chapter on the nature of humour and had collected her pound which she planned to spend on a pair of trousers – a new fashion for women – and she and Mama were searching Oxford Street for a suitable pair.

In spite of the clouds it was still hot, and each of the big stores they went into seemed stickier and more airless than the last. The trousers on offer were all too expensive and it was not until just before closing time that they found a pair that would do. They were navy blue and made of some unidentifiable substance which Mama said would probably melt at the sound of an air-raid warning, but they were the right size and only cost nineteen shillings, elevenpence and three farthings, so they bought them – Anna triumphantly and Mama wearily.

Mama was depressed. She had had a letter that morning from Mr Chetwin full of kindness and concern for Max, but reporting no progress at all, and she was beginning to feel that this, her last hope, was going to fail like all the rest.

They had to queue a long time for a bus and when it finally came she sank into a seat and, instead of admiring Anna's trousers, picked up a newspaper which someone had left behind and began to read. The bus moved only slowly to save petrol and she had time to read the paper from cover to cover.

Suddenly she cried, 'Look at this!'

Anna peered over her shoulder and wondered why a film review should have excited her so.

'Read it!' cried Mama.

It was a very sympathetic account of a film about the difficulties and disasters which beset an anti-Nazi family trying to escape from Germany. It was written not by a film critic but by a politician.

'You see?' cried Mama. 'They can be sympathetic when the people are stuck in Germany, but what happens when they get to England? They put them in internment camps.'

She hastily folded the paper and crammed it into her handbag.

'I'm going to write to this man,' she said.

As soon as they got back she showed the article to Papa. At first Papa was not sure if they should write to the paper. He said, 'We are guests in this country – one should not criticize one's host.' But Mama got very excited and shouted that it was not a question of etiquette but of Max's whole life, and in the end they composed a letter between them.

They explained about Papa's long fight against Hitler and about Max's scholarships and about Mr Chetwin who wanted him to teach at his school. Then they gave a list of all the people at Cambridge who had protested about Max's internment, and ended up by asking whether this was not an absurd situation. Then they all walked down to Russell Square together and posted it.

The reply came two days later.

Anna had been awake half the night because there had been so many air-raid warnings, and for the first time a few bombs had fallen not in the distant suburbs but frighteningly near, in the middle of London. She was tired and depressed and eyed the letter warily, feeling that this was not the sort of day on which people received good news.

Mama, too, seemed almost afraid to open it, but finally ripped at it so clumsily that a corner of the letter tore off with the envelope. Then she read it and burst into tears.

Papa took it from her and he and Anna read it together.

It was from the editor of the paper. He said that his paper had long protested against the government's policy which had caused some of the most brilliant and dedicated anti-Nazis to be put into internment camps. He had been much moved by Mama's and Papa's letter and had passed it on to the Home Secretary who had promised to look into Max's case himself, immediately.

'Does that mean they'll release him?' asked Anna.

'Yes,' said Papa. 'Yes, it does.'

They sat in the cramped breakfast room and looked at each other. Suddenly everything was different. There had been bombs in the night, a new air-raid warning had already sounded, the headline in the morning paper said 'Invasion Barges Massing In Channel Ports' – but none of it mattered because Max was going to be released.

At last Papa said slowly, 'The English really are extraordinary. Here they are, threatened with invasion at any moment, and yet the Home Secretary can find time to right an injustice to an unknown boy who wasn't even born here.'

Mama blew her nose.

'But of course,' she said, 'Max is a very remarkable boy !'

CHAPTER 8

Max arrived home about a week later, unannounced, in the middle of an air raid. It was in the late afternoon. Mama was not yet back from work, Papa had walked to Russell Square to meet her, and Anna had just washed her hair in the bathroom at the end of the passage. She came back to her room with a towel wrapped round her head, and there he was standing in the corridor.

'Max!' she cried and was about to throw her arms round him, but then she stopped, in case he might not like it, in case it was too sudden.

'Hullo, little man,' said Max. It was a nickname he had had for her since they were both quite small. 'I'm glad to see you're keeping clean.'

'Oh, Max,' cried Anna, throwing her arms around him after all, 'you haven't changed!'

'What did you think?' said Max. 'That I'd be hard and embittered? Never smile again? I don't change.' He followed her into her room. 'But I learn from experience,' he said. 'And I'm going to make sure that nothing like the last four months ever happens to me again.'

'How can you?' asked Anna.

Max moved some clothes off the only chair and sat down. 'I'm going to teach for a year,' he said. 'Old Chetwin wants me to, and I owe it him after all he tried to do. Then I'm going into the Forces.'

'But, Max,' said Anna, 'do they take Germans in the British Forces?'

Max's mouth tightened. 'We'll see,' he said.

Then the door flew open and there was Mama, with Papa behind her.

'Max!' she cried, and at the same time there was a thud and a rumble and Max looked startled and said, 'Was that a bomb?'

'Yes,' said Anna apologetically, 'but it was a long way off.'

'Good God,' said Max, and as Mama rushed to embrace him he added reproachfully, 'Really, Mama – so this is what you've brought me back to!'

At supper they drank a bottle of wine that someone had given Papa months before and which he had kept specially. It did not taste quite right – perhaps, said Papa, the bottom of the clothes cupboard had not been the best place to store it – but they drank to Max, to Mr Chetwin and to the Home Secretary, and at the end of it all Anna felt pleasantly muzzy.

Mama could hardly take her eyes off Max. She heaped his plate with food and hung on his every word, but he did not talk much. Mostly he was worried about Otto who, he said, would be lost without him and who was thinking of going on a transport to Canada. 'His professor is going,' he said, 'but what's he going to do in Canada? And anyway, the last transport that went got sunk by a U-boat.'

The All Clear had sounded shortly after Max's arrival, but there was another air-raid warning a little while later and the sound of planes and distant bombs continued throughout the evening. After dark it got worse rather than better and Mama said, 'I don't know what they're up to,' quite crossly to Max, like a hostess whose arrangements for the evening had broken down.

'Is there anything to see?' asked Max. 'I'll just take a look.' And in spite of Mama's and Papa's warnings about shrapnel, he and Anna edged aside the heavy blackout material round the door and went out into the street.

It was not dark at all outside and the sky was bright pink, so that for a moment Anna thought stupidly that she had made a mistake about the time. Then there was a whistling, tearing sound and a crash as a bomb fell, not so very far away, and a man in a tin hat shouted at them, 'Get inside!'

'Where's the fire?' asked Max.

Of course, thought Anna, it must be a fire, that was why the sky was so bright.

The man backed against a wall as another bomb came down, but farther away. 'In the docks,' he said. 'And Jerry's dropping everything and the kitchen sink into it. Now stop messing about and get in!' And he pushed them back into the hotel.

Max looked bemused. 'Is it always like this?' he asked.

'No,' said Anna. 'This is the worst we've had.' She

thought of the pink sky and added, 'It must be a very big fire.'

By bedtime there was no sign of the raid abating and Frau Gruber, the manageress, said that anyone who wished could sleep in the lounge. She bustled about with rugs, and everyone helped to move the tables so as to make more room, and soon the lounge looked like a camp. There were people curled up with pillows in the brown leatherette chairs and people stretched out on blankets on the floor. Some had changed into pyjamas and dressing-gowns, but others had kept on their ordinary clothes and covered themselves with their coats, in case a bomb dropped and they might suddenly have to rush out into the street. The author of the book on the nature of humour wore striped pyjamas, a tweed jacket and his hat.

When everyone was more or less settled, Frau Gruber appeared in her dressing-gown with cups and a jug of cocoa on a tray, as though they were having some kind of dormitory feast. At last the lights were put out, all except one small one in a corner, and Frau Gruber who had become astonishingly cheerful as a result of all this activity, said, 'I hope you all have a very good night,' which Anna thought funny in the circumstances.

She was lying on the floor with her head under one of the tables, next to Max – Mama and Papa were in two chairs the other side of the lounge – and as soon as the room darkened, the thumps and bangs outside became impossible to ignore. She could hear the sound of the planes, a quivering hum like having a mosquito in the room with you only many octaves lower, and every so often the thud of a bomb. The bombs were mostly some distance away, but even so the explosions were quite loud. Some people, she knew, could tell the difference between German planes and British ones, but they all sounded the same to her. They all sounded German.

All round her she could sense people moving and whispering – no one was finding it easy to go to sleep.

'Max?' she said very quietly.

He turned towards her, wide awake. 'Are you all right?'

'Yes,' she whispered. 'Are you?'

He nodded.

Suddenly she remembered how, when she was quite small and frightened of thunderstorms, Max had kept her heart up by pretending that they were caused by God having indigestion.

'Do you remember . . .' she said, and Max said, 'Yes, I was just thinking – God's indigestion. He's really got himself upset this time.'

She laughed and then they both stopped talking to listen to the buzzing of a plane, as it seemed right above their heads.

'To think I could be peacefully in bed on the Isle of Man with Otto reading Wodehouse,' said Max.

The sound of the plane grew fainter, then louder again – it must be circling, thought Anna – and finally faded away in the distance.

'Max,' she said, 'was it very bad in the camp?'

'No,' said Max. 'Not once we'd got settled. I mean, nobody was beastly or anything like that. The thing that got me was simply the fact of being there at all. I didn't belong there.'

Anna wondered where she belonged. Here, in the hotel, among the other refugees? Probably as much as anywhere, she thought.

'You see,' said Max, 'I know it sounds arrogant to say so, but I know I belong in this country. I've known it ever since my first year at school – a feeling of everything being suddenly absolutely right. And it wasn't only me. Other people like George and Bill thought so too.'

'Yes,' said Anna.

'All I want,' said Max, 'is just to be allowed to do the same things as everyone else. Do you know, there were some people in the camp who thought they were lucky to be there because it was safe. Well, I'm not a particularly warlike person and God knows I don't want to be killed – but I'd a thousand times rather be in the Army with George or in the Air Force with Bill. I'm sick to death of always having to be different!'

There was a crash, closer than the rest, which shook the building and as Anna felt the floor move a little beneath her the word 'bombardment' came into her mind. I'm in a bombardment, she thought. I'm lying on the floor of the Hotel Continental in my pink pyjamas in the middle of a bombardment.

'Max,' she said, 'are you frightened?'

'Not really,' he said.

'Nor me.'

'I suppose,' said Max, 'it's a relief just for once to have the same worries as everyone else!'

The raid lasted all through the night. Anna slept fitfully, lulled to sleep by the drone of the planes and startled awake again by distant thuds and crashes, until the All Clear went at half-past five in the morning and Frau Gruber, who seemed to see this new development in Hitler's air warfare as a personal challenge, appeared with cups of tea. She had pulled the blackout curtains aside and Anna saw, somehow to her surprise, that Bedford Terrace looked just as usual. The street was empty and the shabby houses stood silent under the pale sky, as though it had been a night like any other. While she watched, a door opened opposite and a woman dressed in trousers and a pyjama top appeared. She looked up searchingly at the sky, as Anna had done before. Then she yawned, stretched and went back inside to go back to bed or to start cooking breakfast.

Max was anxious to get off to his new job as soon as possible. He had managed with difficulty to get through to Euston Station on the telephone and had been told that due to enemy action there would be long delays on all lines. So Anna and Mama said goodbye to him as he packed his suitcase, with Papa sitting on the bed to keep him company, and went to work as usual.

It was a beautiful clear morning and as Anna walked through the back streets to Tottenham Court Road she was again amazed at how ordinary everything looked. Only there were more cars and taxis about than usual, often with luggage piled high on roof-racks – more people leaving London. While she was waiting to cross a road, a man just opening up his greengrocer's shop smiled at her and called out, 'Noisy last night!' and she answered, 'Yes,' and smiled back.

She hurried past the back of the British Museum – this was the dullest part of her daily journey – and turned into a more interesting street with shops. There was some glass on the pavement in front of her – someone must have broken a window, she thought. And then she looked up and saw the rest of the street.

There was glass everywhere, doors hanging on their hinges, bits of rubble all over the road. And in the terrace opposite where there should have been a house there was a gap. The entire top floor had gone, and so had most of the front wall. They had subsided into a pile of bricks and stone which filled the road, and some men in overalls were shovelling them into the back of a lorry.

You could see right inside what remained of the house. It had had green wallpaper and the bathroom had been painted yellow. You could tell it was the bathroom because, even though most of the floor had gone, the part supporting the bath tub appeared to be suspended in space. Immediately above it was a hook with a flannel still hanging from it and a toothmug in the shape of Mickey Mouse.

'Horrible, isn't it?' said an old man next to Anna. 'Lucky there was no one in it – she'd taken the kids to her sister's. I'd like to give that Hitler a piece of my mind!'

Then he went back to sweeping up the glass outside his shop.

Anna walked slowly down the street. The part closest to the bombed house had been cordoned off, in case any more of it fell down, and on one side of it a man and a woman were already nailing up sheets of cardboard in place of their broken windows. She was glad there had been nobody in the house when the bomb fell. One of the men shovelling rubble shouted to her to keep away and she turned down a side street.

There was only little damage here – broken windows and some dust and plaster underfoot – and as she picked her way among the fragments of glass scattered on the pavement she noticed how the sun sparkled on them. A little breeze blew the dust into swirls round her feet. Her legs were brown from the endless fine weather and she suddenly wanted to run and jump. How awful to feel like this, she thought, when there had been an air raid and people had been killed – but another part of her didn't care. The sky was blue and the sun was warm on her bare arms and there were sparrows hopping about in the gutter and cars hooting and people walking about and talking, and suddenly she could feel nothing but a huge happiness at still being alive. Those poor people who lost their house, she thought, but the thought had hardly time to emerge before it was swallowed up by her happiness.

She took a deep breath – the air smelled of brickdust and plaster – and then she ran to the end of the street and down Tottenham Court Road and all the way to the secretarial school.

CHAPTER 9

After this there were air raids every night. The sirens went at dusk, to be followed a few minutes later by the drone of German bombers, and the All Clear did not go until first light. They were so regular you could almost set your watch by them.

'Mama,' Anna would say, 'can I go and buy some sweets for the air raid?'

Mama would say, 'All right, but be quick – they'll be here in ten minutes.' And Anna would run through the warm, darkening streets to the sweet shop next to the tube station for two ounces of toffees which the woman in the shop would weigh out hastily, with one eye on the clock, and then she would race back to the hotel, arriving together with the first wail of the sirens.

Each night she and Mama and Papa slept in the lounge. There was plenty of room, for a lot of people had left after the first big raid, and more went every day. It was unnerving just lying there in the dark and waiting for the Germans to drop their bombs. There seemed to be nothing at all to stop them. But after a few nights the din of the raids suddenly increased with a series of bangs, like a great drum being blown full of air and exploding, and Frau Gruber, who had become an expert overnight, at once identified this as anti-aircraft fire. It made sleep even more difficult than before, but even so, everyone rejoiced in it.

It was curious, thought Anna, how quickly one could get used to sleeping on the floor. It was really quite snug. There were plenty of blankets, and the heavy wooden shutters over the lounge windows not only muffled the noise but gave her a feeling of security. She never got enough sleep, but nor did anyone else, and this was another thing one got used to. Everywhere you went during the day there were people having little catnaps to catch up – in the parks, on the buses and tubes, in the corners of tea-shops. One girl even fell asleep over her shorthand machine at the secretarial school. When they talked to each other they would yawn hugely in the middle of a sentence and go straight on with what they were saying without even bothering to apologize.

During the third week of the raids a bomb fell in Russell Square, making a crater in the soft earth and breaking most of the windows in Bedford Terrace. Anna was asleep at the time and fortunately for her the blast sucked everything out into the street, so that the glass and the shutters (which had not been so safe after all) landed on the pavement instead of on the people in the lounge.

She leapt up from the floor, hardly awake and unable to understand what had happened. There was a curtain fluttering round her face and she could see straight into the street where an air-raid warden was blowing his whistle. All round her people were stumbling in the darkness and asking what had happened and above it all came Mama's voice shouting, 'Anna! Are you all right?'

She shouted back, 'Yes!' and then Frau Gruber arrived with a torch.

Afterwards she found to her surprise that she was trembling.

After this no one slept in the lounge any more. The man from the Council who came to board up the gaps where the windows had been told Frau Gruber that it was not safe and that it would be better, in future, to use the basement.

Anna boasted a little at the secretarial school about her escape, but no one was very impressed. By now most of the people still remaining in London had a bomb story of some sort. If they hadn't lost any windows they had just failed, by some remarkable coincidence, to be in some building which had received a direct hit. Madame Laroche had returned from a public shelter at dawn to find that a land-mine had somehow got through her roof without exploding and was now dangling from its parachute at the top of the staircase, ready to go off at the slightest tremor. This had so unnerved her, on top of the worry about her family in Belgium, that her doctor had ordered her to rest in the country.

The school hardly missed her. It had almost run down, anyway. There were scarcely a dozen students left and it had become impossible to take down dictation and read it back, for the special paper for the machines had come from Belgium and there was no more to be had. So the students practised by moving their fingers on empty keyboards while the one remaining teacher read out light novels to them. It was perfectly logical, but sometimes, as Anna listened to yet another chapter of Dorothy Sayers or Agatha Christie after walking through the broken streets, it occurred to her that this was a strange way of spending what might be the last days of her life.

At night everyone now slept in the basement. Its stone floor was cold and hard, so if you wanted to be at all comfortable you had to drag the mattress down from your bed. But it always seemed like the last straw, after a largely sleepless night, to have to drag it all the way up again when the All Clear went at dawn.

The cellar they slept in had been a storage room and Anna hated it. To reach it you had to go down a narrow flight of stone steps from the dining-room to the kitchen and then down a few further steps beyond it. It was little more than six feet high and both damp and stuffy. Once you were installed on your mattress listening to the air raid outside and staring up at the low ceiling it was easy to imagine everything collapsing above you, and Anna had an unreasonable wish, even when no bombs had fallen nearby, to keep checking that the stairs to the dining-room were still there.

Sometimes when she could not bear it any longer she would whisper to Mama, 'I'm going to the lavatory,' and in spite of the grumbles of the other sleepers she would pick her way across them and go up into the deserted main part of the hotel. She would climb up the four flights to her room and stay there, with the sound of the bombs and the guns, until she felt ready to brave the basement again.

One night when she entered her room she was startled to see a figure outlined against the window which, by some freak of the blast, had remained unbroken.

'Who is it?' she cried.

Then it turned and she recognized Papa.

'Look,' he said, and she joined him in the darkness.

The night outside was brilliant. The sky was red, reflecting the fires on the ground, and in it hung clusters of orange flares which lit up everything for miles around. They looked like gigantic Christmas decorations floating slowly, slowly down through the night air, and though Anna knew that they were there to help the Germans aim their bombs she was filled with admiration at the sight. It was so bright that she could see the church clock (which had long been stopped) and a place on the rooftop opposite where some of the tiles had been ripped off by the blast. In the distance yellow flashes like lightning were followed by muffled bangs – the anti-aircraft guns in Hyde Park.

Suddenly a searchlight swept across the sky. It was joined by another and another, crossing and re-crossing each other, and then a great orange flash blotted out everything else. A bomb or a plane exploding in mid-air – Anna did not know which – but the accompanying crash sent her and Papa scuttling away from the window.

When it was over they looked out again at the illuminated night. The orange flares had been joined by some pink ones and they were drifting slowly down together.

'It may be the end of the civilized world,' said Papa, 'but it is certainly very beautiful.'

As the days grew shorter the air raids grew longer. By mid-October the All Clear did not sound until half-past six in the morning and it was hardly worth trying to get to sleep afterwards.

'If only this fine weather would stop!' cried Mama, for when the weather was bad enough the bombers did not come and they had the incredible, marvellous experience of sleeping all night in their beds. But one bright day followed another, and though it was exhilarating, each morning, to go out in the crisp autumn air and find that one was still alive, each night the bombers came back and with them the closeness and the fear in the basement.

One night the sirens sounded earlier than usual, while everyone was still having supper. They were followed almost immediately by the drone of planes and a succession of crashes as bombs fell not far away.

One of the Poles stopped with a forkful of shepherd's pie half-way to his mouth.

'Bang-bang!' he said. 'It is not nice when people are eating.' He was a large middle-aged man with an unpronounceable name and everyone called him the Wood-pigeon because of his passion for imitating a pair of scraggy birds which haunted the yard behind the hotel.

'They're going for the stations again,' said Frau Gruber.

'Oh surely not!' cried the German lady whose husband had been killed by the Nazis. 'They went for the stations yesterday.'

The Hotel Continental lay half-way between Euston and St Pancras and when the Germans tried to bomb the stations it always meant a bad night.

'But not did they hit them,' said the Woodpigeon, and then everyone froze as a tearing, whistling sound was followed by an explosion which rocked the room. A glass slid off one of the tables and broke on the floor.

'That was quite close,' said Mama.

Frau Gruber started in a matter of fact way to collect the dishes.

'It's prunes and custard for pudding,' she said, 'but I think we'd better leave it and go to the shelter.'

While Anna went to fetch her mattress from her room there was another crash and the whole building – walls, floors, ceiling – moved perceptibly around her. She grabbed the mattress quickly and rushed down the stairs with it bumping behind her. For once she was glad to get down into the basement – at least it didn't move.

Frau Gruber had hung up a blanket in the middle of the storage room, so that the men could sleep on one side and the women on the other. Anna pushed her mattress into an empty space and found herself next to the German lady whose husband had been killed by the Nazis. Mama was somewhere behind her. Before she had time even to lie down there was another shattering crash and Frau Gruber, who had been tinkering with the prunes and custard in the kitchen, abandoned them and made for the storage room.

'Oh dear,' said the German lady, 'I do hope it's not going to be one of those awful nights.'

This was followed by an even louder crash and then a third, fortunately farther away.

'It's all right,' said Anna. 'He's passed us.'

The Germans always dropped sticks of six or more bombs in a row. As long as the explosions were coming towards you it was terrifying, but once they had moved past you knew that you were safe.

'Thank God!' said the German lady, but Anna could already hear the drone of another plane.

'They're coming in on a different flight-path,' said Frau Gruber. Mama added, 'Straight overhead,' and then the next lot of bombs began to fall. They listened to them screaming down from the sky. One . . . two . . . three . . . four very close – five and six, thank goodness, receding. Then there was another plane – it can't go on like this, thought Anna, but it did.

Next to her the German lady was lying with her eyes shut and her hands clenched on her chest, and on the other side of the blanket she could hear the Woodpigeon muttering, 'Why you not hit the station and go home? You stupid, silly Germans, why you not can hit it?'

At last, after what seemed an eternity, there was a lull. The last bomb dropped by one plane was not followed immediately by the sound of another plane approaching.

It was quiet.

For a few moments everyone waited and when nothing happened they began to move and relax. Anna looked at her watch. It was still only ten o'clock.

'That was the worst we've had,' said Mama.

Papa lifted a corner of the blanket and looked through. 'Are you all right?' he asked, and Anna nodded. Curiously enough she did not feel her usual urge to see if the stairs were still there. How silly, she thought – if they really collapsed one would hear it.

'Well, we may as well try and get some sleep,' said Frau Gruber and at the same moment there was a distant thud and the light went out.

'They've hit a cable,' said Frau Gruber, snapping on her torch.

'The kind Germans have switched off for us the light,' said the Woodpigeon, and everyone laughed.

'Well, I won't waste the battery,' said Frau Gruber and the cellar was plunged into darkness.

Anna closed her eyes so as not to see it. She had been frightened of the dark when she was small and still was. It was quiet except for some bumps in the distance. There was nothing to see, nothing to hear, and she drifted off into sleep.

Suddenly everything seemed to explode. The cellar shook around her and before she could collect herself in the darkness another bomb came screaming down, the loudest she had ever heard, it burst with a huge roaring reverberation that was almost too loud to hear and something came down on top of her and covered her, she could not see or breathe, it was what she had always dreaded . . .

And then she moved and found that it was only the blanket which had fallen on her, and the white faces of Papa and the Woodpigeon appeared with a click of Frau Gruber's torch.

'Are you all right?' said Papa.

She said, 'Yes,' and lay where she was without moving, still filled with the terror of it. Next to her the German lady was crying.

Mama began to say something but stopped because there was another plane above them and the bombs came tearing down again.

'I'll just take a look,' said Frau Gruber after the last one, and the cellar leapt and darkened as she moved with her torch into the kitchen.

'All right,' she said. 'We're still standing.'

Anna lay quite still.

'I mustn't panic,' she thought. But she wished the German lady would stop crying as the cellar shook with another explosion.

At the rate they're bombing us, she thought, we're bound to be hit.

A wave of terror swept over her, but she managed to contain it. If she could just get used to the idea, she thought. If she could manage to keep calm when it happened. Because they always came to dig you out, and if you didn't panic you didn't use up so much oxygen, and then you could last until they came.

Mama leaned over to her in the darkness. 'Would you like to come next to me?' she said.

'I'm all right here,' said Anna.

Mama could not help her.

Another plane came over and another stick of bombs tore down.

If I think about it now, thought Anna, if I imagine it, then when it happens, when I'm trapped in a little hole with tons of rubble on top of me . . .

Again the terror surged over her.

She tried to fight it down. I mustn't fight and scrabble to get out, she thought, I must keep quite still. There may not be much room, much air . . .

Suddenly she could almost feel the tight, black cavity shutting her in and it was so frightful that she leapt into a sitting position as though she had been stung, to make sure it hadn't happened. She was panting for breath and Mama said, 'Anna?' again.

'I'm all right,' she said.

The German lady was moaning and beyond her two Czech voices were murmuring some kind of prayer.

I have to get used to it, she thought, I must! But before she had even finished the thought such terror engulfed her that she almost cried out. It was no good. She couldn't do it. She lay with clenched teeth and clenched hands, waiting for it to subside.

Perhaps it won't be so bad when it happens, she thought. Perhaps it's worse thinking about it. But she knew that it wasn't.

The planes kept coming and the bombs kept bursting while the German lady wept beside her. Once Mama shouted at the German lady to control herself and at some time during the night Papa moved his mattress over to Mama so that they were all near each other, but it made no difference.

She lay alone in the dark, trying to shut out the terrible picture of herself screaming mutely in a black hole.

At last she became so exhausted that a kind of calm came over her. I've got used to it, she thought, but she knew that she hadn't. And when at last the shuddering crashes stopped and a little light filtered into the cellar with the sound of the All Clear, she thought, well, after all, it wasn't so bad. But she knew that this, too, was untrue.

When they inspected the damage they found that the few remaining windows had gone. The top of the church tower which Anna had been able to see from her room had collapsed and there was a ragged hole in the roof of the church. And on the other side of Bedford Terrace, only a few yards along, where there should have been a house, there was only a heap of rubble in which nobody and nothing could have survived.

'Direct hit,' said the porter.

'Who lived there?' asked Anna.

83

She was standing in the cold morning air in her trousers and an old sweater. The wind blew through her clothes and she had wrapped a handkerchief round her hand where she had cut herself on a piece of broken window glass.

'Refugees from Malta,' said the porter. 'But they always went to the public shelter.'

Anna remembered them – frail, dark-skinned people in clothes far too thin for an English autumn. As soon as the air-raid warning sounded they would pour out of the house with a curious twittering sound and hurry fearfully down the street.

'All of them?' she asked. 'Did all of them go to the public shelter?'

'Nearly all of them,' said the porter.

Then a large blue car swept round the corner from Russell Square, negotiated some rubble in the road and stopped inexplicably outside the hotel. The driver opened the door and a little round man climbed out. It was Professor Rosenberg.

'I heard it was bad last night,' he said. 'Are you all right?'

Anna nodded and he swept her ahead of him into the lounge where Mama and Papa were drinking some tea which Frau Gruber had made.

'I think the girl should get out of all this for a bit,' he said. 'I'm driving back to the country this evening. I'll pick her up and take her with me.'

Anna demurred. 'I'm all right,' she said, but tears kept coming into her eyes for no reason and Mama and Papa both wanted her to go.

In the end Mama decided it by shouting, 'I can't stand another night like the last with you here – I wouldn't mind if I knew you were safe!' and Papa said, 'Please go!' So Mama helped her to pack, and about five o'clock she drove off in the back of the Professor's great car.

She leaned out of the window, waving farewell until the car had turned the corner. All the way to the country she carried with her the picture of Mama and Papa waving back as they stood among the rubble of the shattered street.

CHAPTER 10

It was night when they arrived. Already as the car had zig-zagged out of London, detouring round blocked streets and unexploded bombs, dusk had begun to fall, and the Professor had urged the driver to hurry so as to get clear of the city before the bombers came. Anna climbed out into the country darkness, sensed rather than saw great bushy trees surrounding a large house and caught a whiff of acorns and autumn leaves before the Professor propelled her through the front door. While she was still getting adjusted to the brightness of the hall a gong sounded somewhere in the depths of the house. The Professor said, 'Go and find your Aunt Louise,' and disappeared upstairs.

Anna wondered where Aunt Louise could be and, for lack of a better idea, decided to follow the sound of the gong. She went through a large drawing-room furnished with soft chairs, sofas and elaborately shaded lamps, into an equally large dining-room where the long lace-covered table was laid for about a dozen people. There she found another door covered in green baize and had just decided to open it when the gonging stopped and Aunt Louise, dressed in a long velvet gown, burst into the dining-room with the stick still in her hand.

'There will be no dinner . . .' she cried.

Then she saw Anna and threw her arms round her, accidentally hitting her with the padded end of the stick.

'My dear!' she cried. 'Are you all right? I told Sam to bring you. Are your parents all right?'

'We're all all right,' said Anna.

'Thank God,' cried Aunt Louise. 'We heard that last night was terrible. Oh, it must be so awful in London — though here, too, there are problems. The dinner . . .' She drew Anna through the green baize door. 'Come,' she cried, 'you can help me!'

In the narrow corridor beyond they met two maids in frilly aprons.

'Now, Lotte! Inge!' said Aunt Louise. 'Surely you must see reason!' But they looked at her sulkily and the one called Inge sniffed. 'What's said can't be unsaid,' she remarked, and the one called Lotte added, 'That goes for me too.'

'Oh really,' wailed Aunt Louise. 'Who would have thought, just because of some kippers!'

They passed the kitchen with five or six saucepans steaming on the range.

'Look at it!' cried Aunt Louise, 'it will all spoil,' and she almost ran to a room beyond. 'Fraulein Pimke!' she shouted and tried to open the door, but it was locked and Anna could hear someone weeping noisily inside. 'Fraulein Pimke!' Aunt Louise cried again, rattling the door handle. 'Listen to me! I never said anything against your cooking.'

There were some unintelligible sounds from within.

'Yes I know,' cried Aunt Louise. 'I know you cooked for the Kaiser. And for all the highest in the land. And I wouldn't dream of criticizing, only how was I to know that the maids wouldn't eat kippers? And then, when the butter ration . . . Fraulein Pimke, please come out!'

There was a shuffling sound followed at length by a click. The door opened a crack and an ancient, tear-stained face peered out.

'. . . never had my food refused before,' it quavered. 'And then to be shouted at on top of it . . . eighty-two years old and still trying to do my best . . .' The corners of the mouth turned down and more tears ran down the wrinkled cheeks.

'Now, Fraulein Pimke,' said Aunt Louise, cunningly inserting an arm through the crack and drawing her through the door (very much, thought Anna, like extracting a snail from its shell). 'What would the Kaiser say to see you weeping like this?'

Fraulein Pimke, deprived of the shelter of her room, blinked and looked confused, and Aunt Louise weighed in quickly while she had the chance.

'I didn't mean to shout at you,' she said. 'It's just that I was taken aback. When I found that the butter ration had gone on the kippers. And then, when the maids gave notice . . . Fraulein Pimke, you're the only one I can rely on!'

Fraulein Pimke, slightly mollified, blinked at Anna. 'Who's this?' she said.

Aunt Louise saw her chance and took it.

'A bomb victim!' she cried. 'A little victim of the London blitz!' She caught sight of the handkerchief round Anna's hand and pointed to it dramatically. 'Wounded!' she cried. 'Surely, Fraulein Pimke, you cannot let this child go without her dinner!'

By this time she had somehow manoeuvred the group towards the kitchen door, and Fraulein Pimke went in like a lamb.

'Thank you, thank you!' cried Aunt Louise. 'I knew I could count on you – the Professor will be so pleased!'

Then she led Anna back into the drawing-room which was now filled with people in evening dress. Anna's lack of sleep was catching up with her and after the terrors of the previous night everything was beginning to feel like a dream. She was introduced to various people, most of whom seemed to be related to the Professor, but it was difficult to remember who they all were.

There was a little cross-looking woman who was the Professor's sister and two boys younger than Anna who might or might not be her sons. But what was a man dressed in a silk suit and turban doing there, and was he really a maharajah as someone seemed to have said? She was uncomfortably conscious of her trousers and old sweater, but a red-haired woman in a black dress kindly told her that she looked very nice and even appealed to her husband for confirmation, and he said something about the battlefront and asked her what it was like being in the blitz.

It turned out that no one in the house had spent a night in London since the beginning of the air raids, and they asked her endless questions as though she were some strange creature from another world. The maharajah, if he was one, kept saying, terrible, terrible, and how did people survive, which was silly, thought Anna, for what else could you do if you had no choice, and an old lady with an ear-trumpet said, 'Tell me, my dear, is it true that there is a great deal of noise?'

Dinner, served sulkily by Inge and Lotte, was unbelievably good and with her stomach delightfully full Anna almost fell asleep during the ritual listening to the nine o'clock news which followed it.

The Professor put a proper bandage on her cut hand, which everyone insisted on referring to as a wound, and by this time the dreamlike quality of the evening had so far taken over that she was not in the least surprised when Fraulein Pimke appeared in dressing-gown, slippers and hairnet to kiss everyone good night. 'Was the dinner good?' she whispered to each guest, and even the maharajah said, 'Yes,' and let her kiss his hand.

Anna was almost staggering on her feet when at last Aunt Louise took her to her room. It was clean and pretty with new sheets on the bed. Outside the window there were trees and a great calm sky. No bombs, no planes, no noise. Mama and Papa . . . she thought as her head sank into the pillows, but she was so tired and the bed was so soft that she could not finish the thought and fell asleep.

It was bright daylight when she woke up. For a moment she looked in astonishment at the white walls and flowery curtains. Then she stretched out again in the bed with a marvellous sense of well-being. She felt as though she had just recovered from a severe illness – it must be having slept all night without interruption, she thought. When she looked at her watch she found that it was nearly noon.

She got up quickly, putting on her skirt instead of her trousers (but it had been difficult to wash anything in London and it did not look much better) and went downstairs. The drawing-room was empty except for the old lady with the ear-trumpet. When she saw Anna she smiled and shouted, 'A great deal of noise, eh?'

'Yes, but not here,' Anna shouted back.

Outside the french windows she could see grey clouds moving across the sky. With luck Mama and Papa would have had a fairly quiet night. She was not hungry and anyway it was too late for breakfast, so she went outside.

The wind was strong but not cold and whirls of leaves skimmed across the terrace in front of her. At the end of the terrace was what had been a lawn, but now the damp grass coiled round her calves and even her knees as she walked through it. It was a very large lawn, and somewhere about the middle she stopped for a moment with the wind blowing round her face and the grass swaying below her. It was like being at sea and, perhaps because she had had no breakfast, she felt almost giddy with the motion.

Beyond her the grass sloped down towards a row of trees

and when she reached them she discovered a stream running beneath them. She squatted down to look at it, and
just as she did so the sun came out and the water, which
had been mud-coloured, turned a bright greeny-blue. A
small fish appeared, hardly moving above the sandy bottom
and very clear in the sudden light. She could see every
shiny scale fitting round the plump body, the round, astonished eyes, the shape of the delicate tail and fins. As it
stood among the currents it looked sometimes green and
sometimes silver and its spade-shaped mouth stretched
and shrank as it opened and closed. She sat staring at it,
almost feeling it with her eyes, but she must have moved,
for it suddenly darted away, and a moment later the sun
went in and the stream turned brown and dull again.

Some leaves floated down from the trees above her and
after a moment she got up and walked back towards the
house. She could still see the fish in her mind. If one could
paint that, she thought. The wind blew through her hair
and through the grass and, suddenly intoxicated, she
thought, and giraffes and tigers and trees and people and
all the beauty of the world!

She found most of the house-guests assembled in the
drawing-room and they all asked her if she was feeling
better, except for the old lady with the ear-trumpet who
was too busy peering through the dining-room door to see
if lunch was ready yet. Aunt Louise, worn out with the
domestic dramas of the previous night, was resting in her
room, and the maharajah was nowhere to be seen.

The Professor was talking about the old days in Berlin.

'Grandmother's birthday,' he said. 'Do you remember
how all the children use to come?'

His sister nodded. 'She used to give them all presents,'
she said.

'Thank God she didn't live to see how it all ended,' said
the Professor.

Then the door opened and the maharajah appeared,
rather to Anna's relief, for she half-thought she might
have dreamed him. He was still wearing his turban but
an ordinary dark suit, and everyone at once tried to speak
English for his sake. Only the old lady with the ear-trumpet
suddenly said loudly in German, 'She used to serve the best
gefilte fish in Prussia.'

Anna wondered whether the maids who had given notice would be serving lunch, but to her surprise they were both in the dining-room, all smiles and attention. (She discovered later that Aunt Louise had simply raised their wages.) She sat next to the maharajah who asked her again about the air raids and told her that he had been so frightened by the first one that it had made him ill, and that the Professor had brought him out to stay in the country until he could get a passage back to India.

'You are my benefactor,' he said to the Professor, pressing his hand.

'And all of us in this house,' said the red-haired lady, and the Professor looked pleased, but in a worried way, and said a little later that it was awful how food prices had risen since the war.

Anna asked where the two boys were, and the Professor's sister told her that they went to a grammar school in the nearby town but were not learning anything because all the good teachers had been called up.

'Nonsense, you fuss too much,' said the red-haired lady, which made the Professor's sister very angry, and within minutes, to Anna's surprise, everyone had been drawn into a fierce quarrel. Only the maharajah contented himself with saying, 'Education is the finest jewel in a young man's crown,' with which no one could disagree, and the old lady asked Anna to pass the gravy and quietly ate everything in sight.

On the whole it was a relief when lunch was over and most of the house-guests announced that they were going to their rooms to rest. From what? wondered Anna. It had begun to drizzle and she did not feel like going out again, so she wrote a note to Mama and washed some of her clothes in a laundry room she discovered beyond the kitchen.

When she returned to the drawing-room it was still only half-past three and there was no one in it except the old lady who had fallen asleep in her chair with her mouth open. There was a magazine on a table and Anna leafed through it, but it was all about horses and in the end she just sat. The old lady emitted a faint snore. There was a bit of fluff on her dress quite close to her mouth and every time she breathed it moved very slightly. For a while Anna watched it in the hope that something might happen –

the old lady might swallow it, or sneeze, or something—but nothing did.

The room grew slowly darker. The old lady snored and the bit of fluff moved with her breath, and Anna was beginning to feel that she had been there for ever when there was a sudden flurry of activity.

First Lotte came in with the tea trolley. The old lady who must have smelled the tea in her sleep immediately woke up. Aunt Louise, followed by the other house-guests, appeared in her long velvet gown and drew the curtains and switched on the lamps, and then the two boys burst in from school. Their mother at once began to cross-question them. Had they learned anything? What about their homework? Perhaps Anna could help them with it? But they brushed her aside with a quick look of dislike at Anna, and turned on the radio very loud.

Aunt Louise clapped her hands over her delicate ears. 'Must we have that frightful din?' she cried.

One of the boys shouted, 'I want to hear Forces' Favourites!'

Their mother, suddenly changing sides, said, 'Surely the children can have *some* pleasure!' and at once everyone became involved in another argument which continued long after the boys had crept out to listen to their programme in the kitchen. Aunt Louise said they were spoiled. Their mother said that Aunt Louise, having no children of her own, knew nothing about it. The red-haired lady said that there was a terrible atmosphere in the house—you couldn't breathe—and the old lady made a long speech which no one could understand, but which seemed to accuse some unspecified person of interfering with her sugar ration.

Anna could not think what to do, so she went over to the window and peered out into the dusk. The sun had not quite set and she could see that the sky was still overcast. If it was like this in London it shouldn't be too bad. She thought of Mama and Papa getting ready for the night. They would be wondering whether to spend it in the cellar or to risk sleeping in their beds.

Behind her, a voice cried, 'And it was just the same last week over the wellington boots!' and suddenly she wondered what on earth she was doing in this house, at this time, among these people.

All the days at the Professor's house, Anna discovered, were much like the first one. There were long periods of boredom which she filled as best she could with walks and attempts to draw, interspersed with violent rows. Except for the Professor none of the house-guests had anything to do except to wait for the next meal, the news, the end of the blitz, and as only the two boys ever seemed to leave the house they all got on each other's nerves.

It was extraordinary, thought Anna, what little things could start an argument – for instance the business over 'God Save The King'. This cropped up almost every time the radio was on and seemed quite insoluble.

It began one evening when Aunt Louise leapt to her feet and stood to attention while 'God Save The King' was being played after the news. Afterwards she told all the people who had remained seated that they were guilty of rudeness and ingratitude to the country that was giving them shelter. The Professor's sister said her sons had reliably informed her that no Englishman would ever dream of standing up for 'God Save The King' in his own home, and as usual there was a row and everyone took sides.

Anna tried to avoid the whole issue by arranging not to be in the drawing-room after the news when 'God Save The King' was most likely to be played, but the situation was made more complicated by the fact that Aunt Louise was tone-deaf. She was never quite sure whether any rousing tune she heard was really 'God Save The King' or not, and once tried to make everyone stand up for 'Rule Britannia', and twice for 'Land Of Hope And Glory'.

Then there was the great mystery of the sugar ration. This was started, needless to say, by the old lady who had been complaining for some time that her sugar ration was being tampered with, but no one took any notice until she gave a triumphant cry one morning at breakfast and said that she had proof.

To avoid arguments, the sugar rations, like the butter and margarine rations, were carefully weighed out once a week into separate little dishes, each marked with the owner's name, and the dishes were put out by Lotte on the breakfast table for people either to eke out day by day or devour all at once in one greedy feast. The old lady had cunningly marked the level of her sugar with pencil on the side of the dish, and now here it was, a good quarter of an inch lower. Roused to suspicion, the others marked their sugar also and, lo and behold, next day both the Professor's sister and the red-haired lady's husband had lost some, though everyone else's remained untouched.

The ensuing row was bitterer than any Anna had yet witnessed. The red-haired lady accused the two boys, the Professor's sister cried, 'Are you suggesting that they'd steal from their own mother?' which, Anna thought, showed a strange attitude, and Aunt Louise insisted that the Professor must interrogate the servants, as a result of which Lotte and Inge gave notice again.

The mystery was eventually cleared up. Fraulein Pimke, in the course of providing sweet puddings for dinner, had helped herself to the nearest dishes at hand. But so many unforgivable things had been said that almost no one was on speaking terms with anyone else for two days. The maharajah, as the only member of the household to remain aloof from the battle, found it very depressing. He and Anna walked glumly round the park under the dripping trees and Anna listened while he talked wistfully about India, until the cold autumn air drove them back into the house.

It was after the row about the sugar that Anna decided to return to London. She put it as tactfully as she could to Aunt Louise.

'Mama needs me,' she said, though Mama hadn't actually said so.

Even so, Aunt Louise was quite distressed. She did not want Anna to go back into the air raids and also she thought it might upset Fraulein Pimke who had become used to seeing her about the house. And what about the maids? she said. If they really left she would need all the help she could get. But characteristically, just as Anna was beginning to feel rather cross, she flung her arms about her, crying, 'I'm a fool, don't take any notice of me,' and insisted on giving her a pound for the journey.

The Professor was not driving up to London that week, so Anna went by train, which took four and a half hours instead of the scheduled fifty minutes. She had deliberately not told Mama that she was coming because Mama and Papa had both urged her in their letters to stay in the country as long as possible, and she did not want to give them the chance to argue with her.

As the train drew into London she could see gaps in almost every street where bombs had fallen, and there were no windows left in any of the houses backing on to the railway line. Paddington Station had lost all the grimy glass in its roof and it was strange to be able to see sky and clouds beyond the blackened girders. Some sparrows were fluttering in and out among them, swooping down every so often to the platforms in search of crumbs.

The streets were empty – it was early afternoon and everyone was at work – and from her bus crawling along the Euston Road Anna noticed that weeds had begun to grow on some of the bomb-sites, which made them look as though they had been there for years. Altogether the city looked scarred but undramatic, as though it had become used to being bombed.

In Bedford Terrace almost half the houses had been boarded up and abandoned, but the Hotel Continental did not seem to have suffered any further damage and some of the windows had even been repaired. She found Papa in his room – Mama was still at her office – in the middle of typing something on his shaky typewriter.

'Why didn't you stay in the country?' he cried, but since she was there and there was nothing he could do about it, he was clearly delighted to see her. Mama's reaction, an hour or two later, was much the same. Neither of them seemed altogether surprised. Of course, thought Anna, they knew the Rosenbergs a good deal better than she did.

There were fewer people than ever in the hotel. The German lady, Mama told her, had not been able to stop crying after that very bad night in the cellar, and in the end a doctor had sent her to a charitable institution in the country where she would be looked after until her nerves recovered. The porter, too, had left, to stay with his brother in Leicester, and so had many of the staff and guests. The ones who remained looked grey-faced and weary, even though Mama and Papa insisted that since the changeable autumn weather they were getting quite a lot of sleep.

Supper was almost a family affair. The Woodpigeon made a little speech to welcome Anna back. 'Though you are a foolish girl,' he said, 'for not staying in the beautiful countryside with the sheeps and the grasses.'

'Really, Mr Woodpigeon,' said Frau Gruber who could pronounce his name no more than anyone else, 'your English is getting worse each day.'

The air-raid warning did not sound until some time after dark and Mama waved it aside contemptuously.

'They won't come tonight,' she said. 'There's too much cloud.'

'I don't see how you can be so sure,' said Papa, but everyone else seemed ready to accept Mama as an expert, and it was decided not to sleep in the cellar.

Anna found that she had been given a room on the first floor, next to Mama. ('No point in sleeping under the roof when the whole hotel is empty,' said Frau Gruber.) She had been worried that she might get very frightened again during the night, but her rest in the country must have done her good, for the few bumps which woke her did not trouble her at all, and even the following night which had to be spent in the cellar was not too bad.

When she returned to the secretarial school she found that it had acquired a new air of purposeful activity. Madame Laroche, thinner and more excitable than ever, had taken over the reins again and her incomprehensible Belgian accents could be heard in every classroom. There was paper for the machines again – someone had unearthed an English source of supply – and there were even some new students.

No one talked about air raids any more. They had become part of everyday life and were no longer interesting. Instead, all the talk was about jobs. There was a sudden demand for shorthand typists since London had come to terms with the bombing, and Madame Laroche had pinned up a list of vacant positions on a notice board in the corridor.

'How soon do you think I could get a job?' Anna asked her, and to her delight she replied something that sounded like 'get back into practice' followed by 'a few weeks'. In fact Anna's shorthand came back to her very quickly and one morning about ten days after her return she said proudly to Mama, 'I'm going to ring up about a job from school today. So if anyone asks me to go for an interview I may be home late.' She felt very grand saying this, and as soon as the first lesson was over she made for the school telephone with a copy of Madame Laroche's list and a shilling's worth of pennies.

The best jobs were at the War Office. A girl Anna knew had just been taken on there at three pounds ten shillings a week, and she only spoke mediocre French. So what wouldn't they pay someone like herself, thought Anna, with perfect French and German? And indeed, when she rang up and explained her qualifications the voice at the other end sounded enthusiastic.

'Absolutely splendid,' it cried in a military sort of way. 'Can you come round at o-eleven hundred hours for an interview?'

'Yes,' said Anna, and one part of her was still trying to work out what on earth was meant by o-eleven hundred hours while another part was announcing to Mama that she had a job at four pounds or even four pounds ten a week, when the voice said as an afterthought, 'I take it that you're British-born?'

'No,' said Anna, 'I was born in Germany, but my father . . .'

'Sorry,' said the voice, several degrees cooler. 'Only British-born applicants can be considered.'

'But we're anti-Nazi!' cried Anna. 'We've been anti-Nazis long before anyone else!'

'Sorry,' said the voice. 'Regulations – nothing I can do.' And it rang off.

How idiotic, thought Anna. She was so disappointed that it took her some time before she could rouse herself to ring up the Ministry of Information, which was her second choice, but the reply she received was the same. No one could be considered unless they were British-born.

Surely, she thought with a sinking feeling in her stomach, everyone can't have that rule, but it appeared that they did. There were six large organizations on Madame Laroche's list, all appealing for secretaries, and none would even grant her an interview. After the last one had refused her she stood for a moment by the telephone, completely at a loss. Then she went to see Madame Laroche.

'Madame,' she said, 'you told me that I would get a job

at the end of this course, but none of the people on your list will even see me because I'm not British.'

Madame Laroche's reply was difficult to follow as usual. The regulations about British nationality were new – or perhaps they were not new, but Madame Laroche had hoped that by now they might have been waived. Whatever it was, the one thing to emerge clearly was that it was hopeless for Anna to go on trying.

'But, Madame,' said Anna, 'I must have a job. That was my one reason for coming here. You told me that I would get a job, and I told my mother this morning . . .' She stopped, for what she had told Mama was really nothing to do with it, but even so she had the greatest difficulty in keeping her composure.

'Well, there's nothing I can do about it now,' said Madame Laroche unhelpfully in French, whereupon Anna, to her surprise, heard herself say, 'But you'll have to !'

'*Comment?*' said Madame Laroche, looking at her with dislike.

Anna stared back at her.

Madame Laroche mumbled something under her breath and began to rummage among the papers on her desk. Finally she extracted one and muttered something about a cross, red colonel.

'Won't he object to my nationality?' asked Anna, but Madame Laroche thrust the piece of paper into her hand and cried, 'Go ! Go ! Ring up at once !'

Back at the telephone Anna looked at the paper. It said 'The Hon. Mrs Hammond, Colonel of the British Red Cross Society', and gave an address off the Vauxhall Bridge Road. She borrowed two more pennies and dialled the number. The voice that answered was gruff and brisk, but it did not ask whether she was British-born and suggested that she should come for an interview that afternoon.

She spent the rest of the day in fidgety anticipation. She wondered whether to ring Mama and let her know that she was going for an interview but decided not to, in case nothing came of it. At lunch she could not face her usual meal of a bun and a cup of tea at Lyons and wandered about the streets instead, eyeing her reflection in the few remaining shop windows and worrying whether she looked sufficiently like a secretary. At last, when the time arrived, she got there far too early and had to walk up and down the Vauxhall Bridge Road for the best part of half an hour.

It was not a very attractive neighbourhood. There was a brewery at one end and the sour smell of hops pervaded the entire district. Trams shrieked and clattered along the middle of the road. All the shops had been boarded up and abandoned.

Mrs Hammond's office turned out to be a little apart from all this, in a bomb-damaged hospital overlooking a large square, and after the noise of the main road it seemed very quiet when Anna finally rang her bell. She was admitted by a woman in an overall who led her through a vast, dark place which must have been one of the wards, through a smaller brightly-lit room where half a dozen elderly women were rattling away on sewing machines and to a tiny office where the Hon. Mrs Hammond was sitting stoutly behind a desk surrounded by skeins of wool. Her grey hair was covered with fluff and the wool seemed to have climbed all over her, hanging from her chair and her blue-uniformed lap and lying in coils on the floor.

'Damn these things!' she cried as Anna came in. 'I've lost count of them again. Are you any good at arithmetic?'

Anna said she thought so and Mrs Hammond said, 'Jolly good. And what else can you do?' causing Anna to list her accomplishments from her School Certificate results to her ability to take down shorthand in three languages. As she went nervously through them Mrs Hammond's face fell.

'It won't do!' she cried. 'You'd hate it – you'd be bored stiff!'

'I don't see why,' said Anna, but Mrs Hammond shook her head.

'Languages,' she cried. 'Got no use for them here. You want somewhere like the War Office. Crazy for girls like you – French, German, Hindustani – all that.'

'I've tried the War Office,' said Anna, 'but they won't have me.'

Mrs Hammond absent-mindedly tried to unfasten a loop of wool which had wound itself round a button on her tunic. 'Why?' she said. 'What's wrong with you?'

Anna took a deep breath. 'I'm not English,' she said.

'Ha! Irish!' cried Mrs Hammond and added reproachfully, 'You've got green eyes.'

'No,' said Anna, 'German.'

'German?'

'German-Jewish. My father is an anti-Nazi writer. We left Germany in 1933 . . .' She was suddenly sick of explaining, having to justify herself. 'My father's name was on the first black list published by the Nazis,' she said quite loudly. 'After we'd escaped from Germany they offered a reward for his capture, dead or alive. I'm hardly likely, therefore, to sabotage the British war effort. But it's extraordinary how difficult it is to convince anyone of this.'

There was a pause. Then Mrs Hammond said, 'How old are you?'

'Sixteen,' said Anna.

'I see,' said Mrs Hammond. She stood up, scattering wool in all directions like a dog shaking water out of its fur. 'Well now,' she said. 'Why don't we have a look at what the job consists of?'

She led Anna to some shelves stacked with bulky packets up to the ceiling.

'Wool,' she said.

Then she pointed to a filing cabinet and flicked open a drawer full of record cards.

'Little women,' she said, and as Anna looked puzzled, 'They knit. All over the country.'

'I see,' said Anna.

'Send the wool to the little women. Little women knit it up into scarves, socks, Balaclava helmets, what have you. Send them back to us. We send them to chaps in the Forces who need them. That's all.'

'I see,' said Anna again.

'Not very difficult, you see,' said Mrs Hammond. 'No need for languages – unless of course we sent some to the Free French. Never heard of them being short of woollies, though.' She gestured towards the room with the sewing machines. 'Then there's the old ladies out there. Bit more responsibility.'

'What do they do?' asked Anna.

'Make pyjamas, bandages, all that, for hospitals. They live round about and come in. All voluntary, you understand. Have to give them Bovril in the morning and tea and biscuits in the afternoon.'

Anna nodded.

'Fact is,' said Mrs Hammond, 'it's all jolly useful. Found

out from my own son in the Air Force — never got any woollies, always cold. And I do need someone to help. Think you could do it?'

'I think so,' said Anna. It was not exactly what she had hoped for, but she liked Mrs Hammond and it was a job. 'How . . .' she stammered, 'I mean, how much . . . ?'

Mrs Hammond smote her forehead. 'Most important part of the business!' she cried. 'I was going to pay three pounds, but reckon you could get more with all those languages. Say three pounds ten a week — that suit you?'

'Oh yes!' cried Anna. 'That would be fine.'

'Start on Monday, then,' said Mrs Hammond and added, as she ushered her out, 'Look forward to seeing you.'

Anna rode triumphantly down the Vauxhall Bridge Road on one of the clattering trams. It was getting dusk and by the time she had walked to Hyde Park Corner the stairs leading down to the tube were crowded with people seeking shelter for the night. Quite a few had already spread out their bedding on the platform, and you had to be careful where you stepped. At Holborn there were people sitting on bunks against the walls as well as on the floor and a woman in green uniform was selling cups of tea from a trolley. At one end a knot of people had gathered round a man with a mouth organ to sing 'Roll Out The Barrel' and an old man in a peaked cap called out, 'Good night, lovely!' as she passed.

The sirens sounded just as she turned into Bedford Terrace and she raced them to the door of the Hotel Continental, through the lounge and up the stairs, to burst breathlessly into Mama's room. There was a droning sound, announcing the approach of the bombers.

'Mama!' she cried as the first bomb burst, some distance away, 'Mama! I've got a job!'

CHAPTER 12

Anna almost did not start her job on the following Monday after all, because something happened.

It was on the Friday. Max had come on one of his rare visits and was staying the night, and though there had not been very much to eat for supper – food rationing was getting stricter – they had sat over it a long time with Max talking about his life as a schoolmaster which he quite enjoyed, and Anna talking about her job.

'The lady is called the Hon. Mrs Hammond,' she said proudly. 'She must be related to some kind of a lord. And she's paying me three pounds ten a week.'

Mama nodded. 'For the first time we can look ahead a little.'

Her face was pinker and more relaxed than Anna had seen it for some time. It was partly because Max was there, but also because the November mists had finally arrived and they had been able to sleep in their beds two nights running. Tonight, too, the sky was heavy with clouds and Max who was not used to London had been much impressed with Mama's careless dismissal of the air-raid warning.

By the time they went to bed it was quite late and Anna fell asleep almost immediately.

She dreamed about the Hon. Mrs Hammond, whose office had inexplicably become entirely filled with wool which Anna and Mrs Hammond were trying to disentangle. Anna had got hold of an end and was trying to see where it led and Mrs Hammond was saying, 'You have to follow the sound,' and then Anna noticed that the wool was giving out a curious humming like a swarm of mosquitoes or an aeroplane. She pulled gently at the piece in her hand and the humming turned at once into a violent screeching.

'I'm sorry, I didn't mean . . .' she began, but the screeching grew louder and louder and came closer and closer and then it drew her right inside itself and she and Mrs Hammond were flying through the air and there was a shattering crash and she found herself on the floor in a corner of her room at the Hotel Continental.

All round her were fragments of glass from the shattered window – that's the third lot of windows gone, she thought – and the floor was grey with plaster from the ceiling. I mustn't cut myself this time, she thought, and felt carefully for her shoes, so as to be able to walk through the broken glass to the door. As she put them on, her hands were shaking – but that's just shock, she thought. There hadn't really been time to be frightened.

The landing was a mess with a lamp hanging from its socket and plaster all over the floor, and Max and Mama appeared on it almost immediately.

Max was furious. 'You said,' he shouted at Mama, 'that the Germans wouldn't come tonight!'

'Well, they didn't!' cried Mama. 'Only just that one!'

'For God's sake!' Max shouted, pointing to the confusion about them. 'Look what he's done!'

'Well, how was I to know,' cried Mama, 'that the one German plane over London tonight would drop a bomb straight on us? I can't be responsible for every madman who takes to the air in the middle of a fog! It's easy for you to criticize . . .'

'For God's sake,' said Max again. 'We might all have been killed!' – and at this the same realization hit all three of them.

'Papa!' cried Anna and rushed along the passage to his room.

The door was jammed, but there was a scuffling sound inside and after a moment the door was wrenched open and Papa appeared. He was black with dust and there was plaster all over his hair and his pyjamas, but he was all right. Behind him, Anna could see that most of his ceiling had collapsed and that it was only the presence of the heavy wardrobe which had prevented it from crashing down on his bed.

'Are you hurt?' cried Mama, close behind her.

'No,' said Papa, and then they all stood and looked at the wreckage that had been his room.

Papa shook his head sadly. 'To think,' he said, 'that I'd just tidied up my desk!'

Miraculously no one was hurt except for cuts and bruises, but the whole hotel was in chaos. There were ceilings down everywhere, the heating no longer worked, and downstairs in the lounge the wind blew through gaps where doorposts and window frames no longer fitted into the walls. The bomb had fallen on the adjoining house, fortunately empty, and fortunately it had been a very small bomb. ('You see!' cried Mama, still smarting from Max's criticism, 'I told you it wasn't a proper one!') But the damage looked to be beyond repair.

The experts from the Council who came round later thought so too.

'No use trying to fit this place up again,' they told Frau Gruber. 'For one thing it wouldn't be safe. You'd best find somewhere else,' and Frau Gruber nodded, sensibly, as though it were the most ordinary thing in the world, and you had to look quite closely to notice the twitching of a muscle near her mouth as she said, 'It was my livelihood, you know.'

'You'll get compensation,' said the man from the Council. 'Best thing would be if you could find another house.'

'Otherwise we all shall be without a roof on our head,' said the Woodpigeon sadly, and the rest of the guests looked hopefully towards Frau Gruber as though she were capable of producing one out of a hat.

It was curious, thought Anna – ever since the beginning of the blitz everyone had known that this might happen, but now that it had no one knew what to do. How did one find a new home in a bomb-shattered city?

In the middle of it all Aunt Louise rang up. She was in London for the day and wanted Mama to have lunch with her. When Mama explained what had happened she cried at once, 'My dear, you must buy the maharajah's place!'

Mama said rather tartly that Frau Gruber was looking for a house in London, not a place in India, but Aunt Louise took no notice.

'I believe,' she said, 'that it's in Putney,' and announced that since the maharajah was with her she would bring him round at once.

'Really,' said Papa when Mama told him, 'couldn't you have stopped her?'

He and Max had been moving his belongings out of the wrecked room into another that was less badly damaged. The hotel had grown very cold and no one had had any sleep since the bomb had fallen. The prospect of having to cope with Aunt Louise on top of everything else seemed too much to be borne.

'You know what Louise is like,' said Mama, and went off to warn Frau Gruber.

When they arrived, the maharajah in his turban and Aunt Louise in a beautiful black fur coat, they looked like visitors from another world, but Frau Gruber received them with no sign of astonishment. Perhaps she felt, since the bomb, that anything could happen.

'You are the first maharajah I have met,' she said in matter of fact tones and led him off to what remained of her office.

'Really, Louise,' said Mama in the freezing lounge, 'this is a mad idea of yours. She could never afford the sort of money he'd want.'

'Oh dear, do you think so?' cried Aunt Louise. 'And I thought it would be such a help. He really wants to sell the house, you know, because he's going back to India at last. And he is,' she added, 'only quite a *small* maharajah, so it might not be so expensive.'

Then she went on to urge all of them and especially Anna to come down to the country for a rest, but Anna explained about her job and Mama said wearily that they must first find a new home, as it was clearly impossible to stay on in the hotel for more than a few days.

'Just when Anna had got settled,' she said. 'Why does something always have to go wrong!'

Aunt Louise patted her hand and said, 'Don't worry,' and just then Frau Gruber and the maharajah came back into the lounge smiling.

'Well,' said the maharajah, tucking his hand under Frau Gruber's arm, 'shall we go and have a look at the place?'

'What did I tell you?' cried Aunt Louise, and added quickly, 'First we must have lunch.'

They ate at a restaurant which Aunt Louise knew and even had a bottle of wine which made everyone feel more cheerful – in fact Frau Gruber became quite merry – and the maharajah paid the bill. Afterwards Max had to go back to his school, but the rest of them went to see the house in Aunt Louise's car.

Anna was surprised to see how far away it was. They seemed to drive past endless rows of little houses all looking the same, until they crossed the Thames to reach a narrow road lined with shops.

The maharajah pointed fondly. 'Putney High Street,' he said.

It was a dark afternoon, even though it was nowhere near sunset, and the shops were lit up, which gave the street an almost peace-time look. Anna caught a whiff of frying as they drove past a chip shop, there was a Woolworth's and a Marks and Spencer's and people everywhere were doing their weekend shopping. There was far less bomb damage than in the centre of London, and as the car left the High Street and drove up a hill flanked by large houses and gardens it began to smell almost like the country.

The maharajah's house was in a tree-lined side street – very big and spacious with about a dozen bedrooms and surrounded by a neglected garden. For a single person it must have been enormous, but for a hotel or a guest house Anna supposed it would be quite modest. It was empty except for the curtains on the windows and a few forgotten objects – a tall brass vase, a carved stool and, astonishingly, a flight of plaster ducks carefully pinned above a mantelpiece.

They walked slowly from room to room in the fading light and the maharajah explained the workings of the electricity, the blackout arrangements, the hot-water boiler, and every so often Frau Gruber would query something and they would go back and look at it all over again.

'I must say, it all seems very convenient,' she said several times, and then the maharajah would cry, 'Wait till you see the kitchen!' – or the scullery, or the second bathroom. All the downstairs rooms were dominated by the wild garden which lay outside the french windows, and when Frau Gruber said, for the third time, 'I just want to have another look at the kitchen range,' Papa and Anna left the rest of them to it and went out into the wintry dampness.

Mist was hanging like a sheet in the trees and there were fallen leaves everywhere. They clung to Anna's feet as she followed Papa along a path which led them to a wooden bench at the edge of what had once been a lawn. Papa wiped the seat with his handkerchief and they sat down.

'It's a big garden,' said Anna and Papa nodded.

The mist was drifting across the long grass and the bushes, making everything beyond them uncertain, so that it seemed as though there were no end to it. Anna felt suddenly unreal.

'To think . . .' she said.

'What?' said Papa.

There was a clump of leaves stuck to one of her shoes and she removed it carefully with the other before she answered, 'Last night must have been about the closest we've been to getting killed.'

'Yes,' said Papa. 'If that German airman had dropped his bomb a fraction of a second earlier or later – we wouldn't be sitting in this garden.'

It was strange, thought Anna. The garden would still be there in the mist, but she would not know about it.

'It's difficult to imagine,' she said, 'everything going on without one.'

Papa nodded. 'But it does,' he said. 'If we were dead, people would still have breakfast and ride on buses and there would still be birds and trees and children going to school and misty gardens like this one. It's a kind of comfort.'

'But one would miss it so,' said Anna.

Papa looked at her fondly. 'You wouldn't exist.'

'I know,' said Anna. 'But I can't imagine it. I can't imagine being so dead that I wouldn't be able to think about it all – the way it looks and smells and feels – and missing it all quite terribly.'

They sat in silence and Anna watched a leaf drift slowly, slowly down from a tree until it settled among the others in the grass.

'For quite a long time last summer,' she said, 'I didn't think we'd live even till now. Did you?'

'No,' said Papa.

'I didn't see how we could. And it seemed so awful to die before one had even had time to find out what one could do – before one had really had time to try. But now . . .'

'Now it's November,' said Papa, 'and the invasion hasn't happened.' He put his hand over hers. 'Now,' he said, 'I think there's a chance.'

Then the gravel crunched behind them and Mama appeared through the mist.

'There you are!' she cried. 'Louise wants to leave, so as to get out of town before dark. But the maharajah is coming back tomorrow to fix the final details with Frau Gruber. She's going to take the house. Don't you think it's a nice place?'

Anna got up from the seat and Papa followed her.

'We've been appreciating it,' he said.

There seemed to be less room in the car on the way back. Anna sat squeezed between Papa and the driver, and it was hot and stuffy. Behind her the maharajah and Frau Gruber were talking about the house, with Mama and Aunt Louise chipping in. As the car crawled through the dusky suburbs the street names mingled with scraps of conversation into a hypnotic mixture which almost sent her to sleep. Walham Crescent . . . St Anne's Villas . . . Parsons Green Road . . . '. . . such a very useful sink,' said Frau Gruber, and Mama replied, '. . . and in the summer, the garden . . .'

There was a spatter of rain on the windscreen. She rested her head on Papa's shoulder, and the grey road and the grey houses sped past.

Everything is going to be different, she thought. I'm going to have a job, and we'll live in a house in Putney, and we'll have enough money to pay the bills, and perhaps we'll all survive the war and I shall grow up, and then . . .

But it was too difficult to imagine what would happen then, and probably rather unlucky, too, she thought, with the next air raid not far away, and as the strain of the previous night caught up with her she fell asleep.

Part Two

CHAPTER 13

Compared with the summer, the winter was almost cosy. For one thing, the air raids abated. There were several nights in December when the sirens did not sound at all, and when the Germans did come over bombs rarely fell on Putney. As a result you could sleep in your bed every night, and though some nights were noisier than others, the desperate tiredness that had been part of everyday life gradually receded.

The house in Putney was friendlier than the Hotel Continental and it seemed a great luxury to have a garden.

'In the summer we'll get some deck-chairs,' said Frau Gruber, but even in the winter the Woodpigeon and the other Poles, Czechs and Germans walked admiringly among the dead leaves and on the overgrown lawn.

The only thing Anna did not like was that she had to share a room with Mama. There were almost no single rooms in the house, and she could see that Papa, who was home all day, needed a place of his own to write in – but she still hated never being alone. However, there was nothing to be done about it, so she tried not to think about it more than she could help.

Most of the time her mind was on her job. It was not difficult, but she was nervous about it to begin with. Her first day had been an agony – not only because she was afraid of making some disastrous mistake, but because she had discovered two days before that she had caught lice in the tube. This was not uncommon – there was an epidemic of lice among the shelterers and it was only too easy to pick them up. But just before starting a new job!

Mama had rushed to get her some evil-smelling brown liquid from the chemist and she had spent the weekend trying to wash the lice out of her hair in the bombed hotel. At the end her hair had seemed to be clear, but just the same she had been haunted, the whole of her first day as a secretary, by the possibility that one louse – just one – might have escaped, and that it would emerge from her hair and walk across her ear or her neck just as the Hon. Mrs Hammond was looking at her. She was so worried about this that she kept rushing to the lavatory to examine her hair in the mirror, until one of the old ladies on the sewing machines asked her quite kindly if she had a tummy upset. Fortunately the Hon. Mrs Hammond put down her nervousness to the fact that she had so recently been bombed, and once Anna was convinced that all the lice had really been exterminated she was able to concentrate on the job and do it quite well.

There was not really much to it. First thing in the morning she would go through the post, unpack whatever woollies had arrived and send off more wool to the knitters. Then she would put out the half-made pyjamas and bandages for the old ladies who came in about ten, and the sewing machines would begin to hum.

She had to be careful about allocating the work, for the old ladies were quick to take offence. Different ones came on different days, but the most regular were Miss Clinton-Brown who was tall and religious, little Miss Potter who talked only about her budgie, and Mrs Riley who said she was a retired actress but had really been in music hall and who wore a frightful fringed shawl and smelled, causing the more genteel ladies to avert their noses.

They were always trying to persuade Mrs Hammond to get rid of her, but she was too good a worker.

'Bit niffy, I agree,' said Mrs Hammond, 'but chaps in hospital won't mind that. Pyjamas get washed before they wear them, anyway.'

Mrs Hammond's arrival about eleven was the high point of the morning. As soon as they heard her taxi draw up the old ladies began to twitter and to preen themselves, and as she walked into the sewing-room their heads would be bent over their work and the machines would be racing along at twice their normal speed.

'Morning, ladies!' she would cry, and this was Anna's cue to pour the boiling water on the Bovril and hand it round. Mrs Hammond's mug went in her office, but to the ladies' delight she often carried it back into the sewing-room and chatted with them while she drank it. She lived at Claridge's Hotel during the week – at weekends she went back to her estate in the country – and met all sorts of famous people and her careless mention of their names turned the old ladies quite dizzy with excitement.

'Met Queen Wilhelmina last night,' she would say. 'Poor old thing – quite dotty.' Or, 'Heard Mr Churchill speak at a dinner – marvellous man, but no taller than I am, you know,' and the ladies would repeat the information to each other, rolling it round their tongues and enjoying the dottiness of the Dutch queen and the small stature of Mr Churchill for the rest of the week.

After the Bovril she would call Anna into her office and dictate letters to her until lunch time, and Anna would spend the afternoon typing them. The letters were mostly to high-ranking officers in the Forces, all of whom Mrs Hammond appeared to have known since childhood, and who wanted her to send them woollies for the men in their command. She nearly always managed to give them what they wanted.

Once or twice there was a note to her son Dickie who was in the Air Force, trying to become a navigator and finding it very difficult.

'Poor fellow's got enough to do working out sums without deciphering my scrawl,' she would say, and dictate a brief, affectionate message of encouragement, to be accompanied by a small gift like a pair of Air Force blue socks or gloves.

Once he came to the office and Mrs Hammond introduced him to Anna – a stocky, open-faced boy of about nineteen, with a stammer. He was taking an exam the next day and was worried about it.

'You'll pass all right,' cried Mrs Hammond. 'You always do, in the end!' and he grinned at her ruefully. 'T-trouble is,' he said, 'I have t-to work t-twice as hard as everyone else.'

Mrs Hammond slapped his back affectionately. 'Poor old chap!' she shouted. 'No head for scholarship – but jolly good with animals, I can tell you. No one better than Dickie,' she explained to Anna, 'with a sick cow!'

At the end of every week Anna collected her wages and paid Frau Gruber two pounds five shillings for her room. Fifteen shillings went on fares, lunches and necessities like toothpaste and shoe repairs, five shillings to Madame Laroche to pay for the shorthand machine which had not been included in the tuition fees, and the remaining five shillings she saved. By May, she calculated, she would have paid Madame Laroche back and she would be able to save ten shillings a week. It seemed to her a wonderfully lavish income.

Mrs Hammond was kind to her in an amused sort of way. Sometimes she asked Anna if she was all right, if she liked the new boarding-house in Putney, if Papa had any work. But she insisted on keeping her German background a secret, especially from the old ladies.

'Old biddies wouldn't understand,' she said. 'Probably suspect you of sabotaging the Balaclava helmets.'

Once, when Max was in London during the Easter holidays she took them both to a film.

Afterwards he said, 'I like your Mrs Hammond. But don't you ever get bored?'

He had had to wait for Anna at the office and had watched her typing letters and parcelling up wool.

She looked at him without comprehension. 'No,' she said. She was wearing a new green sweater, bought with her own money. She had nearly paid back the money for the shorthand machine, and that morning Mrs Hammond had introduced her to a visiting colonel as 'my young assistant – practically runs this place single-handed'. What could be boring about that?

As the weather grew warmer the fear of invasion also grew again – until one day in June, soon after Anna's seventeenth birthday, when there was an announcement on the radio which staggered everyone. The Germans had attacked Russia.

'But I thought the Russians and the Germans were allies!' cried Anna.

Papa raised one eyebrow. 'So did the Russians,' he said.

It was clear that if the Germans had opened up a new Russian front they could not at the same time invade England, and there was a great rejoicing in the office. The Bovril session was extended to nearly an hour while Mrs Hammond quoted a general who had told her that the Germans could not last a month against Stalin. Miss Clinton-Brown thanked God; Miss Potter said she had taught her budgie to say, 'Down with Stalin,' and was worried whether this might now be misunderstood; and Mrs Riley rose suddenly from her chair, grabbed a pole used for putting up the blackout and demonstrated how she had posed as Britannia at the Old Bedford Music Hall in 1918.

After this Anna and Mrs Hammond retired to her office, but they had scarcely got through half a dozen letters when they were again interrupted. This time it was Dickie, on unexpected leave, wearing a brand-new officer's uniform.

'P-passed all my exams, Ma,' he said. 'Second from the b-bottom, but I p-passed. F-fully f-fledged navigating Officer Hammond!'

At this Mrs Hammond was so delighted that she gave up all thoughts of further work and invited Anna to join them for lunch.

'We'll go home,' she said, which meant Claridge's.

Anna had only been there once before, to deliver some letters which Mrs Hammond had forgotten at the office, and then she had only got as far as the hall porter. Now she was swept along in Mrs Hammond's wake, across the heavily carpeted foyer, through the swing doors and into the pillared dining-room, where they were met by the head waiter ('Good morning, Mrs Hammond, good morning, Mr Richard') and escorted to their table. All round them were people in uniform, mostly very grand ones, talking, eating and drinking, and the hum of their conversation filled the room.

'Drinkies!' cried Mrs Hammond, and a glass of what Anna decided must be gin appeared in front of her. She did not like it much, but she drank it, and then the waiter brought the food and as she worked her way through a large piece of chicken she began to feel very happy. There was no need for her to say anything, for Mrs Hammond and Dickie were talking about the estate and about a dog of Dickie's in particular ('Are you sure,' he was asking, 'that W-Wilson has w-wormed him?'), so she looked around the room and was the first to notice a thin man in Air Force uniform bearing down on them. There was a great deal of gold braid about him and as soon as Dickie saw him he leapt from his chair and saluted. The man nodded and smiled briefly, but his attention was on Mrs Hammond.

'Boots!' he cried, and she answered delightedly, 'Jack! How lovely! Come and sit down!'

She introduced him to Dickie and Anna as an Air Chief Marshal of whom even Anna had heard, and ordered another round of gin, and then the Air Chief Marshal ordered a third, to celebrate the news about Russia.

'Best thing that's happened in the war,' he said, 'since we beat the bastards off last September,' and plunged into a long conversation with Mrs Hammond about the effects of this new development.

Anna's feeling of happiness had increased with each gin, until now it was like a vast smile in which she was entirely enveloped, but Dickie was looking at her and she felt she ought to say something.

'I'm so sorry your dog isn't well,' she brought out at last, a little indistinctly, and immediately found a wave of pity sweep over her for the poor animal which perhaps hadn't been wormed when it needed to be.

Dickie looked at her gratefully. 'B-bit of a worry,' he admitted, and started to tell her about the dog's lack of appetite, the state of its coat (why does it have a coat? thought Anna, until she remembered that he must mean its fur), and his lack of confidence in Wilson's judgment. Then there were the horses, too, and the cows. It was difficult, nowadays, to find chaps who looked after them properly. He sat there in his new officer's tunic, fretting about it all, and Anna listened and nodded and thought how nice he was and how nice to have lunch at Claridge's with an Air Chief Marshal, and how nice that the Germans had attacked the Russians and would not now be invading England.

And when the Air Chief Marshal, on leaving, congratulated Dickie on his attractive girl-friend, that was nice too, and rather funny, but an even funnier thing happened after he had gone.

'Ma,' said Dickie reproachfully, 'that m-man is in charge of a third of the Air F-force. Why does he call you Boots?' And Mrs Hammond answered in an astonished voice, 'Always has done. Ever since we went to dancing lessons together when we were five and I used to trample all over his feet.'

At this Anna laughed so much that she found it difficult to stop and Mrs Hammond said, 'Good God – we've made the poor child tight!'

She gave her some black coffee and then she drove her to Bond Street tube station, where she told her to take the afternoon off.

'My apologies to your Mama,' she said. 'But what with the Russian front and Dickie getting his commission . . .'

The rest of the sentence seemed somehow to have escaped her, and Anna suddenly noticed that Mrs Hammond's speech, too, was less precise than usual.

'Anyway,' cried Mrs Hammond, retreating a little unsteadily into the car, 'it was a damned good party!'

Anna still thought the story about the Air Chief Marshal quite funny after the effects of the gin had worn off, and she told Max about it the next time she saw him. By this time it was July and Max was in deep gloom. The summer term was nearly over and he did not want to embark on a second year's teaching, but all his enquiries about getting into the Forces had brought only discouraging replies.

The Army and the Navy had firm rules forbidding the acceptance of foreign nationals. The Air Force, being a younger Service, had no such rule but didn't accept them anyway. Max had more or less given up hope, but when he heard the Air Chief Marshal's name he pricked up his ears.

'If I could talk to him —' he said. 'Do you think Mrs Hammond would give me an introduction?'

'Well, I could ask her,' said Anna doubtfully, but in fact Mrs Hammond did much more.

On the following Monday, after Anna had explained the situation to her, she rang the Air Chief Marshal in her presence, cutting through secretaries, adjutants and personal assistants as a ship cuts through the waves.

'Jack,' she said. 'Got a rather special young man I want you to meet. Can you have lunch?' Then, in answer to a question from the other end of the telephone, 'I should think very bright indeed.' This was followed by some chat about the war, a reference to Dickie who had just been posted to his first operational squadron, and a joke about the dancing class, until the conversation ended with a laugh and an inexplicable shout of 'Tally-ho!'

'Well, that's settled,' said Mrs Hammond. 'Max and I are having lunch with Jack.'

The appointment had been fixed for a day nearly a fortnight away and Max was very nervous about it. He decided to learn as much as possible about aeroplanes in the meantime, and his pupils were set endless essays to write in class while he studied the characteristics of everything from Tiger Moths to Messerschmitts, and a book about the theory of flight for good measure.

Papa encouraged him in this. 'Such an Air Chief Marshal,' he said, 'will expect you to be well informed.' But Mama refused to consider that there might be any difficulty.

'Of course the Air Chief Marshal will make an exception for you,' she said, to Max's rage.

'But you don't know that!' he cried. 'And if he doesn't, I don't know what I'll do!'

Anna just kept her fingers crossed. She knew that if Max didn't get into the Air Force he would feel it was the end of the world.

A few days before Max's appointment she was unpacking some woollies in the office. One of them was an Air Force sweater and she was holding it up, wondering whether Max would soon be wearing one like it, when Mrs Riley came in with a face wrapped in gloom.

'Terrible news,' she said.

'About what?' said Anna. There had been nothing special on the radio.

Mrs Riley waved a tragic hand. 'Poor lady,' she said. 'Poor, poor Mrs Hammond. And there she was yesterday, as happy as a sandboy.'

Mrs Riley was always making dramas out of nothing, so Anna said irritably, 'What's happened to her?' not expecting to hear anything that mattered.

She was shattered when Mrs Riley replied, 'Her son has been killed in his aeroplane.'

Dickie, she thought, with his nice, not-too-bright face and his worries about the cows and the horses. It hadn't even been an operational flight, just a practice one. The plane had stalled and crashed, and all the crew had died. Mr Hammond had brought the news late the previous afternoon – Anna had already left to post some parcels – and then he had taken Mrs Hammond home.

'Their only child,' said Miss Clinton-Brown, who had arrived just after Mrs Riley.

Anna tried to think of something to say, but there was nothing. What could you say about the death of this decent, simple person?

'He was the glory of his squadron,' said Mrs Riley,

striking an attitude. But that was just what he hadn't been and for some reason it made it worse.

There was nothing to do but to carry on as usual. The old ladies hardly spoke while they raced their machines up and down the seams, as though a larger turn-out of pyjamas would somehow make up to Mrs Hammond for her loss. Anna decided to tidy up the stock of knitting wool and it was not until half-way through the morning that she remembered about Max. What would happen about that now?

When no news came from Mrs Hammond except a message through her chauffeur asking everyone to keep going in her absence, she decided to ring Max at the end of the day.

'I don't think she'll want to keep the appointment,' she said, and could feel Max's depression like a miasma leaking down the telephone. 'And I think that's a very good thing!' she cried, with a sudden vivid memory of Dickie smiling and talking about his dog only such a short time ago.

Max said blankly, 'If you speak to Mrs Hammond please tell her how sorry I am. But if I don't hear from you I'll come anyway, just in case.'

The next few days in the office were full of gloom. The Bovril sessions were the worst times. The old ladies would sit sipping their hot drinks in silence and return to their work as soon as possible. Only once little Miss Potter paused while handing Anna her empty mug. 'Why should it have been him?' she asked, and added with no sense of anti-climax, 'He always used to ask me about my budgie.'

There was no news of Mrs Hammond, and on the day of Max's appointment Anna felt more and more depressed at the thought that he was coming all the way from the country to no purpose. He was due to arrive at twelve, and a little before this she waited for him in the disused ward, so that they would not have to talk in the sewing-room.

'No news?' he said at once, and she shook her head, taking in his shining shoes and carefully brushed suit.

'I didn't really think there would be.' He looked suddenly somehow crumpled. 'Poor woman,' he said and added apologetically, 'It's just that I knew this was my only chance.'

They stood in the half-darkness, wondering what to do

next. They'd better have some lunch, thought Anna, as soon as the old ladies had gone – perhaps she could hurry them up.

'I'll just go into the sewing-room,' she began, when she heard a car door slam.

They looked at each other.

'Do you suppose . . . ?' said Max.

There were footsteps outside – not like Mrs Hammond's, thought Anna, these were slower and more slurred – but a moment later the door opened and there she was. She blinked a little at seeing them unexpectedly in this dim place, but otherwise she seemed just as usual with not a hair out of place and her face carefully made up. Only her eyes were different and her voice, when she spoke, was hoarse, as though she were having to force it to work.

She shook her head as they stumbled into some attempt at condolences.

'It's all right,' she said. 'I know.'

For a moment her glance rested on Max as though she were trying, through him, to recreate poor Dickie who might even have stood in the same spot only a week or two before. Then she said, 'I can't face the old ladies. We may as well go.'

She started towards the door with Max following, but stopped before she reached it.

'Max,' she said in her strange, hoarse voice, 'you know you don't have to do this. Are you sure it's really what you want?'

Max nodded and she stared at him with something almost like contempt. 'Like a bloody lamb to the slaughter!' she shouted. Then she shook her head and told him to take no notice.

'Come along,' she said. 'We'll go and see Jack.'

CHAPTER 14

Two weeks later Max was accepted by the Air Force.

Mama said, 'I told you so,' and he was sent to a training camp in the Midlands where conditions were rough and he spent most of his time marching and drilling, but when he came home on leave in his uniform he looked happier than he had done for a long time.

The very first time he had a day in London he came to the office to thank Mrs Hammond, but she was not there. Since Dickie's death she had come in less and less, and Anna found herself almost running the place on her own. It was not difficult, but it was dull. She had not realized how much her interest had depended on Mrs Hammond's presence, and the old ladies missed her even more than Anna did.

They looked at Anna glumly when she poured out the Bovril, as though it were hardly worth drinking without Mrs Hammond to tell them about Mr Churchill and Queen Wilhelmina, and quarrelled a good deal among themselves. Miss Clinton-Brown had been put in charge of cutting out pyjamas (which had previously been supervised by Mrs Hammond) and endlessly thanked God for having made her the sort of person others could rely on, while Miss Potter and Mrs Riley sat together and said nasty things about her under cover of the hum of their sewing machines.

There were fewer letters to type and Anna spent much of her time checking through the card index and keeping the peace. Sometimes when she could think of nothing else to do she made drawings of the old ladies on a pad under her desk. Some of them came out well, but she always felt guilty afterwards because after all that was not what she was getting paid for.

Winter came early and almost at once it got quite cold. Anna first noticed it while she was waiting at the bus stop in the mornings. Her coat suddenly seemed too thin to keep out the wind and when she got to the office she had to thaw out her feet over the gas fire. On Sundays when the weather was fine she would walk across Putney Heath with

Mama and Papa. The grass crunched frostily under their feet, the pond at Wimbledon Parkside was frozen even though it was barely November, and the ducks stood gloomily about on the ice.

Sometimes, if they were feeling rich, they would stop at the Telegraph Inn and Papa would have a beer while Anna and Mama drank cider, before returning to the hotel for lunch. They tended to delay until the last possible minute, for once you were back, there was nothing much to do.

After lunch everyone sat in the lounge, now filled with the tables and leatherette chairs which Frau Gruber had brought from the Hotel Continental, because it was the only room with heating. It had an open fire and in the maharajah's day, when you could get as much coal as you liked, there must have been a great blaze which would have warmed every corner. But now, with fuel hard to come by, it never seemed to get quite as warm as one would have liked.

It was not very exciting sitting in the lukewarm room with nothing to do except wait for supper, but people occupied themselves as best they could. They read, the two Czech ladies knitted endless scarves, and for a while the Woodpigeon tried to teach Anna Polish. He had a book which she tried to read, but one day when he was feeling depressed he took it from her in the middle of a sentence.

'What is the good?' he said. 'None of us will ever see Poland again.'

Everyone knew that no matter whether the Germans or the Russians won the war, neither would ever give Poland back her independence.

Sometimes a couple called Poznanski organized group discussions about it. They never reached any conclusions, but just talking about Poland seemed to cheer them up. Anna quite enjoyed these, for the Poznanskis handed out paper and pencils in case anyone should wish to make notes, and instead of listening she would surreptitiously draw the other people.

Once she made a funny drawing of the two Czech ladies knitting in unison. She carried it with her to the dining-room when the gong went for supper and Mama picked it up while they were waiting for the trayloads of mince and cabbage to reach them.

'Look,' she said, and showed it to Papa.

Papa looked at it carefully. 'This is very good,' he said at last. 'Like an early Daumier. You ought to draw far more.'

'She ought to have lessons,' said Mama in a worried voice.

'But, Mama,' said Anna, 'I've got my job.'

'Well, perhaps in the evenings or at weekends,' said Mama. 'If only we had some money . . .'

It would be nice, thought Anna, to have something to do in the evenings, for they were very dull. She and Mama had already read their way through half the books in the public library and the only other distraction was bridge, which Anna disliked. She was glad, therefore, when Mama announced that they had been invited to spend an evening with Mama's Aunt Dainty.

Aunt Dainty was Cousin Otto's mother, and the invitation was to celebrate Otto's return from Canada where he had been first interned, then released and finally sent home for some special purpose which Aunt Dainty was vague about.

'Are you coming, Papa?' said Anna.

But Papa had finally persuaded the BBC to broadcast one of his pieces to Germany and was busy writing a second one in the hope that they would take this, too – so Mama and Anna went on their own.

As their bus crawled through the blackout towards Golders Green, Anna asked, 'Why is she called Aunt Dainty?'

'It was a nickname when she was a child,' said Mama. 'Somehow it stuck, even though it hardly suits her now.' Then she said, 'She's had a bad time. Her husband was in a concentration camp. They got him out before the war, but he's never been the same.'

It was difficult finding the address – a basement in a long street of houses which all looked the same – but as soon as Mama pressed the bell the door was flung open by one of the largest and plainest women Anna had ever seen. She was wrapped in a long black skirt almost down to the ground and there were various sweaters, cardigans and shawls on top of it.

'Ach hullo – come in !' she cried in German, revealing a

mouthful of irregular teeth, but the eyes half-buried in the heavy face were friendly and warm and she embraced Mama enthusiastically.

'Hullo, Dainty,' said Mama. 'How lovely to see you.'

Aunt Dainty swept them down some steps and into a large room which must have been a cellar but had been so draped with curtains and hangings of every kind that it had acquired a certain grandeur.

'Sit down, sit down,' she cried, waving them towards a sofa piled high with cushions, and added, 'Goodness, Anna, you're so grown up – you look just like your father.'

'Do I?' said Anna, pleased, and while she warmed her hands over the oil stove which heated the room, Mama and Aunt Dainty embarked on the usual conversation of how many years was it, and don't you remember that time at Lyons in Oxford Street, and oh no perhaps she was at school then but I'm sure you must have seen her – until Otto came in.

He looked better dressed than Anna had ever seen him and Aunt Dainty at once put her arm round his shoulder as though she had not yet got used to having him home.

'He's leaving again quite soon,' she said. 'Back to Canada.'

'Canada?' cried Mama. 'But he's only just left there.'

'I came home to see some people and get some things cleared up – papers and so forth,' said Otto. 'Then I'm going back to Canada to do a job of research. Touch wood,' he added, just to be on the safe side.

'To and fro across the Atlantic like a pendulum,' wailed Aunt Dainty. 'And with German U-boats everywhere waiting to catch him.'

She pronounced them ooh-boats, which made them sound as though they had their mouths open ready to swallow him up.

'What sort of research?' asked Mama who had been good at physics at school. 'Anything interesting?'

Otto nodded. 'Rather hush-hush, I'm afraid,' he said. 'You remember the Cambridge professor who was interned with me – he's in it too, with a few other men. It could be quite important.'

'But do you know,' cried Aunt Dainty, 'when he came home his father didn't recognize him. I talked to him. I said, "Victor, this is your son – don't you remember?" But we're not sure if he realizes even now.'

'I'm sorry,' said Mama. 'How is Victor?'

Aunt Dainty sighed. 'Not good,' she said. 'In bed most of the time.' Then she cried, 'The soup – we must eat!' and rushed out of the room.

Otto pulled some chairs round a table which was laid in a corner and then helped his mother carry in the food. There were hunks of brown bread and soup with dumplings.

'Knoedel!' cried Mama, munching one. 'You always were a wonderful cook, Dainty!'

'Well, I've always liked it,' said Aunt Dainty. 'Even in Germany when we had a cook and six maids. But I've learned something new now – how do you like my curtains?'

'Dainty!' cried Mama. 'You didn't make them!'

Aunt Dainty nodded. 'And the cushions on the sofa, and this skirt, and a whole lot of bits and pieces for the lodgers.'

'She saved the money for a sewing machine out of the rent,' said Otto. 'She had to let the rooms upstairs when I was interned – with Father the way he was. And now,' he said fondly, 'she's turning the place into a palace.'

'Ach Otto – a palace!' said Aunt Dainty, and for someone so large she looked quite girlish.

Mama, who could hardly sew on a button, couldn't get over it. 'But how did you do it?' she cried. 'Who showed you?'

'Evening classes,' said Aunt Dainty, 'at the London County Council. They cost practically nothing – you should try them.'

While she was talking she had cleared away the soup dishes and brought in an apple tart. She cut a piece for Otto to take to his father and doled out the rest.

'Do you think Victor would like me to go in and see him?' asked Mama, but Aunt Dainty shook her head.

'It would be no use, dear,' she said. 'He wouldn't know who you were.'

After supper they moved back to the oil stove and Otto talked about Canada. He had had a bad time on the way there, locked in the overcrowded hold of a boat, but it had not shaken his faith in the English.

'It wasn't their fault,' he said. 'They had to lock us up. For all they knew we might have been Nazis. Most of the English Tommies were very decent.'

The Canadians, too, had been very decent, though not quite as decent, he implied, as the English, and he was particularly pleased that his new job was an English venture. 'But I'll get paid in Canadian dollars,' he said, 'and I'll be able to send some home.'

Mama questioned him again about his work, but he would only smile and say that it was very small.

'And Otto so clumsy with his fingers!' cried Aunt Dainty. 'Just like his cousin Bonzo.'

'Whatever happened to him?' asked Mama, and they quickly slid into the kind of conversation which Anna had heard at every meeting of grown-ups since she had left Berlin at the age of nine. It was an endless listing of relatives, friends and acquaintances who had been part of the old life in Germany and who were now strewn all over the world. Some had done well for themselves, some had been caught by the Nazis, and most of them were struggling to survive.

Anna had either never known or forgotten nearly all these people, and the conversation meant little to her. Her eyes wandered round the room, from Aunt Dainty's curtains past Otto's books piled high on a shelf to the table with its bright cover and to the door beyond it.

It was half-open and she suddenly realized that there was someone standing outside, staring in. This was so unexpected that it frightened her and she glanced quickly at Aunt Dainty, but she was pouring coffee and Mama and Otto were both facing the other way.

The figure at the door was old and quite bald and there was a curious lopsided look about the head which had a scar running down one side. It was dressed in a kind of shift and as Anna looked at it, it moved one hand in a vague gesture of silence or farewell. Like a ghost, thought Anna, but the eyes that stared back at her were human. Then it tugged its shift closer about its body and a moment later it was gone. It could not even have been wearing shoes, thought Anna, for there had been no sound.

'Black or white?' said Aunt Dainty.

'White, please,' said Anna, and as Aunt Dainty handed her the cup she heard the front door close.

Aunt Dainty started. 'Excuse me,' she said and hurried out of the room. She was back almost at once, looking distraught.

'Otto!' she cried. 'It's your father. Quickly!'

Otto leapt up from the sofa and rushed for the front door while Aunt Dainty stood helplessly among the coffee cups.

'He runs away,' she said. 'He keeps doing it. Once he got right to the end of the street – in his nightshirt. Luckily a neighbour saw him and brought him back.'

'What makes him do it?' said Mama.

Aunt Dainty tried to speak in a matter-of-fact voice.

'Well, you know,' she said, 'when he first came out of the concentration camp it was happening all the time. We couldn't make him understand that he was no longer there, and I suppose he had some idea of escaping. Then it got better, but lately –' she looked at Mama unhappily. 'Well, the brain was damaged, you see, and as people get older these things get worse.'

There were muffled voices outside and Aunt Dainty said, 'Otto has found him.'

The voices sorted themselves into Otto's, trying to soothe, and a kind of thin crying.

'Oh dear,' said Aunt Dainty. She looked anxiously at Anna. 'Now you mustn't let this upset you.' Suddenly she began to talk very fast. 'You see, when he gets like this he doesn't know any of us, especially Otto because he hasn't seen him for so long. He thinks he's still in the concentration camp, you see, and he thinks we're . . . God knows who he thinks we are, and poor Otto gets very distressed.'

The front door slammed and Anna could hear them on the stairs, Otto talking and the old man's voice faintly pleading. There was a bump at the bottom of the stairs – someone must have slipped – and then Otto appeared at the open door with his arms round his father, trying to guide him back to his bedroom, but the old man broke away and tottered towards Mama who involuntarily stepped back.

'Let me go!' he cried in his thin voice. 'Let me go! Please, for God's sake, let me go!'

Otto and Aunt Dainty looked at each other.

'Did he get far?' she asked, and he shook his head.

'Only two doors away.'

The old man had found some apple tart on the table and began absently to eat it.

'Father –' said Otto.

'My dear, it's no use,' said Aunt Dainty, but Otto ignored her. He moved a few steps towards his father – carefully, so as not to frighten him.

'Father,' he said, 'it's me – Otto.'

The old man went on eating.

'You're no longer in the concentration camp,' said Otto. 'We got you out – don't you remember? You're safe now, in England. You're home.'

His father turned his face towards him. The cake was still in his hand and his nightshirt had somehow got caught round one of his bare ankles. He stared at Otto intensely with his old man's eyes. Then he screamed.

'Ring the doctor,' said Aunt Dainty.

'Father –' said Otto again, but it was no use.

Aunt Dainty went quickly over to the old man and took him by the shoulders. He tried to struggle, but he was no match for her, and she led him back to bed while Otto went to the telephone. Anna saw his face as he passed her and it looked as though he were dead.

She and Mama did not speak at all until Aunt Dainty came back into the room. 'I'm sorry,' she said. 'I wish it hadn't happened while you were here.'

Mama put her arm round her large shoulders. 'My dear Dainty,' she cried, 'I didn't know!'

'It's all right,' said Aunt Dainty. 'I'm used to it now – as far as one ever gets used . . .' Suddenly tears were running down her face. 'It's Otto,' she cried. 'I can't bear to see him. He's always been so fond of his father. I remember when he was small he used to talk about him all the time.' She looked towards the bedroom where the old man was battering feebly on the door. 'How can people do such things?' she asked. 'How can they do them?'

When they were sitting on the bus on the long ride home Anna asked, 'How did they get Uncle Victor out of the concentration camp?'

'It was a kind of ransom,' said Mama. 'Dainty sold all her possessions – she was quite rich – and gave the money to the Nazis. And Otto was already in England. He talked to someone at the Home Office and got them to agree that Victor could come here – otherwise the Nazis would never have let him go.'

'That's why he always says the English are wonderful,' said Anna.

She wondered what it would feel like to be Otto. Supposing it had been Papa in the concentration camp . . . It did not bear even thinking about. She was glad that at least Otto had his job. She could imagine him in Canada, throwing himself into the work with no thought of anything else, to blot out what had been done to his father, to help the wonderful English win their war. Whatever research Otto was given to do, she thought he would do it extremely well.

'Mama,' she said, 'what's very small in physics?'

Mama was cold and tired. 'Oh, you must know,' she said. 'Molecules – atoms – things like that.'

Atoms, thought Anna – what a pity. It did not sound as though Otto's research would be very important.

A few days later Otto came to say goodbye. His father was better, he said. The doctor had prescribed some new sedatives and he now slept most of the time.

'Keep an eye on my mother,' he asked Mama, who promised to do so.

Just before he left he handed her a leaflet. 'My mother asked me to give it to you,' he said, a little embarrassed. 'She thought you might be interested – it's all about her evening classes.'

Anna glanced through it after he had gone. It was extraordinary what you could learn for a modest fee – anything from book-keeping through Ancient Greek to upholstery. Suddenly she noticed something.

'Look, Mama,' she said. 'There are even classes in drawing.'

'So there are,' said Mama.

Unbelievingly they checked the fee. Eight shillings and sixpence a term.

'We'll ring up first thing in the morning,' said Mama.

CHAPTER 15

They spent Christmas in the country with the Rosenbergs. The Professor's sister and her two boys had gone to stay with another relative in Manchester, where the schooling was better, and the atmosphere was much more peaceful than when Anna had been there before. Everyone was happy because the Americans had finally come into the war, and the Professor even said it might all be over by the end of 1942.

Aunt Louise had decorated a Christmas tree which filled a corner of the dining-room, and on Christmas Day Max managed to come for lunch by dint of hitching lifts both ways. He was learning to fly and had almost completed his training as a pilot. As usual, he had emerged top of all the exams and had already been recommended for a commission.

Anna told him that she was going to drawing lessons after the holidays.

'A life class,' she said, 'at a proper art school.'

'Good show,' said Max because that was what people said in the Air Force, but Aunt Louise flew into a flutter of amazement.

'A life class!' she cried. 'Oh dear! You'll meet all sorts of people there!'

It was impossible to tell whether she considered the prospect dangerous or attractive, but she clearly thought it fraught with excitement. As a result Anna was a little disappointed when, a week or two later, she went to her first evening class at the Holborn School of Art.

She was directed to a large, bare room with a wooden platform and a screen at one end. A few people were sitting about, some with drawing-boards propped up in front of them, some reading newspapers. Nearly all of them had kept their coats on, for the room was very cold.

Just after she had come in a little woman with a shopping bag arrived and hurried behind the screen. There was a thump as she put the bag down and a potato rolled out from under the screen, but she retrieved it quickly and emerged a moment later in a pink dressing-gown.

'Christ, it's freezing,' she said, switched on an electric fire aimed at the platform and crouched in front of it.

By this time Anna had helped herself to some drawing paper from a stack marked one penny a sheet and pinned it to one of the boards which seemed to be for general use. She got out her pencil and rubber and sat astride one of the wooden forms provided, propping up her board against the easel-shaped front like the other students. She was ready to learn to draw, but nothing happened. On one side of her an elderly woman was knitting a sock and on the other a youth of sixteen or so was finishing a sandwich.

At last the door opened again and a man in a duffel coat appeared.

'Late again, John!' sang out the youth next to Anna in a strong Welsh accent.

The man looked across the room with absent-minded blue eyes before his attention focused.

'Don't be cheeky, William,' he said. 'And you'd better do me a good drawing today, or I'll tell your father what I really think of you!'

The Welsh boy laughed and said, 'Yes sir,' with mock respect, while the man threw off his duffel and went to confer with the model.

Anna heard him say something about a standing pose, but the model shook her head.

'Not tonight, Mr Cotmore,' she cried. 'My feet aren't up to it.'

She had taken off the pink dressing-gown and was standing there with no clothes on at all and with the electric fire casting a red glow on her rather tubby stomach.

Anna had been a little nervous of this moment. She had wondered what it would feel like to be in a roomful of people all looking at someone naked. But everyone else took it so much for granted that after a minute or two it seemed quite normal.

'I've been queueing an hour for fish,' said the model and indeed, even without her clothes, it was only too easy to imagine her with a shopping bag in her hand.

'A sitting pose, then,' said the man called Cotmore and covered a chair on the platform with what looked like an old curtain for the model to sit on. When he had arranged her to his satisfaction he said, 'We'll keep this pose for the whole evening.' There was a rustle of newspapers being put down; the woman with the sock reluctantly rolled up her wool, and everyone began to draw.

Anna looked at the model and at her blank sheet of paper and wondered where to start. She had never spent more than a few minutes drawing anyone, and now she would have two and a half hours. How could one possibly fill in the time? She glanced at a girl in front of her who seemed to be covering her entire paper with pencil strokes. Of course, she thought – if you made the drawing bigger it was bound to take longer and you could put in more detail. She grasped her pencil and began.

After an hour she had worked down from the model's head to her middle. There was something not quite right about the shoulders, but she was pleased with the way she had drawn each of the many curls in the model's hair and was just about to start on the hands which were folded on one side of the stomach, when the man called Cotmore said, 'Rest!'

The model stretched, stood up and wrapped herself in her dressing-gown and all the students put down their pencils. How annoying, thought Anna – just when she was getting into her stride.

A murmur of conversation went up from the class, newspapers were unfolded, and the woman next to her went back to her knitting. Anna found that in spite of having kept her coat on, her feet and hands were frozen.

'Chilly tonight,' said a man with a muffler and offered her a toffee out of a paper bag.

The model came down from her throne and walked slowly from one drawing-board to the next, inspecting the different versions of herself all round the room.

'Have we done you justice?' called Mr Cotmore. He was surrounded by a small group of students, the Welsh boy among them, and they were all chatting and laughing.

The model shook her head. 'They've all made me look fat,' she said, and went glumly back to her chair.

When Anna returned to her drawing at the end of the rest it did not seem quite as good as before. The shoulders were definitely wrong : the trouble, she realized, was that she had drawn the right shoulder higher than the left, whereas the way the model was sitting it was the other way round. How could she not have seen this before? But it was too late to change it, so she concentrated on the hands.

They were folded together in a complicated way, with the fingers interlaced, and as she tried to copy all the joints and knuckles and fingernails she became increasingly confused. Also she could not help noticing that as a result of the mistake over the shoulders, one arm had come out longer than the other. She was staring at it all, wondering what to do, when a voice behind her said, 'May I?'

It was Mr Cotmore.

He motioned to her to get up and sat down in her place. 'Don't draw it all in bits,' he said, and began a drawing of his own at the side of the paper.

Anna watched him, and at first she could not think what he was drawing. There were straight lines like scaffolding in different directions, then a round shape which turned out to be the model's head and then, gradually, the rest of her appeared among the scaffolding, supported by the straight lines which indicated, Anna now realized, the angle of the shoulders, the hips, the hands in relation to the arms. It was all finished in a few minutes and although there were no details – no curls and no fingernails – it looked far more like the model than Anna's drawing.

'See?' said Mr Cotmore, as he stood up and walked away.

Anna was left staring at his work. Well, of course it was easier to do it small, she thought. And she wasn't sure that putting in all those guide-lines wasn't a kind of cheating. All the same . . .

She could hardly bear to look at her own drawing after his. It rambled all over the paper with its funny shoulders and its one long arm and one short arm and its fingers like sausages. She wanted to crumple it up and throw it away but had just decided that this would attract too much attention, when she became aware of the Welsh boy looking down at it.

'Not bad,' he said.

For a moment her heart leapt. Perhaps after all . . .?

'One of Cotmore's best,' said the boy. 'He's in form tonight.' He must have sensed her disappointment, for he added, 'Your first attempt?'

Anna nodded.

'Yes, well –' The Welsh boy averted his eyes from her

drawing and searched for a kindly comment. 'It's often difficult to start with,' he said.

When Anna got home Mama was waiting to hear how it had all gone. 'I think it's very good,' she cried when she saw the drawing, 'for someone who's never done anything like that before!'

Papa was more interested in Mr Cotmore's version. 'John Cotmore,' he said. 'I've read something about him recently. An exhibition, I think – very well reviewed.'

'Really?' said Mama. 'He must be good then.'

'Oh yes,' said Papa, 'he's quite distinguished.'

They were sitting on the beds in the room which Anna and Mama shared, and Mama was trying to re-heat the supper Anna had missed earlier in the dining-room. She had lit the gas-ring which Frau Gruber had provided in each of the bedrooms and was stirring up some unidentifiable meat, boiled potatoes and turnips in a saucepan she had bought from Woolworth's.

'It's a bit burned,' she said. 'I don't know – perhaps next time it might be better to eat it cold.'

Anna said nothing.

It was nearly ten o'clock and she was tired. Her appalling drawing lay on the floor beside her. Next time? she thought. There did not seem much point.

However, by the following week she was anxious to try again. Surely, she thought, she was bound to do better this time.

It turned out that the model was the same, but this time Mr Cotmore had persuaded her into a standing pose. Divested of her pink dressing-gown, she leaned with one hand on the back of the chair to steady herself and stared gloomily at her feet.

Anna, remembering the lesson of the previous week, at once attacked her paper with scaffolding lines in every direction. She tried not to be distracted by details, and the upper part of her drawing came out better than before, but all her new-found skill deserted her when she reached the legs and feet.

She could not make her drawing stand. The feet were at the bottom, but the figure appeared to float or hang on the paper with no weight and nothing to support it. Again and again she rubbed out and re-drew, but it was no use until, towards the end of the evening, Mr Cotmore came round to her. He sat down without a word and drew a foot at the side of her paper. It was facing straight forward like the model's, but instead of drawing a line round it, as Anna had tried to do, he built up section by section from the foreshortened toes at the front, through the arch of the foot, to the heel at the back, each piece fitting solidly behind the other, until there on the paper was a sturdy foot standing firmly on an invisible floor.

'See?' he said.

'Yes,' said Anna and he smiled slightly.

He must be about forty, she thought, with intelligent eyes and a curious wide mouth.

'Difficult things, feet,' he said, and walked away.

After this Anna went to art school every Tuesday night. She became obsessed with learning to draw. If she could just do one drawing, she thought, that looked as she wanted it to – but each time she mastered one difficulty she seemed to become aware of two or three more whose existence she had not even suspected. Sometimes Mr Cotmore helped her, but often she spent the whole evening struggling alone.

'You're getting better, though,' said the Welsh boy. His name was Ward but everyone called him Welsh William. 'Remember the first drawing you did? It was bloody awful.'

'Were your drawings awful when you first started?' asked Anna.

Welsh William shook his head. 'I've always found it easy – perhaps too easy. John Cotmore says I'm facile.'

Anna sighed as she looked at the beautiful fluid drawing which he had produced apparently without effort.

'I wish I was,' she said. Her own work was black with being redrawn and almost in holes with being rubbed out.

Sometimes, as she travelled home on the half-empty tube after the class had finished, she despaired at her lack of talent. But the following week she would be back with a new pencil and another sheet of paper, thinking, 'Perhaps this time . . .'

She came home from the classes looking so peaky that Mama worried about her.

'It can't be good for you, sitting for hours in the cold like that,' she said, for there was a fuel shortage and often the art school was entirely without heating, but Anna said impatiently, 'I'm all right – I keep my coat on.'

There was heavy snow in February and again in March. Everyone was depressed because Singapore had fallen to the Japanese, and the German army, far from succumbing to the Russians, seemed about to enter Moscow. At the office Mrs Hammond caught 'flu and did not come in for nearly three weeks, so the old ladies were steeped in even deeper gloom. Miss Clinton-Brown no longer thanked God for letting her cut out the pyjamas, but instead had formed a new alliance with Miss Potter against Mrs Riley who upset them all with her Japanese atrocity stories.

She knew an amazing number and always told them with all possible drama. Leaning on the table with one hand, she would peer over her Bovril with narrowed eyes to impersonate a Japanese commander of unspeakable cruelty, and then open them wide for the noble, well-spoken replies from his English captives who were, however, invariably doomed. Miss Potter always became very distressed by these dramatics and once had to go home in the middle of a pyjama jacket to see, she said confusedly, if her budgie was safe.

When Mrs Hammond recovered from her bout of 'flu she told Mrs Riley very firmly to stop repeating such ill-founded rumours about the fate of British prisoners. Mrs Riley sulked for two days and Miss Clinton-Brown thanked God that there were still some sensible people left in the world who were not afraid to speak their mind. It would all have been quite funny, thought Anna, if one hadn't suspected that most of Mrs Riley's stories were probably true.

Going to art school after all this was a relief. Anna had discovered that there was another life class on Thursdays which, for an extra three shillings and sixpence, she was entitled to attend, so she now went twice a week. All the classes had shrunk, for the intense cold kept the knitters and the newspaper-readers away, and Mr Cotmore had more time to teach those students who remained. He corrected most of their drawings every night and during the rest period he would sit in a corner of the life-room with a favoured few and talk. Anna watched them from a distance. They always seemed to have a good time, arguing and laughing, and she thought how splendid it must be to belong to that inner circle. But she was too shy to go anywhere near them, and after school they always left very quickly in a bunch.

One night she was packing up her things at the end of the class. She had worked with a kind of despair all evening and had managed at last to produce a drawing that bore some faint resemblance to what she had in mind. In the struggle a lot of pencil had got on her hands and somehow from her hands on to her face.

Welsh William looked at her with interest.

'Did you get any of it on the paper?' he asked.

'Certainly,' she said, and showed him.

He was quite impressed. 'Very forceful,' he said. 'We may make something of you yet. Why don't you wash your face and come and have a coffee?'

She scrubbed her face at the sink and they walked a few doors down the road to a café. As they opened the door there were welcoming cries from inside. She blinked in the sudden light and saw Mr Cotmore and his regular crowd of students looking back at her. They were sitting at two tables pushed together, with coffee cups in front of them, and occupied most of the narrow room.

'It's the little girl who gets pencil all over herself,' cried one of them, a small man of about Mr Cotmore's age.

'But to good purpose,' said Mr Cotmore before she had time to blush. 'It's Anna, isn't it?'

She nodded, and they made room for her and Welsh William at the tables. Some coffee appeared before her and, half-excited and half-apprehensive, she buried herself in the cup, so that no one else should ask her any questions. Gradually the conversation resumed around her.

'You're wrong about Cezanne, John,' said the small man and John Cotmore rounded on him with 'Nonsense, Harry, you're just trying to start something!'

Two girls at the other side of the table laughed, but Harry had evidently been trying to do just that, for soon everyone was disagreeing about the French Impressionists, the Italian Primitives, Giotto, Matisse, Mark Gertler, Samuel Palmer – who on earth were they all? thought Anna, listening in silence for fear of revealing her ignorance. On one side of her Harry was waving his arms in argument, on the other Welsh William was absently drawing something on the edge of a newspaper. A pale man with a pale tie whispered intensely about form and content, one of the girls ordered a portion of chips and passed them round, everyone drank more coffee, and John Cotmore with his warm deep voice somehow kept the whole thing going. He spoke only little, but whenever he did everyone else stopped to listen.

Once he addressed her directly. 'What do *you* think?' he asked. They had been talking about styles in drawing, some students extolling the sensitive line of someone Anna had never heard of and others defending another painter with a more chunky approach.

She stared at him, horrified.

'I don't know,' she stammered. 'I just want to draw it the way it looks. But I find it very difficult.'

What a stupid answer, she thought, but he said seriously, 'That's not a bad start,' and she noticed that the others looked at her with new respect.

Later, when everyone else was talking, she plucked up courage to ask him something that had worried her for weeks.

'If someone was going to be any good at drawing,' she said, 'surely they wouldn't find it so difficult?'

'I don't think that follows,' he said. 'It might just mean that they had high standards. In your case,' he added, smiling a little, 'I would say that the situation looks very promising.'

Very promising, she thought, and while he was drawn back into the general conversation she turned his answer over and over, inspecting it for alternate meanings. But there were none. He must really mean that her work was very promising. It was unbelievable, and she sat hugging the thought to herself until it was time to go home.

They sorted out how many coffees had been drunk by whom and then stood for a moment in the cold outside the café.

'See you on Thursday, Anna,' said Welsh William, and several other voices echoed, 'See you on Thursday.' They sounded strangely disembodied in the dark. Good night, Harry. Good night, Doreen. Then the sound of footsteps as unidentifiable figures melted into the blackout.

Anna buttoned up her coat against the wind when a voice, deeper than the rest, called out, 'Good night, Anna!'

'Good night . . . John!' she called back after a moment's hesitation, and as the happiness welled up inside her she broke away from the group into the invisible street beyond.

John Cotmore had said good night to her. And her work was very promising. The pavement rang under her feet and the darkness shone all about her, like something that she could almost touch. She was surprised to find Holborn tube station looking just as usual.

Something tremendous, she felt, had happened in her life.

CHAPTER 16

When Anna arrived at the office a few weeks later she found Mrs Hammond already there. It was embarrassing because Anna was late as usual – there seemed no point in hurrying to work when there was so little to do – but luckily Mrs Hammond had not noticed. She was standing in the disused hospital ward, examining dusty shelves and cupboards, and as soon as she saw Anna she said, 'Got a new job for you.'

'What?' asked Anna.

Mrs Hammond was looking more positive than she had done since Dickie's death.

'Sad job, really,' she said. 'But jolly useful. Officers' clothing.' And as Anna looked puzzled, she suddenly said, 'Dead men's shoes! Can't call it that, of course – upset people. But that's what it comes to. Pass on uniforms – all sorts of clothes – from chaps who've been killed to chaps who are still alive and need them.'

Anna noticed for the first time that on a dust-sheet in a corner of the ward was a pile of garments. There were suits, shirts, ties, bits of Air Force uniform. A used kitbag had P/O Richard Hammond stencilled on it in large white letters. Mrs Hammond followed her glance.

'Silly to hang on to them,' she said, 'when there are other boys who'd be glad of them.' Then she said, 'After all, he wasn't the only one.'

It turned out that she had a partner in this new enterprise – a Mrs James who had lost both her sons, one in the Army in the African desert and the other in the Air Force over Germany. Anna met her briefly later that day, a gaunt, elderly woman with huge tragic eyes and an almost inaudible voice.

She had brought with her a little pug-faced man of great energy who proceeded at once to turn the empty ward into a store-room for the clothing they hoped to receive. He cleaned and hammered and moved furniture and by the end of the week it was ready, with a little office for Mrs James in one corner. '

This consisted only of a table and chair behind two screens, and there was no heating in the whole freezing place except one bar of an electric fire directed at her feet, but she did not seem to notice. She just sat there, staring into space, as though it was as good a place to be as any other.

Mrs Hammond had kept her office next to the sewing-room but spent a good deal of time running in and out to see how everything was getting on. It was she who composed the advertisement in *The Times,* appealing for clothes to the wives and parents of the young men who had been killed. Anna typed it out and by the following week the clothes began to come in.

They varied from single, pathetic garments to whole trunkfuls and they all had to be acknowledged and sorted. It was strangely distressing work. Some trunks, arriving directly from Service stations, seemed to contain nearly all the dead men's possessions, and there were golf-clubs, paperbacks and writing-cases which no one knew what to do with. Once when Anna was pulling an RAF tunic out of a suitcase a ping-pong ball flew out with it and bounced all over the floor of the empty ward. For some reason this upset her more than anything else.

At the same time the old ladies still needed attention – more than before, for they were jealous of Mrs Hammond's new interest – and the wool still had to be sent out to the knitters, and suddenly Anna found that she was very busy. She no longer arrived late in the mornings and barely had time for lunch. Sometimes when she finished at six o'clock she wondered if she wasn't too tired to go on to art school, but she always went in the end.

In the meantime Mrs Hammond had informed all the generals, admirals and air marshals she knew of her new scheme to help servicemen, and at last, less than three weeks after its inception, the first young man arrived to be kitted out. He was a naval lieutenant who had lost all his possessions when his ship had been sunk by a U-boat, and Mrs Hammond and Mrs James vied with each other to give him everything he wanted.

Mrs Hammond had been all a-bustle since the new scheme had started, so it was not surprising to see her turning over stacks of clothes to find trousers exactly the right length or a cap with the correct insignia. But it was astonishing, thought Anna, to see the change in Mrs James.

For the first time her huge eyes stopped staring into the distance, and as she questioned the young man, gently and sensibly, about his needs, it was as though he were providing some kind of vitamin of which she had been deprived. She smiled and talked and even made a little joke, until Mrs Hammond led him away to try on some shoes, when she relapsed into inactivity like a wind-up toy that had run down.

After this there was a steady stream of young men in need and an equally steady supply of clothes from the relatives of other young men who had been killed in action. Anna sometimes wondered how it would feel to wear these garments, but the young men seemed to look on them in purely practical terms. Since rationing had been introduced the previous summer every kind of clothing was hard to come by, and it did not do to be too sensitive.

They were surprisingly cheerful on the whole and sometimes, intoxicated by the money they had saved, they asked Anna out for the evening. They took her to films and theatres and to West End restaurants, and it was fun to dress up in Judy's and Jinny's more elegant cast-offs for these grand places, just as though she were really the nice English girl they took her for. Afterwards they usually wanted to kiss her, and this, too, was exciting. I must really be quite attractive, she thought in wonder, but she did not find any one of them more interesting than the rest and she never went out with them on her art school nights.

'Why not?' cried Mama. 'It's much better for you than those old evening classes!'

Anna shook her head. 'It's an awful waste of time, really,' she said in the special knowing-her-own-mind voice she had recently acquired. 'And, honestly, Mama, they seem so *young*!'

'I hear you're living in a social whirl,' said Max. 'Well, it looks as though the war is going to go on for ever, so you may as well enjoy it.'

He was depressed again, for although he had come out top of his course and was now a Pilot Officer, the Air Force had decided that he could fly neither bombers nor fighters.

'Just because of my background,' he said. 'They're afraid that if I was shot down and the Germans found out about me they wouldn't treat me as a prisoner of war. So I've got to be a flying instructor.'

'Surely that's important too,' said Papa, but Max was too annoyed to listen.

'You don't understand,' he said. 'Nearly everybody else is going to fly on operations. It's the same old thing – I'm always stuck with something different.'

At this Mama, normally so sympathetic to his longing for equality, blew her top.

'For God's sake, are you determined to be killed?' she shouted, and added incongruously, 'As though we hadn't got enough to worry about!'

'There's no need to get excited,' said Max, 'especially as I've got no choice.'

Mama had been increasingly nervous of late, and a few days later Anna discovered why. It was when she came home from work. Nowadays she did not have many evenings at home, and she had planned this one exactly. First she was going to paint over the cracks in her shoes with some brown dye she had bought in her lunch-hour. Then, if there was any hot water, she would wash her hair, and after supper she would mend her two remaining pairs of stockings, so as to have some to wear the following day.

As she passed Papa's room she heard voices and went in. Mama was half-sitting, half-lying on the bed and Papa was holding her hand. Her blue eyes were swimming, her mouth was dragged down at the corners, and her whole face was soaked with tears.

'What's happened?' cried Anna, but Papa shook his head.

'It's all right,' he said. 'Nothing terrible. Mama has lost her job.'

Mama at once leapt into a sitting position.

'What do you mean, nothing terrible,' she cried. 'How are we going to live?'

'We'll manage somehow,' said Papa, and gradually Anna found out what had happened. It was not that Mama had been sacked, but that the job had simply come to an end.

'Of course I hated it anyway,' cried Mama through her tears. 'It was never meant to be more than a stop-gap after Lord Parker died.'

Anna remembered once going to see Mama when she was still Lady Parker's social secretary. Mama had sat in a pretty, white-painted room with a fire, and a footman had brought her tea and biscuits, returning with an extra cup for Anna. Mama had never seemed to have much to do except answer the telephone and send out invitations, and in the evenings she and Anna had marvelled at the way Lady Parker lived.

'Her stockings cost a guinea a pair,' Mama had told her. 'And they can only be worn once because they are so fine.'

Since Lord Parker's death Mama had worked in a basement entirely filled with his papers – such stacks and stacks of them that it had not occurred to her until recently that the task of sorting them could ever come to an end.

'What shall I do?' she cried. 'I have to get a job somehow!'

'Perhaps you'll find something more interesting,' said Anna.

Mama brightened.

'Yes,' she said, 'I suppose I might, now that so many people have been called up. And since you've been self-supporting I've been able to save a little, so we can last a while – I could pick and choose a bit.' But then despair overcame her again. 'Oh God!' she cried, 'I'm so sick of always having to start again!' She looked at Papa who was still holding her hand. 'How much easier it would be,' she said, 'if the BBC would only use some of your stuff and broadcast it to Germany.'

Papa's face tightened. He had not been able to sell anything to the BBC since that first piece, and though he sat at his table and wrote each day, he was earning almost no money at all.

'I'll ring them again,' he said, but they all knew that it would be no use.

The weekend after Mama had gone to her office for the last time she was quite cheerful. It was summer weather and everyone was sitting in the garden. The Woodpigeon had cut the grass with an ancient lawnmower he had discovered in a shed and the Czech ladies both wore triangles of stiff white paper over their noses to protect them from sunburn.

Mama was sitting in a deck-chair with a pile of newspapers beside her. She was checking through the 'situations vacant' columns and writing letters of application for any that seemed possible. Every time she had finished one she

would say, 'Do you think that's all right?' and show it to
Anna and Papa. The jobs were all secretarial, and as Anna
and Papa read through them, Mama would say, 'I didn't
mention that I can't do shorthand because once they gave
me the job I'm sure I could manage,' or 'I know it says
British-born, but I thought if they just saw me . . .'

She looked so determined, sitting there in the sunshine
with her blue eyes frowning at the paper while she attacked
it with her pen, that it was easy to imagine her talking
anyone into giving her any job she wanted.

However, by the following Thursday she had only had
one request for an interview. This turned out to be with
a little man in the City who said that actually they were
looking for someone younger – just a girl, really – and sent
Mama home in deep depression.

She wrote another batch of letters and waited for replies,
but nothing happened. The weather continued lovely and
hot, so she sat in the garden and wrote more letters and
read books from the library. After all, she said, she had
earned a holiday.

When the weather changed and the garden became
chilly Mama cleared out her wardrobe. She walked down
to Putney High Street with Papa to spend the shilling and
sixpence they had allocated for their joint lunch and then
they ate it together in his room. In the evening she played
bridge with the Woodpigeon and the Poznanskis and, on
special occasions, with Miss Thwaites, a new arrival in the
hotel. In fact Miss Thwaites did not play very well, but
since she was English – not just half-English or naturalized
English or English by marriage, but real, genuine born-
and-bred English – she was the most sought-after person
there. She was a withered-looking spinster with a grey
pudding-bowl hair-cut who worked in the local bank, and
she accepted the respect accorded to her as her due.

It was not until Mama had been out of work for four
weeks that she became really frightened. She calculated
that in that time she had had only four replies to her
letters, and two interviews, and when she checked her
savings she found that, as always, they were dwindling
faster than she had expected. She began to haunt the telephone and hang about the hall, waiting for the postman.
When Anna came home in the evenings she would say,
tight-lipped, 'I still haven't heard anything,' before Anna

had even time to ask, and at night she tossed and turned in her bed, unable to sleep.

'What are we going to do?' she cried one Sunday when the three of them were sitting in Papa's room after lunch. Papa had been reading them a poem he had written the previous day. It was addressed to his sister who was now somewhere in Palestine, and in it he remembered their childhood together in Silesia and wondered if they would ever meet again except perhaps in Paradise. If there were such a place, thought Papa, it would probably look rather like the woods and meadows among which they had grown up. It was a beautiful poem.

When Mama asked him what they were to do he looked at her, full of affection and confidence.

'You'll think of something,' he said.

Mama who had been nervously clutching a newspaper suddenly flung it on the floor.

'But I don't want to have to think of something!' she cried. 'Why should it always be me? Why can't you think of something for a change?'

Papa, one hand still holding the poem, seemed to be considering deeply and for a moment Anna thought he was going to come up with the solution to the whole thing. Then he put his other hand over Mama's.

'But you're so much better at it than I am,' he said.

At this Mama burst into tears and Anna said, 'I'm sure I could manage five shillings a week, or even seven-and-sixpence,' but Mama shouted, 'It wouldn't be enough!' Then she blew her nose and said, 'I'll try and talk to Louise.'

'Louise?' said Papa and made a face, but then he caught sight of Mama's expression and said, 'Very well, then, Louise.'

Aunt Louise willingly gave Mama fifteen pounds to help eke out her savings.

'I'm sorry it isn't more,' she said, 'but I don't like to ask Sam at the moment.'

The Professor had become anxious about money since his sister had unexpectedly returned to him with her two boys. He spent each meal-time watching expensive food disappear down the throats of his many impecunious relatives.

'And he worries,' said Aunt Louise, 'what is to become of us all.'

Anna insisted on contributing her five shillings a week and Max sent a cheque for ten pounds from his RAF pay, so they were safe for a while at least. But Mama's anxiety continued. It was difficult to be in her company, for as she sat with her hands clenched in her lap and her blue eyes staring the tension was like a physical presence in the room and nothing could alleviate it.

'Do you really think so?' she would cry when Anna suggested that some particular application for a job looked hopeful and, five minutes later, again, 'Do you really think they'll give me that job?'

The only thing that took her mind off her worries was playing bridge in the evenings. Then her fierce concentration would switch to the cards and as she argued about Culbertson, overtricks and bungled grand-slams the anxiety about her job receded.

Anna occasionally got dragged into these games – Papa couldn't tell a club from a spade – but only if there was no one else at all, for she was so bored by them that she cast a blight on the other players. She would sit there, making mistakes and drawing all over her score-pad, to escape gratefully at the end, irrespective of whether she had won or lost. She felt sorry for Mama and wished to help her, but she also found it a strain sharing one small bedroom with her and so was guiltily relieved whenever there was a reason for her to stay out late.

One morning just as Anna was leaving for work Mama caught her at the door.

'Miss Thwaites wants to play bridge tonight,' she said. 'The Woodpigeon is free, but we need a fourth.'

'I can't,' said Anna. 'I've got my evening class.'

Mama had slept badly and the morning post had failed, yet again, to produce the job she was hoping for.

'Oh, come on,' she said. 'It won't matter if you miss it just once.'

'But I don't want to miss it,' said Anna. 'Can't the Poznanskis play?'

Mama said that they couldn't, and Anna could see the tension rising in her, like a kettle coming to the boil. She said, 'Look, I'm sorry, Mama, but I really don't want to miss my evening class. I'm sure you'll find someone else.'

She edged nervously towards the bedroom door, but before she could reach it Mama exploded.

'Surely,' Mama cried, 'you could do this one little thing for me! I don't ask you much! God knows if one of your boy-friends asked you out you'd give up your evening class quick enough!'

'That's not true!' cried Anna. She had always refused invitations on art school nights. But Mama was now in full flood.

'It's my one pleasure in life,' she cried. 'The only thing that takes my mind off the endless worrying about money. And it's not as though anyone else in this family ever worried about how we're going to live. You just go off to your nice little job each morning and Papa sits in his room writing poems, and I am left with everything – everything!'

'Mama . . .' said Anna, but Mama cut straight through her.

'Who went and asked Louise for money?' she cried. 'Did you? Did Papa? No, as always, it was left to me. Do you suppose I enjoyed that? And who arranged for you to learn shorthand-typing and found a way of paying your fees? And who got Max out of the internment camp? It wasn't you or Papa. Don't you think that in the circumstances you could give up one evening – just one single evening – to make my life a little easier?'

Anna looked at Mama's desperate scarlet face and had a curious, panicky sensation of being sucked into it. She backed away, feeling pale and cold.

'I'm sorry, Mama,' she said, 'but I must go to my evening class.'

Mama glared at her.

'After all,' cried Anna, 'it's only a game of bridge!'

'And you, I suppose,' yelled Mama, 'are going to produce a masterpiece!'

Anna made for the door.

'If I did,' she heard herself yell back, 'you wouldn't even know that it was one!'

Then she escaped, trembling, into the corridor.

She worried about it all day at the office. She thought of ringing Mama up, but there always seemed to be someone near the telephone and, anyway, she wouldn't have known what to say. At six o'clock she still had not made up her mind whether to go home or to the art school. She decided to leave it to chance. If a tram passed her before she reached Victoria she would go home – otherwise not. The tram came almost at once, but she ignored it and took the bus to Holborn, arriving just in time for the class.

And why shouldn't I? she thought. After all, it wasn't as though she'd been out a lot lately. Two of the young men who most frequently invited her had been posted away from London, so she'd had almost no social life at all. I was absolutely right, she thought, but it did not help, for she could not concentrate on her work and produced a drawing so poor that she crumpled it up and threw it away. At the end of the class she did not go to the café but made straight for the tube. If I get home quickly, she thought, there might still be time for a game or two of bridge.

Suddenly, on the train, she had a vision of Mama crying on the bed after she had lost her job. How could I? she thought, and was overwhelmed by pity and guilt. As she hurried down the street she thought of Mama in Paris, Mama helping her buy her first pair of slacks, Mama taking her out on her sixteenth birthday.

'Mama!' she cried as she burst into the lounge – and there was Mama playing bridge with Miss Thwaites against the Woodpigeon and Mrs Poznanski.

'You're early,' said Mama, and Miss Thwaites added, 'Mrs Poznanski found she didn't have to go out after all.'

'But, Mama . . .' cried Anna.

Then rage filled her and she turned on her heel and walked out of the room.

'I couldn't help it,' she said later to Papa. 'I've got a right to my own life. I can't just throw it all up to play bridge whenever Mama wants me to.'

'No, of course not,' said Papa. He was looking tired, and Anna realized that the day could not have been easy for him either.

'Mama is having a difficult time,' he said after a moment. 'I wish we could all live very differently from the way we do. I wish I could be more help.'

There was a pile of closely-written sheets on his desk and Anna asked, 'What are you writing?'

'Something about us – a kind of diary. I've been working on it for a long time.' He shook his head at Anna's look of hope. 'No,' he said, 'I don't think anyone would buy it.'

He had some bread left over from lunch and as Anna couldn't face her cold supper he made her some toast. He suspended a slice of bread from a large paper clip and Anna watched as he held it over the gas fire at the end of a stick from the garden.

'It's so difficult,' she said, 'sharing a room.'

Papa looked worried. 'I wish I could . . .'

'No,' she said. 'I know you need yours to write in.'

Outside on the landing a door slammed and there were voices and footsteps on the stairs. The bridge game must have broken up.

Suddenly Papa said, 'Be nice to her. Be very, very nice to her. She is your mother and it's quite true what she says – life is not easy for her.'

'I am,' said Anna. 'I always have been.'

As she got up to leave him he said, 'Try to forget all about today.'

But she could not quite forget and nor, she suspected, could Mama. There was a carefulness between them which had not been there before. One side of Anna was saddened by this, but another secret, steely side, whose existence she had never even suspected, half-welcomed it for the increased privacy it brought her. All because I wanted to go to art school that one night, she thought. How complicated life became if there was something you really wanted to do.

The following week at the café she said to John Cotmore, 'Do you think art, if one takes it seriously, is bad for personal relationships?'

She had never used so many abstractions before in one sentence, and his mouth twitched as he looked at her.

'Well,' he said at last, 'I think it probably makes them more difficult.'

She nodded and then blushed, overcome by embarrassment. She had just remembered what someone had told her – that he did not get on with his wife.

CHAPTER 17

In the autumn the National Gallery put on an exhibition of French Impressionist paintings. It was a great event, for all valuable pictures had been hidden away since the beginning of the war to save them from being bombed. But there had been only few air raids on London recently – the Luftwaffe must have been too busy fighting in Russia – and so it was considered worth taking a chance to show them again.

Anna had never seen them. There was a book about them in the library, but it had only black and white reproductions and you could not really tell from them what the paintings were like. So, on the first Sunday after the opening of the exhibition, she went along to look at it.

It was a brilliant cold day and she was feeling happy because it was the weekend, and because she had done two good drawings during the week, and because Mama had at last got a job – not a very good job, but after the worry of the past few months it was a relief for her to have got anything at all. As she crossed Trafalgar Square the stone lions cast hard shadows on the pavement and there were more people than usual milling round Nelson's column in the sharp air. The fountains had not worked since the beginning of the war, but as she passed between them a cluster of pigeons took off at her feet and she watched the spatter of their wings turn dark as they rose up into the shining sky. Suddenly she felt a great surge of joy, as though she were flying up with them. Something marvellous is going to happen, she thought – but what?

The National Gallery was crowded and she had a struggle to make her way up the steps and into one of the main rooms. This, too, was full of people, so that at first she could only see parts of the paintings between bobbing heads. She knew at once that she liked them. They looked like the square outside, brilliant with light and a kind of joyful promise.

They were hung in no particular order and as she walked from room to room she was bewildered by the profusion.

She did not know what to look at first, since it was all unfamiliar, and stared at landscapes, figures and interiors indiscriminately between the shifting bodies of the crowd. When she got to the end she went round again and this time some things leapt out at her – a mass of green water lilies in a green pond, a woman in a garden, a miraculously drawn dancer tying her shoe.

But when she went round a third time she had already changed. The water lilies which had so dazzled her before now seemed less remarkable, and she was fascinated, instead, by some bathers painted entirely in tiny spots of brilliant colour. She looked and looked and finally, when she could see no more, she fought her way to the office near the main door in the hope of buying some postcard reproductions which she could look at at home, but the gallery was about to close and there were none left. She must have been looking at the pictures for nearly three hours, she thought in surprise.

As she emerged on to the steps above Trafalgar Square, now purple in the dusk, she stopped for a moment. Suddenly she did not want the bother of catching buses and tubes and of sitting through supper at home. She stood and stared across the darkening square, feeling vaguely afloat.

A voice behind her said, 'Hullo,' and she turned to see John Cotmore in his old duffel coat.

'Well,' he said, joining her at the balustrade, 'and what did you think of the Impressionists?'

'I loved them,' she said.

He smiled. 'First time you've seen them?'

She nodded.

'First time I saw them was twenty years ago,' he said. 'In Paris. I was quite a dashing young man then.'

She could not think what to answer. Finally she said, 'I used to live in Paris. I went to school there.'

'What, finishing school?' he asked, and she laughed.

'No, the *école communale* – elementary school.'

There was a sudden exodus from the gallery and people streamed past them down the steps, hemming them in.

'I'm a German refugee,' she said, and immediately wondered why on earth she had said it. But he seemed interested and not too surprised, so she went on to explain about Max and Mama and Papa and their life together since they had left Berlin.

'I don't usually tell people about it,' she said at last.

This did surprise him. 'Why not?' he asked.

'Well—' It seemed obvious to her. 'People think it's odd.'

He frowned. 'I don't think it's odd.'

Perhaps it isn't, she thought, as the darkness closed round them and the last footsteps clattered past. It was suddenly cold, but he seemed in no hurry to leave.

'You mustn't go round pretending you're something you aren't,' he said. 'Where you come from is part of you, just like your talent for drawing.'

She smiled, hearing only the word 'talent'.

'So no more of this pretence.' He took her arm. 'Come on, I'm going to walk you to the tube.'

They made their way along the narrow pavements of a side street, and as they reached the Embankment she was again filled with the happiness that she had felt earlier that afternoon. But this time, instead of being shapeless, it seemed to contain the paintings she had seen and the fact that she was walking through the dusk with John Cotmore, as well as a huge and mysterious sense of expectancy.

The feeling was so strong that she smiled involuntarily, and he said, 'What's funny?' looking put out.

He had been talking, but she had hardly listened. Something about living alone, cooking his own supper. Had his wife moved out, then?

Hurriedly, she said, 'I'm sorry, nothing's funny, it's just ...' She hesitated because it seemed so idiotic.

'I've been feeling terribly happy all day,' she brought out at last.

'Oh!' He nodded. 'I suppose at your age ... How old are you, anyway?'

'Eighteen,' she said.

'Really,' he said to her annoyance. 'You seem much younger.'

They had arrived at the tube station and stood together for a moment before she bought her ticket. Then, as she stepped into the lift, he called after her, 'See you on Tuesday!'

'See you on Tuesday!' she called back, and the happiness welled up again inside her and lasted all the way home to Putney.

The cold, sunny weather persisted, and so did Anna's

happiness. She felt almost painfully aware of all the sounds, shapes and colours around her and wanted to draw everything in sight. She drew on the tube and in her lunch-hour and when she got home in the evenings. She filled one notebook after another with drawings of people strap-hanging, sitting, eating and talking, and when she was not drawing she thought about it.

She loved everything. She felt as though she had been asleep for years and had just woken up. In the mornings when she took the bus down Putney Hill to the tube station she stood outside on the platform, so as not to miss a moment of the view as the bus crossed the river in the early light. She spent hours looking at a book about the French Impressionists which John Cotmore had lent her, and some of the reproductions so delighted her that it was almost as though she could feel them with her eyes. When there was music on the radio in the lounge it seemed to her unbearably beautiful, and the sight of the dead men's clothes at work made her unbearably sad. (But even this was curiously agreeable.) She joined the local firewatchers, which meant turning out at night whenever there was an air-raid warning, and stood endlessly in the dark, admiring the dim shapes of the suburban landscape in the starlight.

One night she was on duty with Mr Cudderford, who was the leader of the group. There had been a few bombs, but nothing close, and some anti-aircraft fire from the guns on Putney Heath. No incendiaries, which was what Anna and Mr Cudderford were watching for. It was very cold and the All Clear was a long time coming, and Mr Cudderford began to talk about his experiences in the previous world war.

He had been in the trenches where there had been a lot of suffering and Mr Cudderford, especially, had suffered with his legs. Other men had been wounded and others yet had had trench feet, but Mr Cudderford had varicose veins. In case Anna did not know what varicose veins were, he explained them to her, and exactly how they felt, and what the doctor had thought about them.

Like everything else during the past weeks, Mr Cudderford's varicose veins were very vivid to Anna, and as he proceeded with his description she found herself feeling slightly sick. How silly, she thought, but the feeling grew alarmingly until suddenly, when Mr Cudderford said, 'So the doctor told me, "We'll have to cut those out," ' she was overwhelmed by a stifling wave of nausea.

She mumbled, 'I'm sorry, but I'm feeling rather ill,' and then, amazingly, the sky shifted sideways and the ground lurched up towards her and she was lying in some wet leaves and Mr Cudderford was blowing his whistle.

'I'm all right,' she said, but he had told her to lie still and almost at once the boots of another firewatcher appeared on the ground beside her.

'Passed out,' said Mr Cudderford with a certain satisfaction. 'I reckon it's the cold.'

'No, really –' said Anna, but suddenly they had a stretcher and were loading her on to it.

'Heave-ho,' said Mr Cudderford, they lifted her up and the stretcher began to move through the darkness. Trees and clouds passed erratically above her and for a while she watched them with pleasure, but as they approached the hotel she suddenly realized what her arrival would look like to Mama and Papa.

'Honestly,' she said, 'I can walk now.'

But the firewatchers had seen no action for months, and there was no stopping them. They carried her through the front door and Mama, who must have seen them from the window, came rushing down the stairs in her dressing-gown.

'Anna!' she shouted so loudly that various doors opened and the Woodpigeon appeared behind her, followed by the two Czech ladies and the Poznanskis.

'Where is she hurted?' cried the Woodpigeon.

'Yes, where?' cried Mama, and Mr Poznanski, amazingly wearing a hairnet, suddenly called from the top of the stairs, 'I will a doctor fetch.'

'No!' shouted Anna, and Mr Cudderford at last let her off the stretcher so that she could prove to everyone that she was all right.

'It was only Mr Cudderford's varicose veins,' she explained when her rescuers had left, and it seemed ridiculous even to herself.

Once Mama had got over her fright she thought the whole incident very funny, but she said, 'You never used to be so easily upset.'

It was true, thought Anna, and wondered at the change in herself.

The evening classes were the focal point of her world. She now went to three a week and John Cotmore not only helped her with her life drawings but took an interest in the sketches she made out of school.

'These are very good,' he once told her after looking at a series of drawings she had made of workmen shifting rubble on a bomb-site, and she felt as though she had suddenly grown wings.

It was disturbing and yet exciting to be absorbed in something of which Mama and Papa knew so little. Neither of them had ever had the slightest wish to draw. Once, while John Cotmore was talking at the café, Anna suddenly understood about abstract painting, which had always been a bit of a joke at home, and her feeling of elation was followed by a twist of something like regret.

How far away I am moving from them, she thought, and Mama must have sensed it too, for although she admired Anna's sketches she became increasingly irritated with the evening classes.

'Always that cold art school,' she would say. 'Surely you don't have to go *again*!' And she would ask Anna about the people she met there and what on earth they found to talk about all that time.

Sometimes Anna tried to explain and Mama would listen, her blue eyes bright with concentration, while Anna expounded some thought she had about drawing.

'Oh yes, I understand that, it's quite simple,' Mama would say at the end, and expound it all back to Anna to prove that she had indeed understood.

But Anna always felt that somehow during the explanation some essential ingredient had escaped, so that not only had Mama not *quite* understood, but the thought itself had somehow shrunk in the process and had been returned to her poorer and more meagre than before.

Talking to Papa was more satisfying. There was an initial difficulty to overcome in that she did not know the words for what she wanted to say in German, and Papa did not know them in English. She had to speak in each language in turn, with a bit of French thrown in for good measure, until her meaning came across – more, she sometimes felt, by telepathy than anything else. But then Papa understood completely.

'It's very interesting that you should think this,' he would say, and talk about some comparable aspect of writing, or ask her what she thought of some painter she hadn't mentioned.

Both he and Mama were curious about John Cotmore and the students with whom she spent so much of her time.

'What sort of people are they?' asked Papa, and Mama said, 'What sort of homes do they come from?'

'I suppose they come from all sorts of homes,' said Anna. 'Some of them have cockney accents. Harry, I think, is quite grand. I like them because they all draw.'

'This John Cotmore,' said Mama. 'What sort of age is he?'

(Why did she have to call him *this* John Cotmore?)

'I don't know,' said Anna. 'Quite old – about forty.' Later she said hypocritically, 'It's a pity you can't meet them all,' knowing full well that there was little opportunity for Mama to do so.

However, next time Max was home on leave he suggested coming to the café one day after school. Probably it was Mama's idea, thought Anna, but she did not mind – she had wanted him to come anyway.

At first it was difficult. Max sat there among the cracked coffee cups with his open smile and his uniform, looking like an advertisement for the RAF, while the pale young man and Harry discussed the influence of Cubism and the girls gazed at Max admiringly but dumbly. But then Barbara arrived. She was a recent addition to the group – a big blonde girl in her late twenties with a pleasant, placid face. She settled herself next to Max and asked such intelligent questions about the Air Force that he was delighted. Then she said, 'We all have great hopes for your sister, you know,' which was an exaggeration but made Anna blush with pleasure.

'Isn't that so, John?' asked Barbara, and added to Max, 'John here thinks she's absolutely bursting with talent.'

John Cotmore agreed that he did think Anna very promising, and Anna sat between them feeling pleased but foolish, exactly, she thought, as she had done when Mama came to talk to the teacher at the end of her first term at primary school.

Max must have felt something of the same sort, for he assumed an elderly air while phrases like 'full-time art course' and 'help from the Council' fell between them, and only became himself again when the pale young man asked him if flying wasn't very dangerous and Barbara offered him some chips.

'I like your friends,' he told Anna later. 'Especially that girl Barbara. And John Cotmore seems to think that you can draw.'

They were travelling down the escalator to the tube and she glowed inwardly while he considered the evening.

'Do they all know about your background?' he asked. Harry had made a glancing reference to Germany.

'Yes, well, I told John Cotmore first,' she said eagerly. 'And he said it was wrong to pretend to be someone one wasn't. He said that people who mattered would accept me anyway, so there was no need.'

'He's quite a chap,' said Max.

'Yes, isn't he!' cried Anna. 'Isn't he!'

Max laughed. 'I take it you want me to reassure Mama about him. Don't worry, I'll tell her everything she wants to hear.'

They had reached the bottom of the escalator and were walking down the steps towards the platform. Anna took his arm. 'Did you really like him?' she asked.

'Yes,' said Max. 'Yes, I did.' Then he said, 'He's divorced or something, isn't he?'

CHAPTER 18

There were air raids again in the spring. People called them 'scalded cat' raids because the planes came in low, dropped their bombs and escaped again at top speed. They were not bad raids, but tiresome. Anna had to turn out with the local firewatchers every time the air-raid warning sounded. She still had chilblains left over from the winter and it was agony cramming her feet back into her shoes after the warmth of the bed had made them itch and swell.

However, one night when she was keeping watch with Mr Cudderford he said to her, 'I hear you're artistic.'

Anna admitted that she was, and Mr Cudderford looked pleased and told her that his aunt had just died. At first it was unclear how this could affect Anna, but then it transpired that the aunt had been artistic too – extremely artistic, said Mr Cudderford – and had left a lot of equipment which no one knew what to do with.

'If there's anything there that you'd like, you're welcome to it,' he told Anna, and so, the following weekend, Anna went to look at it.

The equipment was nearly all Victorian, for the aunt who had lived to the age of ninety-three had acquired most of it in her girlhood. There were two easels, several palettes and a clutter of canvases, all enormously heavy and solid. Anna was intoxicated at the sight of it. John Cotmore had been encouraging her for some time to try painting in oils, and here was nearly everything she would need for it.

'I think I could use it all,' she said, 'if you can spare it.'

Mr Cudderford was only too pleased to be rid of it and even lent her a wheelbarrow in which to carry the things home.

The problem now was where to put them. Anna's and Mama's joint bedroom could not possibly accommodate them.

'Perhaps I could use the garage,' said Anna. This was a separate building in the garden at present filled with the old lawnmower and other paraphernalia.

'But you couldn't drag your easel up to the house every

time you wanted to paint,' said Mama. 'And anyway, where would you set it up? You couldn't use oil paints in the lounge.'

Then Frau Gruber had an idea. Above the garage was a small room where, in the maharajah's day, the chauffeur must have slept. It was dusty and unheated but empty, and there was even a basin with a tap in one corner.

'No one ever uses this,' she said. 'You could have it as a studio.'

Anna was delighted. She moved in her equipment, wiping at the dust half-heartedly, for it did not bother her, and took a hard look round. All she needed now was some form of heating and some paints and brushes. She dealt with the heating by buying a second-hand paraffin stove, but after this her money was exhausted. It was difficult, nowadays, to save anything out of her wages, for prices had gone up and her wages hadn't.

'Max,' she said next time she saw him, 'could you lend me eight shillings and ninepence?'

'What for?' he asked, and she explained.

He pulled a ten shilling note from his pocket and handed it to her.

'A gift,' he said, 'not a loan,' and when she thanked him he sighed and said, 'I've always wanted to be a patron of the arts.'

They were sitting in the buffet at Paddington, waiting for his train to take him back to his RAF station. Nowadays he made frequent trips to London, often calling only briefly on Mama and Papa, and always seemed abstracted. She watched him nervously crumbling a bright yellow object described as a bun on his plate.

'Are you all right?' she said. 'Why do you keep getting leave to come to London? Are you up to something?'

'Of course not,' he said quickly. 'I come to London to see you and Sally and Prue and Clarissa and Peggy . . .'

He had a host of girl-friends, but she did not believe that was the reason.

'All right,' he said at last, 'but don't tell anyone. I'm trying to get on ops.'

'You mean you're going to fly on operations?'

Max nodded. 'Only I've had half a dozen interviews so far without getting anywhere, so there seemed no point in talking about it.'

'It would be an awful risk, wouldn't it?' said Anna.

Max shrugged his shoulders. 'No worse than what I'm doing now.'

'But, Max!' she cried. It seemed madness to her.

'Listen,' he said, 'I've been an instructor long enough. I'm bored, and when I'm bored I get careless. The other night –' He stopped.

'What?' said Anna.

'Well, I suppose I nearly killed myself. And my pupil.' He suddenly noticed the bun in his fingers and dropped it on the plate in disgust. 'It was a stupid mistake – something to do with the navigation. I thought I was approaching Manchester . . . Anyway, I almost flew into a Welsh mountain.'

'What did you do?' asked Anna.

He grinned. 'Turned left,' he said. 'Very quickly.' Seeing her face, he added, 'Don't worry – I've been very careful ever since. And don't tell Mama.'

Anna bought the brushes and paints the next day in her lunch-hour. In the evening at art school she asked John Cotmore's advice on how to use them. He told her how to set out the paints on her palette, how to thin them down when necessary and how to clean her brushes. By the weekend she felt she was ready to start painting.

She had decided, since her first painting might not be very good (though one could never tell), that she would not waste her only unused canvas on it. John Cotmore had explained to her that she could paint over a used canvas and she had chosen one that was not too big. It must have been one of Mr Cudderford's aunt's last efforts, she thought, for it was only half-finished. It showed a worried-looking stag peering out of a bush, and there had evidently been some intention of having a whole lot more stags leaping about in the background, but either Mr Cudderford's aunt had become discouraged or old age had gripped her – at any rate this part of the painting was barely sketched in.

Anna picked up a stick of charcoal and, ignoring the stag's reproachful eye, began to map out her design. She planned to paint a group of shelterers. Since the recent air raids many of them had returned to the tube with their bundles and blankets, and the painting was to show not only what they looked like but how they felt. It was to be very sombre and moving. She quickly sketched out the shapes of three women, two sitting and one lying on a bunk above them, so that they just filled the canvas. Then she squeezed some colours on to her palette, and then she stopped.

Were you supposed to thin the colours with turps or linseed oil? She was pretty sure John Cotmore had said turps, but suddenly felt it would be nice to talk to him before actually starting to paint. She flew up to the public telephone, looked up his number in the book, dialled and found herself almost choked with nerves when he replied.

'Hullo?' he said. He sounded half-asleep.

'It's Anna,' she said, and he immediately woke up.

'Well, hullo,' he said. 'What can I do for you?'

'I'm just going to start to paint.' She seemed to have less than her usual amount of breath, so she added as briefly as possible, 'Is it turps or linseed oil that you should use as a thinner?'

'Turps,' he said. 'Linseed oil would make it sticky.'

There was a pause, and then, to make the conversation last longer, 'I thought you'd said turps, but I wasn't sure.'

'Oh yes, definitely turps.'

There was another pause and then he said, 'Well, nice to hear your voice.'

'And yours,' she said with infinite daring.

'Is it?' He laughed. 'Well, good luck with the painting.'

After this she could think of nothing more to say and had to ring off.

She walked back through the garden and it was quite a long time before she could compose herself enough to start work.

She spent most of the day covering up the stag. It was impossible to see her composition properly as long as he was staring out of the middle of it, and in her hurry to get rid of him she quickly painted in the main shapes as best she could. The following morning she concentrated on improving them, and it was not until the afternoon that she began to have doubts. By this time she had painted everything except the bunk, which would be tedious, but the picture still did not look right. I'll leave it, she thought. I'll look at it again next weekend when I'm fresh.

'How's the painting?' John Cotmore asked her at art school the following week. It was the first time he had ever sought her out to speak to her alone.

'I'm not sure,' she said.

The following Saturday she was shocked when she saw it again. Now that the paint had dried not only did the colours look unpleasant, but the whole thing had gone flat. Also, due to some chemical process, the stag's eye had reappeared and glowed faintly through one of the shelterer's faces.

Well, at least I know what's wrong with it, she thought. There's no light on it. She painted out the stag's eye and spent the rest of the weekend changing the colours and putting on dabs of light in various places. It was difficult because, as she gradually realized, she was not at all sure where the light would come. At the end the painting looked different but not much better – a speckled effect rather than a flat one – and she was very depressed.

'I'm having a lot of trouble with my painting,' she told John Cotmore. 'Could I show it to you some time?'

'Of course,' he said. Then he added casually, 'It's difficult to talk properly here. Why don't you bring it round to my house? Come and have tea on Saturday.'

She was at once thrown into confusion.

Girls didn't go alone to men's houses . . . did they? On the other hand, why not? She looked at him, carelessly perched on one of the stools in the art-room. He seemed quite unconcerned, as though he had suggested something very ordinary.

'All right,' she said with a curious sense of excitement, and he wrote down the address for her on a piece of paper. Then he added the telephone number. 'In case you change your mind,' he said.

In case she changed her mind? Did that mean it wasn't so ordinary after all? Oh, she thought, I wish we'd always stayed in one country, then Mama would have been able to tell me what people do and what they don't do, and I'd know!

She worried about it for the rest of the week. She played with the idea of asking Mama's advice, of ringing up at the last moment and saying no, but all the time she knew with mounting excitement that she would go, that she would not tell Mama, and while part of her mind was still inventing excuses for calling the whole thing off another had already decided what she would wear. On Saturday she told Mama, as she had always known she would, that she was meeting a girl-friend from art school, and went.

John Cotmore lived in a quiet road in Hampstead. It was the first warm day of the year and as Anna walked up slowly from the tube station she passed flowering trees, people working in their gardens and open windows everywhere. She was early and had time to make several detours before stopping outside the door. A notice above the bell said Out of Order and after a moment she used the knocker. Nothing happened and panic seized her at the thought that he might have forgotten and gone out – to be replaced by relief and a different kind of panic as the door opened and he appeared.

'Hullo,' he said. He was wearing a blue sweater which she had never seen and was holding a spoon in one hand.

'Just getting the tea ready,' he said.

She waved her painting, wrapped in brown paper, like a passport and followed him into the house.

It was bright and empty and specks of dust danced in the light of his large untidy living-room.

'Sit down,' he said, and she sat in a chair with the painting beside her.

Through the door at the end of the room she could see his studio and there were stacks of drawings everywhere.

'I'm working for another exhibition,' he said. 'These are some of the ones I've done recently.'

'Oh!' she said and stood up again to look at them.

They were mostly figures and a few landscapes in pen and wash, all drawn with his usual perceptive precision. It was embarrassing to go through them while he watched, but she really admired them and so found various suitable things to say. There was one in particular, a wash drawing of trees and a wide expanse of sky, which had such a feeling of wetness and spring that she forgot all her careful phrases and cried instead, 'It's lovely!'

He was looking at it critically over her shoulder.

'You think I should put it in?'

'Oh yes,' she cried. 'You must – it's beautiful.'

He was standing quite close to her and for a moment she felt his hand on her arm.

'You're very sweet,' he said. Then he said, 'Must put the

kettle on,' and disappeared, leaving her alone and slightly light-headed.

She could hear him clattering in the kitchen nearby – he must have found more to do than just the kettle – and after a while she began to look through another stack of drawings on the sofa. These seemed to be mostly unfinished or discarded sketches, but there was one different from the rest. It showed a man working some kind of a machine. The man looked very strong and every bit of the machine, down to the tiniest screw, was carefully drawn and shaded. She was looking at it in surprise when she heard his voice behind her.

'That's not mine,' he said. 'That's my wife's.'

He sounded put out, and she dropped it as though it were red-hot.

'I wondered why it was so different,' she said quickly, and to her relief he smiled.

'Yes, amazing – all those nuts and bolts.' He replaced the drawing and threw some others on top. 'But a lot of precision there. She's very keen on social significance, whereas I – ' He gestured towards his own work and Anna nodded sympathetically. It must be awful for a man of his sensitivity to be tied to someone so fond of nuts and bolts.

'It's easier since we live apart,' he said. 'We each go our own way – quite a friendly arrangement.'

She did not know what to answer, and he added, 'You probably don't know about such things at your age, but people make mistakes and marriages break up. It's no use blaming anyone.'

She nodded again, touched by his generosity.

'Well then,' he said, 'let's have some tea.'

The kitchen was even untidier than the living-room, but he had cleared a space among the clutter of jugs and saucepans and unwashed crockery for a tray laid ready for two. She helped him carry it into the living-room, suddenly less bright, for the sun had moved round a corner, and he lit the gas fire and moved two chairs up close to it. She watched him as he poured the tea into two cups of different shape and then they sat together in the pale glow of the fire.

'I've been working flat out,' he said, and began to tell her about his work, about his frame-maker and the difficulty of finding the right kind of paper in war-time.

Gradually the room grew warmer. She noticed how his sweater wrinkled at the elbows, how his stubby fingers fitted round his cup. A great contentment filled her. His voice droned pleasantly on and she had long ceased to listen to the words when it suddenly stopped.

'What?' she said. She had a feeling that there had been a question.

'What about your painting?' he said.

'My painting!'

She jumped up guiltily to fetch it.

It looked worse than ever as it emerged from its wrapping and there was no mistaking his expression when he saw it.

'It's awful,' she said. 'I know it's awful, but I thought you could help me with it.'

He stared at it in silence. Then he pointed to a misty shape which had appeared in the centre and asked, 'What's that?'

'A stag,' she said.

'A stag?' he asked, startled.

Suddenly she was filled with rage and shame at having spoiled the afternoon with her awful picture.

'Yes,' she cried. 'A bloody great stag that was underneath and keeps coming through, and I don't know how anyone can manage these impossible paints, and I think the only thing is for me to give it all up!'

She glared at him, daring him to laugh, and he put his arm round her shoulders.

'Come on,' he said. 'It's not as bad as all that. There's nothing wrong with what you were trying to do. Only you've got a lot to learn.'

She said nothing.

He dropped the painting on to a chair but left his arm where it was.

'As a matter of fact,' he said, 'I've been offered another evening's teaching. I thought we might make it a painting class rather than a drawing class – what do you think?'

It flashed across her mind that if there was to be a painting class she could have shown him the picture at school instead of coming to his house, but she pushed the thought aside.

'It would be marvellous,' she said faintly.

His face was very close to hers.

'I just wanted to know,' he murmured, 'what you thought.'

And then, as she had always known he would, he put his other arm round her and kissed her gently, slowly and lovingly on the lips.

I'm being kissed! she thought and was horrified to find herself looking past him at the mirror above the fireplace to see what it looked like. Her hands were clasped behind his neck and she hurriedly unclasped them and put them on his shoulders. But at the same time something she had never felt stirred inside her and the happiness which had filled her for so long rose to a climax. This is it, she thought. This was what it was all about. This was the marvellous thing she had always known was going to happen.

After a long time he let her go.

'I'm sorry,' he said. 'I didn't mean to do that.'

She found herself sitting down without quite knowing how she had got there.

'It's all right,' she said. She thought of adding, 'I don't mind,' but it seemed inadequate.

He sat close to her in the other chair and for a long time there was nothing but the room and the fire and her own overwhelming happiness.

'I must talk to you very seriously,' he said at last.

She looked at him.

'No, I mean it,' he said. 'You're very young.'

'Eighteen,' she said. For some reason she could not stop smiling.

'Eighteen,' he nodded. 'And you're quite happy. Aren't you?'

'Oh yes,' she said. 'Of course.'

'Well – how shall I put this – I wouldn't want to disturb you.'

Why did he have to do all this talking? She would have been quite content just to sit. And what did he mean, disturb her? If only I was English, she thought, I would know what he meant.

'Disturb me?' she said.

'If I made love to you now . . .' He waited. 'It would disturb you, wouldn't it?'

But it wouldn't disturb her if he kissed her again, or

held her hand. What did he mean, made love to her?

To cover her confusion, she said carelessly, 'Not necessarily.'

'It wouldn't disturb you if I made love to you?' He seemed very surprised.

An English girl would know, she thought desperately, she would know exactly. Why couldn't she have grown up in one country like everyone else?

He was waiting for her answer, and at last she shrugged her shoulders. 'Well,' she said in as worldly a voice as she could manage, 'it didn't disturb me just now.'

He suddenly sat back in his chair.

'Would you like some more tea?' he asked after a moment.

'No.'

But he poured a cup for himself and drank it slowly. Then he stood up and took her hand.

'Come along,' he said. 'I'm going to send you home.'

'Now?'

'Now.'

Before she could recover from her surprise, he had fetched her coat and put it on her as though she were a child. Then he handed her her painting, back in its paper bag.

'There,' he said. 'You'll just get home before the blackout.'

'But I don't mind . . .' she said, as he propelled her gently out of the room, '. . . about the blackout . . .'

They had reached the front door and the rest of the words went out of her head as he kissed her again.

'You do understand,' he murmured. 'It's just that I don't want to disturb you.'

She nodded, moved by the warmth of his voice. He seemed to expect something more, so she said, 'Thank you.'

All the way home on the tube she thought how wonderful he was. For he must have meant . . . But he loved her too much, he respected her too much. To take advantage of me! she thought, and the phrase seemed to her deliciously funny. Slowly she went over the afternoon look by look, word by word, gesture by gesture. He loves me! she thought incredulously. John Cotmore loves me! She felt that it must show on her somehow, that she must look different. She stared at her reflection, racing dimly down the tunnels in the window beside her, and was surprised to find it looking as usual. He loves me, she thought again, I am sitting here on the Bakerloo line and he loves me.

Then she thought, I must never forget this moment. Because even if nothing good ever happens to me again, it will have been worth living just to feel as I do now.

CHAPTER 19

It was a poor summer, but Anna hardly noticed. She thought only of John Cotmore and of learning to paint. The painting classes had been introduced on Fridays, so she saw him four evenings a week. At school and even at the café afterwards he treated her just like everyone else – well, of course he had to do that, she thought. But when they found themselves alone in a corridor or walking to the tube he would kiss her as he had kissed her at his studio, dispelling any doubts she might have had about his feelings for her. Afterwards he always reproached himself for his weakness which showed, thought Anna, what a marvellous person he was and made her admire him more than ever. She lived in a daze of happiness from Mondays to Fridays (with a little dip on Wednesdays when there was no evening class) and somehow fought her way through the arid desert of the weekends until Monday was once more in sight.

I'm in love, she thought. She had often wondered whether this would ever happen to her and it was satisfying that it had. If people only knew, she thought as she parcelled up wool and listed bits of uniform. If I suddenly said to them, I'm in love with my drawing teacher! Then she thought, how corny – Victorian girls were always falling in love with their drawing teachers. But how witty of her to realize that it was corny. And yet, how strange that knowing it was corny made not a bit of difference to the way she felt! She hugged the whole range of complicated new feelings to herself, posting navy wool to helpless old ladies who had particularly stipulated only Air Force blue, and tried a different track. I'm in love, she thought daringly, with a married man!

Fortunately her new emotions did not affect her work at the art school. On the contrary, she seemed to have developed an added perceptiveness and her drawings and even her newly-acquired skills in painting improved almost visibly from week to week.

'You seem to have struck a very happy patch,' said Welsh

William, and she smiled secretly at the aptness of the phrase.

Even the war was going better at last. The British army had at last won the battle of North Africa, and in August the Russians began to push the Germans back towards their own frontiers. Quite a lot of people thought it might all be over in another year.

Only at home things were worse rather than better. Frau Gruber, who had always tried not to charge too much, had finally had to raise the price for board and lodging by five shillings a week. Anna could just manage this out of her wages, but for Mama and Papa it made solvency suddenly impossible.

In despair Mama asked her new boss for a rise. He was a refugee dress manufacturer with a modest workroom at the back of Oxford Circus. His English was poor and Mama not only typed his letters but corrected them. However, the business brought in very little profit and when she spoke to him about the money he spread his arms wide and said, 'I'm sorry, my dear, but more I cannot!'

At first she consoled herself by laughing with Anna at this strange phraseology, but they both knew it was disaster. It meant that, yet again, every new tube of toothpaste, every shoe repair, would cause a major crisis and that, however much she scraped and saved, she would not be able to pay the bills at the end of the week.

'Do you think perhaps Max . . . ?' said Anna, but Mama shouted, 'No!'

Max had finally succeeded in getting transferred to operational flying and Mama was worried sick about him. He had persuaded Coastal Command to accept him, arguing that, even though RAF rules forbade him to fly over enemy territory, there was nothing to stop him flying over the sea. So far he was still in training, but soon he would be risking his life three, four, five times a week.

'No,' said Mama, 'I'm not asking Max for money.'

In the end Aunt Louise came to the rescue as usual. She gave Mama twenty pounds, and as the weekly deficit was only a matter of shillings, this would last for many months.

'She really is a good friend,' said Mama. She thought it specially touching that Aunt Louise had asked, quite diffidently, whether in return Papa would mind just looking at something the Professor had written. 'It would mean so much to him,' she said, 'to have the views of a great writer.'

Papa sighed and said he could not imagine the Professor writing anything, unless it were a medical book.

'Heaven preserve us if it's poetry!' he said, and Mama said nervously, 'Whatever it is, you've got to be nice about it!'

It turned out that the Professor was writing neither poems nor medical books but his memoirs. He was dictating them to his secretary in the country and so far they had produced two chapters between them.

'What are they like?' Anna asked Papa.

Papa shrugged his shoulders.

'He can't write,' he said, 'but some of it is quite interesting. I didn't know, for instance, that the Minister of Justice under the Weimar republic had stomach ulcers.'

Even this did not sound very interesting to Anna.

'What will you do?' she asked.

He pulled a face. 'I suppose I'll have to go and talk to him about it.'

The Professor was filled with encouragement even by Papa's careful comments. He listened only absently to Papa's advice on keeping sentences short and adjectives to a minimum.

'Wait till you see the next two chapters!' he cried. 'About my social life!' Many of his patients in Berlin had been famous and he had gone to all their parties.

'I'm afraid he's going to write a lot of rubbish,' said Papa when he got back, but Mama said, 'Well, where's the harm in your just looking at it for him?'

The next two chapters must have taken the Professor longer to write, for no more typescript arrived for Papa for some time.

Anna went to the office and to her evening classes and dreamed about John Cotmore. She found it difficult to take an interest in her secretarial work, and once she caused a crisis in the sewing-room when she absent-mindedly put the cutting-out material in front of Miss Potter's place instead of Miss Clinton-Brown's. Miss Potter cut out three pairs of pyjama trousers before she could be stopped, with a total of six right legs and no left ones. When Mrs Riley pointed out her mistake she wept and had to go home to her budgie, and Miss Clinton-Brown was so outraged that she had to appeal to God for patience, with little success.

There was not much to do on the Officers' Clothing side. Fewer things were being sunk, and the sailors who had often needed to be completely re-equipped only rarely came now. In fact, there seemed hardly enough young men to occupy both Mrs Hammond and Mrs James, and rather than embarrass them with their joint attentions they came to a tacit agreement to take it in turns to help them. This meant that both had more time on their hands. Mrs Hammond used it to dictate more letters or to chat with the old ladies in the sewing-room, but Mrs James seemed simply to shrink. She sat in her makeshift office, staring at the piles of dead men's clothing with her huge, empty eyes, and sometimes did not even notice Anna when she came in with a message or a cup of tea.

'I'm worried about her,' said Mrs Hammond, but as soon as a young man in need appeared Mrs James came back to life.

One day Anna was taking down some notes in Mrs Hammond's office. Mrs Hammond had just finished supplying a Flight Lieutenant who had lost his possessions in an air raid. He had been particularly grateful and Mrs Hammond wanted to write to his commanding officer, to offer help to anyone else who might need it. However, she had hardly begun to dictate the letter when the door opened and Mrs James appeared. She looked more grey and gaunt than ever and, ignoring Anna, she looked straight at Mrs Hammond.

'I don't want to make a fuss,' she said, 'but it was my turn to look after that young man.'

'But you looked after the Pilot Officer this morning,' said Mrs Hammond, surprised.

Mrs James just stood there, staring at her with her great eyes, and Mrs Hammond motioned to Anna to go back into the sewing-room. As she went out Mrs James spoke again.

'The Pilot Officer only wanted a cap. He didn't count.'

The old ladies had stopped machining at Mrs James's appearance.

'She strode past those pyjamas just like Lady Macbeth,' declared Mrs Riley.

'Looking ever so poorly,' said Miss Potter, and Miss

Clinton-Brown murmured, 'Such an odd way to behave.'

They all strained their ears for sounds from the office but there was nothing to be heard above a low mumble of voices. Anna had just decided to put on the kettle for tea when one of the voices rose to a higher pitch.

'It's not fair!' cried Mrs James. 'I can't work with someone who isn't fair!'

The door suddenly opened and Mrs James ran out.

'Especially as the whole thing was my idea in the first place!' she shouted and made for the storage room with Mrs Hammond in pursuit. Mrs Hammond tried to close the door behind her but missed, and Anna could see Mrs James stop short at the sight of the uniforms and begin to finger them in the semi-darkness.

'I have to explain to you,' she said in a voice which was both reasonable and somehow alarming, 'that far more young men have now died than remain alive. That's why we have all these clothes which nobody wants.'

Mrs Hammond said something like 'no' or 'nonsense', but Mrs James swept her aside.

'And since there are so few young men left,' she said in the same queer voice, 'they have to be allocated very fairly. And the only fair way is for me to look after twice as many as you.'

Mrs Hammond had been making vaguely soothing noises, but this last sentence so astonished her that she cried, 'For heaven's sake, why?'

Mrs James turned and Anna caught a glimpse of her face which looked quite mad.

'Well, it's obvious, isn't it?' she said. 'After all you only lost one son, but I lost two.'

As Mrs Hammond stared at her, she added matter of factly, 'I knew you wouldn't understand. There is no point in our continuing together.'

Afterwards Mrs Hammond told Anna that Mrs James was suffering from strain and that she hoped to sort things out with her when she was feeling better. But Mrs James never reappeared in the office. A few days later the pug-faced man arrived with a letter explaining that in future Mrs James would run the Officers' Clothing scheme by herself on different premises.

Since it had, indeed, been her idea, there was nothing anyone could do. He loaded up all the uniforms, shoes, handkerchiefs and shirts, the paperbacks and the odd golf-clubs and the writing cases which no one had known what to do with, and drove away, leaving Mrs Hammond alone in the empty store-room.

Many weeks later she heard that Mrs James had become too ill to work and that her scheme had been taken over by a charitable organization.

'What made her suddenly break down after all this time?' wondered Anna.

'Four years of war,' said Mrs Hammond. 'And the news being better.'

When Anna looked at her without understanding she said impatiently, 'The thought of peace – when there's no longer any point.'

Without the Officers' Clothing scheme, the place was very quiet. For a while Mrs Hammond continued to come in every day, as though to prove that it didn't matter, but there really was not much for her to do and gradually she stayed away once, twice and finally three or four times a week. The days grew long and dull again, and Anna found them hard to get through.

Only nine o'clock, she would think when she arrived in the morning. How could she break up those endless, pointless hours which stretched before her until she could go to her art class? Her lunch-hour was the only bright spot and she could hardly wait for the old ladies to pack up their work and go, so as to get out of the place herself.

When the weather was wet she sat in the Lyons tea-shop, drawing everyone in sight, but when it was dry she would eat very quickly and then wander about the streets. She discovered some stables at the back of the Army and Navy stores where the mules that pulled the war-time delivery carts were quartered and spent several weeks trying to draw their gloomy, strangely proportioned faces. Once she saw some girls in Air Force uniform struggling with a barrage balloon in Vincent Square and drew them too. Sometimes she found nothing, or the drawings did not come out as she wanted, and then she returned to her typewriter guilty and depressed, and the afternoon seemed longer than ever.

Wednesdays were her worst days because there was not even an art class at the end of them and she only survived them by making small purchases – a pencil with a pre-war coat of yellow paint from a secret store she had discovered in a shop in Victoria Street, an ounce of unrationed sherbet powder to eat surreptitiously during the afternoon, a packet of saccharine for John Cotmore who liked his tea very sweet and found saccharine hard to get. Just having this in her pocket made her feel better since it was proof that she would be seeing him again soon.

One Wednesday when she came home she met Aunt Louise on the doorstep. She was saying goodbye to Mama and Papa and seemed in high spirits.

'I am sure,' she was saying, 'that we shall all be very happy with this arrangement.'

Then she saw Anna who was wearing her old school coat over her ancient skirt and sweater because Wednesday was such an awful day that it wasn't worth wearing anything better.

'Well, hullo,' she said, and her eyebrows rose at the sight of the dreadful clothes. Then she turned back to Mama. 'It may help Anna as well,' she said.

'What arrangement?' asked Anna after Aunt Louise had climbed into her big blue car and driven away.

'Louise has asked me to revise Sam's memoirs,' said Papa.

'They want to give us another twenty pounds,' said Mama.

Anna looked from one to the other.

'Are you going to do it?' she asked.

Papa said carefully, 'I said I'd look at them.'

At supper that evening Papa was very quiet. To while away the time between the main course – turnip pie – and the pudding, Mama was trying to do *The Times* crossword. Miss Thwaites had introduced her to this, and not only was Mama very good at it but it also made her feel very English. She read out clues, announced triumphant solutions and every so often asked for advice, which Anna gave her, until she noticed how isolated this made Papa.

'How are the Professor's memoirs?' she asked in German.

He raised his eyes to heaven. 'Unbelievable,' he said.

Mama at once came out of her crossword.

'But you're going to revise them!' she cried.

At that moment the waitress arrived with the pudding

and Papa said, 'Let's discuss it upstairs.'

Afterwards, in his room, he leafed through the Professor's latest efforts.

'It's incredibly bad,' he said. 'Listen to this : "He had piercing eyes in a face framed by an ample grey beard." That's Hauptmann the playwright.'

'Well, it's not so bad,' said Mama.

'Wait!' cried Papa. 'This is Marlene Dietrich.' He turned a page and read, ' "She had piercing eyes in a face framed by corn-coloured locks," and again –' He waved Mama into silence – ' "I was surprised by the piercing eyes in the face framed by a small moustache." The last one is Einstein, and I can understand Sam being surprised. I should think Einstein would be surprised as well, seeing where his moustache had got to.'

'Well, of course he's not used –' began Mama, but Anna interrupted her.

'Why does the Professor want you to revise this stuff?' she cried. 'Surely he must know that no one would ever publish it!'

'You don't know anything about it,' said Mama crossly. 'One of his patients is a publisher and Louise says he's very interested. He's even suggested a translator.'

'Gossip writing,' said Papa. 'It seems there's a market for it.'

Anna suddenly remembered the piece Papa had read out at the International Writers' Club long ago, where each word had been exactly right, and how moved she had been and how everyone had clapped.

'I don't think you should have anything to do with it!' she cried. 'I think it's disgusting – someone who can write like you and this . . . this horrible rubbish. I think you should simply refuse!'

'Oh,' cried Mama, 'and what would you suggest I tell Louise? That we're grateful for all her help in the past, that no doubt we'll need it again, but that Papa refuses to do the one thing she's ever asked of us in return?'

'No, of course not!' cried Anna. 'But there must be another way!'

'I'd be glad to hear what it is,' said Mama.

Anna tried to think of one.

'Well, there must be something you can do,' she said at

last and added, to Mama's rage, 'it's just a matter of using a little tact.'

Mama exploded and it was some time before Papa could cut through the stream of angry words to say that it would be best if he and Mama discussed it alone.

Anna swept out and locked herself in the bathroom. For once the water was hot and she soaked herself in a huge bath, glaring defiantly at the line four inches from the bottom which denoted the maximum depth allowed in war-time. I don't care, she thought, but it did not make her feel any better.

Later in their joint bedroom Mama explained in a careful voice that she and Papa had agreed on a compromise. Papa would correct the Professor's worst excesses, but any further changes should be made by the publisher if and when the memoirs were translated into English.

'I see,' said Anna in an equally careful voice, and pretended almost at once to fall asleep. As she lay awake in the close, dark room she could hear Mama crying quietly a few feet away.

'Mama . . .' she said, overwhelmed by pity. But Mama did not hear and she found herself suddenly filled with an equally strong desire not to listen to the sounds from the other bed, not to be involved, to be somewhere else.

John, she thought. The previous evening at art school John Cotmore had shown her sketch book to Barbara. 'Talented little thing, isn't she?' he had said, and later, when they were walking to the tube, he had kissed her secretly behind a pillar. She wished she could be with him now, that she could always be with him.

If I gave myself to him, she thought, and part of her felt full of love and daring while another giggled at the novelettishness of the phrase. But how did one set about it? She imagined herself saying something like 'I am yours.' But then? Suppose he looked embarrassed, or just not very keen? And even if he said exactly the right thing like 'My darling,' or 'I love you,' – how did one manage the rest? And where would they do it? she suddenly thought in alarm. She had never seen his bedroom, but if it was anything like the kitchen . . .

The sounds from the other bed had stopped. Mama must be asleep.

I'll make it up with her in the morning, thought Anna. And as she herself drifted off into sleep, she wished that Papa could suddenly earn a huge sum of money, that they didn't have to be grateful to the Rosenbergs, and that everything were quite, quite different.

CHAPTER 20

'I think it's time you did something,' John Cotmore said
to Anna a few weeks later at art school. 'I mean something
more than drawing from the model or filling up sketch
books.' He was sitting on the edge of the model's throne
with Welsh William and Barbara who nodded in agreement.

'What sort of thing?'

He gestured vaguely. 'Something of your own. Illustrate
a book – paint a wall – anything.'

'A wall!' The idea at once appealed to her. But where
would one find one?

'I did a mural in a school once,' said Barbara. 'It was
great fun. All you need is some oil-bound distemper and a
few large brushes.'

'Not so many walls left, though,' said Welsh William.

1944 had begun, ominously, with the heaviest air raids
in years.

John Cotmore waved him aside. 'All the more reason
for painting them,' he said.

The idea of the wall stuck in Anna's mind and she found
herself examining any large vertical surface with a view
to decorating it. She thought briefly about the disused ward
where the officers' clothing had been stored, but dismissed
it. It was dark and no one would ever see it – there would
be no point.

There was nothing in the hotel either, but then, one day,
she found just the right place. It was pouring with rain
and, rather than get soaked walking to the Lyons tea-shop
which was some distance away, she decided to have lunch
in a café in Victoria Street. The tables were packed with
steaming bodies and she ordered Russian steak (mince
patriotically renamed from the Vienna steak of pre-war
days) with a pleasant sense of extravagance.

While she was waiting for it to arrive she looked round
and suddenly realized that the café was exactly what she
had been looking for. It consisted of several rooms knocked
into one and the result was an irregularly-shaped space
bounded by a great many walls at different angles. They

were all painted pale cream and there was absolutely nothing on them except a few mirrors. Surreptitiously she counted them. Nine. Nine walls all crying out to be painted! She eyed them greedily all through the Russian steak and the eggless, sugarless trifle that followed it. I could really do something here, she thought.

She ate at the café again the following lunch-time, bankrupting herself for the rest of the week, and thought about it for several more days before she summoned up enough courage to do anything about it. Finally, one evening after she had finished work she walked past it twice, peered through the windows and at last went in.

'We're closed,' said a stocky man who was scattering knives and forks over the empty tables.

'Oh, I haven't come for a meal,' said Anna.

'What then?'

She produced the speech she had been rehearsing for three days. 'I'm a painter,' she said, 'and I specialize in murals. I wondered if you'd like me to decorate your restaurant.'

Before the stocky man could answer, a voice called out from the basement.

'Albert,' it cried. 'Who you talkin' to?'

'Little girl,' Albert called back. 'Wants to do some paintin'.'

'What sort o' paintin'?' shouted the voice.

'Yeah, what sort o' paintin'?' said Albert.

'Decorations,' said Anna as grandly as she could manage. 'Pictures. On your walls.'

'Pitchers,' shouted Albert just as the owner of the voice emerged from the basement, saying, 'I 'eard.'

It was a very large woman with a pale face and small, dark eyes like a hedgehog's, and she was carrying a trayful of glasses. She put the tray down on a table and looked from Anna to the walls and back again.

'What wouldyer paint on 'em then?' she asked.

Anna was prepared for this.

'I thought as it's called the Victoria restaurant,' she said, 'it might be nice to have some Victorian scenes. Men in tophats, children playing with hoops – that sort of thing.'

'Bit grand, init?' said Albert.

'Dunno – might brighten it up at that,' said the large woman. 'If it was done nice.' She looked at Anna. 'You don't seem like you was very old.'

Anna by-passed this neatly. 'Well, of course I'd let you see sketches,' she said. 'I'd do it all on paper first, so you could see what it would look like.'

'Sketches,' said the woman. 'That'd be nice. Don't you think that'd be nice, Albert?'

Albert looked doubtful and Anna wanted to kill him. He searched his mind for objections and finally came up with, 'What about me mirrors? I'm not takin' down none o' me mirrors.'

'Young lady'd paint round 'em, wouldn't you, dear?' said the woman trustingly.

Anna had had no such intention.

'Well – ' she said.

'He couldn't take 'em down,' said the woman. 'I mean, Albert paid good money for them mirrors, din you, Albert? He couldn't just waste 'em.'

Nine walls, thought Anna. What did a few mirrors matter?

'All right,' she said and added, to save her dignity, 'I'll incorporate them in the design.'

'That'd be nice,' said the woman. 'Wouldnit, Albert?'

Then they both stood looking at Anna in silence.

Was it settled? She decided to assume that it was.

'Good,' she said as carelessly as she could. 'I'll come and measure up the walls this time tomorrow.'

No one objected.

'See you then,' she said, and managed somehow to walk out of the place as though nothing special had happened.

'I'm going to decorate a restaurant!' she shouted triumphantly as soon as she saw John Cotmore, and he gave her a quantity of advice which ended with kissing her behind the paint cupboard.

It was not until she got home that she realized that she had completely forgotten to mention any payment for her work.

She spent the next three weeks making sketches. A book from the library gave her all the information she needed about Victorian dress, and she worked every weekend and often in the evenings, even giving up some of her life-classes so as to get the drawings done.

The mirrors were not nearly such a nuisance as she had

expected. They were all different shapes and sizes, and she found that she could make them stand for some large object which she then surrounded with people. An upright mirror made the main body of a puppet theatre, with Punch and Judy painted at the top of it and children staring up from both sides. A long thin one, with a few reeds painted round about, suggested a lake. As she finished the design for each wall, she pinned it up in her room above the garage, and both Mama and Papa came to admire them.

At last she rolled them all up together and submitted them to her patrons, spreading them over half the tables in the café. They stared at them in silence. At last the woman said, 'They're quite nice. Don't you think so, Albert?'

Albert looked gloomily at the drawings and at his pure cream walls.

'What's that, then?' he said, pointing to the puppet theatre.

'That's your mirror,' said Anna. 'I'm just going to paint these things round it.'

Albert checked with the wall.

'Yeah,' he said.

'It's the centre of the design,' she explained.

Albert seemed pleased. 'Yeah,' he said. 'It is, init?'

'I think it's ever so nice,' said his wife, warming to it.

Albert made up his mind.

'Yeah,' he said. 'All right then. You can do the place up.'

Anna had been wondering how to get round to the subject of money, but he forestalled her.

'How much was you thinkin' of askin'?' he said, and panicked her into coming out with the first sum she could think of.

'Fifteen pounds,' she said and at once cursed herself for ruining everything with her excessive demands, but Albert remained calm.

'Yeah,' he said. 'All right.'

After this Anna became frantically busy. The café closed for the weekend after lunch on Saturday, and she was there, waiting for the last customer to leave, from two o'clock onwards. Albert had provided a step-ladder, and she spent the first two weekends drawing her designs all over the walls in chalk. There was no heating and spring was late, so she wore two pairs of socks and several sweaters which gradually became covered in chalk dust as she drew, climbed down to view her work from a distance and climbed back again to change it.

It was strange to spend so many hours alone, with her ideas gradually becoming visible around her, and by the end of the second Sunday she was almost giddy with it.

She had drawn in the last shape to her satisfaction and sat exhausted in the middle of the floor. The white outlines of the figures were everywhere, clustered round the puppet theatre, watching the ducks on the lake and moving round the room in a cheerful procession of parasoled ladies, gentlemen on penny-farthings and children with hoops and tops. Some appeared twice over as they were reflected in the mirrors on opposite walls, and the effect was strangely dreamlike.

It looks just as I hoped it would look, she thought, and a great joy welled up in her, but she quickly subdued it to stare at each wall severely in turn, trying to catch it out in some fault of composition or proportion.

She was so absorbed that she hardly noticed the sound of knocking until it became insistent, and she realized with a shock that there was someone at the door.

As long as it isn't Albert who's changed his mind, she thought, and went to open it, but it was not Albert – it was Max in his RAF uniform, radiating warmth and energy.

'Well!' he said, looking round. 'You seem to have found your *ambience.*'

'What's an *ambience*?' she asked, and he grinned.

'What you've found.'

She showed him round and he looked at all the walls and then at her sketches, full of enthusiasm and intelligence. But the parts he liked were not always the best and she was relieved to find that in this one thing, at least, her judgment was better than his.

'I didn't know you were coming up,' she said at last. 'Have you been home?'

He nodded. 'I've got five days' leave. Finished my course.'

That meant he would be posted to an operational squadron.

'Already,' she said, as lightly as possible.

'Yes,' he said, 'and Mama and Papa both said "already" in exactly the same always-keep-a-lamp-in-the-window voice as you. I'm only doing what thousands of others are doing.'

'Oh, I know,' said Anna.

'I'm going to live all my life in this country,' said Max. 'I have to take the same risks as everyone else.'

'Everyone else,' said Anna, 'does not fly on operations.'

Max was unmoved. 'People like me do,' he said.

She began to tidy up, rolling up her drawings and pushing tables and chairs back into place.

'How did you find Mama and Papa?' she asked.

He did not answer at once. Then he said, 'They're not too good, are they?'

She shook her head. 'Seeing them every day – one gets used to it.'

Max pulled out one of the chairs she had just tidied away and sat on it.

'What worries me,' he said, 'is that I can't think of anything that would help even if one could arrange it. I mean, money would help, of course. But I still don't know how they'd live the rest of their lives.'

'I've never thought beyond the money,' said Anna.

There was a chalk mark at the side of the puppet theatre which bothered her and she wiped it off with her sleeve.

'Perhaps after the war . . .' she said vaguely.

'After the war,' said Max, 'if there's anything left in Germany to print books with, and if there are any people left who would want to read them, they'll probably republish Papa's work – in time. But he still wouldn't want to live there.'

'No,' said Anna. It would be impossible, after all that had happened. She had a vision of Mama and Papa floating in a kind of limbo. 'It's funny,' she said. 'When I was small I always used to feel so safe with them. I remember I used to think that as long as I was with them I'd never feel like a refugee. Do you remember Mama in Paris? She was marvellous.'

'Well, she still is,' said Max. 'She does everything, she keeps everything going – only the strain is making her difficult to live with.' He looked round at the chalk figures promenading all over the walls. 'I'm so glad about all this,' he said, 'and about the whole art school thing. You belong here now, just as I do. But Mama and Papa . . .'

She watched him make the face, half-smiling and half-regretful, which he always made when something was difficult, and suddenly remembered the countless times they had talked like this, sharing the worries of their disrupted childhood in four different countries.

'Oh, Max!' she cried, throwing her arms about him. 'For God's sake take care of yourself!'

'There, there,' he said, patting her back – gingerly, because of the chalk on her clothes. 'Nothing is going to happen to me.' And as she still clung to him, he added, 'After all, if it did, Mama would never forgive me!'

It took Anna five more weekends to finish painting her murals. On Barbara's advice, she used white distemper which she mixed with powder paints to get the colours she wanted. She stirred them up together in an ever-expanding collection of old tins and pots and it was a clammy, exhausting job – but she loved it. The murals continued to look as she had hoped, and as she finished the walls one after another and stood staring at them, covered in paint now as well as chalk dust, the same great joy welled up in her as on the day she had finished the drawings. Sometimes when she thought about them at home she imagined some frightful flaw which she had overlooked, and had to rush to the café early next day and peer through the windows to reassure herself. But they were always all right, and the customers as well as Albert and his wife seemed pleased.

Max got his posting and wrote after some time that he had now flown several operations and that nothing ever happened on them. 'And we always get egg and bacon on our return,' he said, 'so it's a great improvement in every way.'

No one was sure whether to believe this, but Mama could not bear to consider any other possibility and insisted that it must be true.

Finally, in May, Anna finished her murals. Albert paid her the fifteen pounds, and since she was now richer than ever before in her life, she decided to invite first Mama and Papa and then her friends from the art school to the café for a meal. Mama and Papa were both full of admiration and Anna sat happily between them in a new sweater, peering at her work through half-closed eyes and wondering only occasionally whether some hand might not have been better drawn or whether a figure on one wall might not have looked better on another.

'But it's so professional!' cried Mama, and Papa said, 'It's delightful!'

But it was the art school outing that really mattered. Anna had hardly been to evening classes while she was working on her murals – there had not been time – but now she was excited at the prospect of seeing John Cotmore again. He'll have missed me, she thought. It seemed to her suddenly that the purpose of decorating the café had been solely to show it to him, and that when he had seen it and spent a whole evening with her something must change, that something extraordinary and quite unprecedented must happen between them. He'll realize that I'm grown-up, she thought, more of an equal, and then he'll . . . She was not sure herself what he would do. But there would be some sign, some way of committing himself, of showing her that from now on things between them would be quite different.

She was in a state of feverish expectancy by the time he arrived. Hiding behind the menu in a corner, she watched him stand for a moment inside the door and saw the sudden concentration in his face as he looked at her murals. He examined each wall in turn, walking slowly round and twice retracing his steps. At last he saw her and sat down beside her.

'Well,' he said, 'you *have* grown up.'

If she'd chosen the words for him she couldn't have done it better.

'I hoped you'd like it,' she said, and then listened in happy confusion while he praised the composition, her drawing and the subtlety of the colours.

'I expected something good,' he said, 'but this is a surprise.'

She could do nothing but sit and smile and watch him as he looked at her work again, and then from her work back to her.

'So this is what you were doing,' he said, 'instead of coming to art school!'

It was all happening just as she had hoped. She nodded and smiled and saw his eyes look back at her with a new seriousness . . . And then the others were upon them.

'It's enchanting!' cried Harry from the door. 'Don't you think it's enchanting, John?'

He was followed by Welsh William who settled himself beside her. 'I was afraid it would be ladies in crinolines,' he said. 'You know, standing about with no feet, the way they used to do on chocolate boxes. How can I eat my food, I asked myself, when it's been paid for by ladies in crinolines with no feet? But now –' he gestured respectfully towards the wall – 'my conscience is clear.'

'By Winterhalter out of Berthe Morrisot,' said Barbara firmly, and Anna blushed with pleasure.

It seemed like the pleasantest evening she had ever spent. Even the food – dried egg omelette, Spam fritters, vegetable pie – seemed to her delicious. She basked in her friends' praises and listened to their news – Barbara had a new job and Welsh William had sold a drawing but was soon to be called up. She ordered food and ate it and glanced surreptitiously at her murals and watched John Cotmore's face, and all the time her excitement grew because she knew that something more was going to happen, that the best part of the evening was still to come.

At last all the food had been eaten and all the coffee had been drunk. Albert had presented her with the bill and she had paid it with a flourish, and they all stood outside the café in the early evening light.

'Well –' said John Cotmore.

Anna waited.

'Thank you for a lovely evening,' he said. 'And thank you for painting such good murals.' He took her hand and suddenly turned to Harry. 'I think one's allowed to kiss a favourite student, isn't one?' And before she had time to think he had kissed her formally on the cheek. 'Congratulations,' he said. 'May you paint many more murals as successful as these.'

Then he turned, called out something that could have been either 'good night' or 'goodbye', and walked away in the direction of Westminster, with Harry and Barbara following.

Anna could not believe that it had happened. She stood there with the smile still on her face, her hand still ready to take his arm, and the dust of Victoria blowing about her feet.

'Went off a bit sharpish, didn't he?' said Welsh William, and they both watched his figure rapidly diminish as it hared off down the street.

'Well,' said Welsh William at last, 'coming?'

She roused herself and, still in a daze, walked with him to the tube. He talked all the way, but she did not hear a word. She could think only of John Cotmore. What on earth had happened? Why had he kissed her like that and rushed away? And was it 'good night' that he had called out or 'goodbye'?

CHAPTER 21

During the next few weeks Anna's mood varied between happiness and profound depression, and the war seemed to echo her state of mind.

In June the Second Front finally became a reality. This was the landing of British and American troops in the North of France, the first step in liberating the countries overrun by the Nazis four years before. To Anna, remembering the fearful summer of 1940, this was far more exciting than any victories in Africa or Russia, and once it became clear that the Allies were firmly established she began to think, with cautious amazement, that the end of the war might really be in sight.

However, hardly had everyone's spirits risen before they were dashed again by the arrival of the flying bombs. They were Hitler's new secret weapon – pilotless planes sent across the Channel with a large charge of explosive. When they ran out of fuel they fell to the ground and blew up everything in the vicinity. Most of them were primed to fall on London.

The first time Anna saw one neither she nor Mr Cudderford could think what it was. They heard a puttering sound and saw a dark, rounded object with flames spurting from its tail move slowly across the sky. Suddenly it disappeared, the puttering had stopped, and a moment later there was a very loud explosion.

'It must have been a plane,' said Anna, but Mr Cudderford shook his head.

'None that I've ever seen,' he said.

Next day, after an air-raid warning that lasted till dawn, the explanation was in all the papers.

At first only a few flying bombs came over and people laughed at them, telling each other how silly they looked bumbling along, and inventing funny names for them like buzz-bombs or doodle-bugs. But soon they began to arrive in large numbers both by day and night. It was unnerving, as you went about your business, to listen to the sound of the engines which might cut out at any moment. You prayed for the buzz-bombs to keep going, but felt guilty while you did so because you knew they would only fall on someone else. And the fact that the war might soon be over made everyone wish, quite desperately, to stay alive.

People again began to leave London. The familiar crocodiles of children with labels reappeared at the railway stations, and every day there was new bomb damage among the old. Since the bombs came over all the time it was useless to go to a shelter, and those who remained in London simply dived into the nearest doorway or under the nearest piece of furniture when they heard a flying bomb cut out, as it seemed, immediately above their heads. Anna was constantly amazed by the agility of the old ladies. One moment they would be sitting at their machines, working away, and the next they would all be under the table, with only Miss Potter's primly overalled bottom sticking out at one side and Miss Clinton-Brown's size eight feet at the other. Mrs Riley, perhaps as a result of her early acrobatic training, always got the whole of herself tucked under.

Anna herself was not as frightened as she had been during the blitz and sometimes almost welcomed the drama of the flying bombs as a distraction from her other worries. John Cotmore had become inexplicably remote since the dinner at her restaurant and she felt as though the rug had been pulled from under her life. Then she thought about Max flying on operations, she did not know how many times a week, and it seemed to her, illogically, that by being in danger herself she must be diverting some of the danger which threatened him.

Mama was even more superstitious. She became meticulous in all her dealings, as though to satisfy some higher agency that might be watching her, and once Anna caught her, after years of only paying her bus fares when they were demanded of her, actually pressing the money into the conductor's hand. When she caught Anna's eye she said, 'I don't think one should take any chances,' and added defiantly, 'with Max flying and everything!'

At the same time, strangely enough, Mama could not bear to admit that Max was in any danger and became furious with Papa for saying that he was.

'But they shoot at him!' said Papa, and Mama cried, 'Not at him specially! And anyway, they'd never hit Max!'

The evening classes continued in spite of the flying bombs and Anna still lived from each one to the next, but they usually left her depressed and bewildered. Nothing was the same. She only spoke to John Cotmore when he formally discussed her work. Because of the bombs everyone hurried home immediately afterwards and there was only one occasion when they went to a café. This was when Welsh William was called up. He had come to show off his soldier's uniform and they plied him with talk and coffee as in the old days, but he looked forlorn and much too young to go to war, and on the whole everyone was relieved when the evening was over.

What had happened to everything? wondered Anna. Only a short time ago it had seemed so promising – the war nearly at an end, her work, and . . . and everything, she thought, unwilling to give even the vaguest shape to whatever she had expected from John Cotmore. And now it was like being back in the blitz and life seemed empty. When, at the end of July, the art school closed for the summer holidays, it seemed the end of an era.

She got a week's leave from Mrs Hammond and spent it in the country with the Rosenbergs. The Professor had abandoned his memoirs after the sixth chapter (so all that emotion had been for nothing, thought Anna) and was now deeply engrossed in growing vegetables for food. Aunt Louise carried on her usual running battle with the maids, and Anna spent much of her time painting a portrait of Fraulein Pimke in a corner of her kitchen. When she wasn't painting she helped with the vegetables and felt herself grow brown and healthy in the process.

Only at night was there nothing to do, and then she thought about John Cotmore. She re-lived her visit to his house, and the different times when he had put his arm round her, or kissed her, or said something affectionate. She even counted the number of times he had kissed her. There were eleven, not including the formal peck after dinner at her restaurant. You surely wouldn't kiss a person eleven times, she argued hopefully, unless you meant it? But what about his strange behaviour during the past weeks? That must be his conscience, she decided – because of his wife.

As she was dropping off to sleep she imagined the most

unlikely situations in which he would be driven to declare his love for her. Sometimes it was when she had done a brilliant drawing in the life class. Sometimes he found her trapped under the rubble of a flying bomb explosion, in pain but terribly brave and of course quite unmarked. Other times it was she who saved him by her courage and cheerfulness when they were buried together under the wreckage of the art school. Part of her despised herself for these imaginings, but another part found them a great comfort.

On her return to London she found a message from Barbara suggesting a meeting, and snatched at the chance at least to talk about him. They ate a modest meal at Lyons Corner House while Anna held forth about his talents and his virtues, and Barbara nodded and agreed, with her pleasant, placid smile. This made Anna feel much better, and they met twice more, once to go to a film and once to a concert. But then Barbara became too busy for further meetings, and Anna was left more lonely than ever.

One day when she was sitting bored at her typewriter Harry rang up. He had been given a batch of tickets for a concert – Beethoven and Mozart, very traditional, he said – and wondered if she'd like to go.

'Bring a friend,' he said. 'I've asked everyone I can think of and I've still got plenty of tickets left.'

Everyone Harry could think of must include John Cotmore, thought Anna, and her lethargy fell away like an old skin.

'I'd love to come!' she cried, surprising him with her enthusiasm, and at once made plans for what she would wear, how she would look, and what she would say.

'I'll be out tomorrow night,' she announced to Mama and Papa at supper. 'I'm going to a concert.'

'Who with?' asked Mama.

Anna frowned at Mama's curiosity. 'No one special,' she said. 'Just some people from the art school. There's a whole lot of tickets, but it's mostly Beethoven and some of them think that's rather old-fashioned, so not very many may turn up.'

Frau Gruber came to clear away the plates.

'No appetite today?' she asked Papa who had left most of his vegetable pie, and he smiled and shook his head.

'Beethoven,' he said, and Anna noticed that he looked pale. 'What are they playing?'

She told him – the Seventh Symphony and something else that she could not remember, and he nodded.

Mama began to say something about the food, but Papa interrupted her.

'I should like,' he said, 'to come with you.'

'To the concert?' cried Anna.

It was impossible.

'They're not proper seats,' she said quickly. 'Not like the ones you used to have in Berlin. These are right up in the gallery, just steps really, that you sit on – only students use them.'

Papa nodded. 'Nevertheless,' he said, 'I should like very much to come.'

She stared at him, horrified.

'Do you really want to go?' asked Mama. 'It does sound a bit spartan.'

Anna waited hopefully, but Papa shook his head.

'The seats are unimportant,' he said. 'I should like to hear the music.'

There was no answer to this.

After searching for one in vain, Anna mumbled some sort of agreement and spent the rest of the meal in deepest gloom. The first time in weeks that she might see John Cotmore, and she was going to be stuck with Papa! During her empty day at the office she had half-fantasized, half-formulated a plan to get him alone, perhaps even to ask him what was wrong, and then perhaps he would explain and he might say . . . But now Papa had made all that impossible.

She tried to believe, against all previous experience, that he might change his mind, but when she arrived at the theatre the following evening Papa was already there. He was looking at a poster in the foyer and in his shabby, foreign-looking coat he had a sad air which filled her with a mixture of love and irritation.

'Hullo,' she said, but before she could say any more her heart leapt at the sight of John Cotmore hurrying past to the gallery entrance. So he had come!

She bustled Papa along to Harry who had the tickets, and could hardly contain her impatience while Harry declared his delight at meeting Papa and Papa replied in his halting English. By the time they reached the gallery entrance John Cotmore had long disappeared. Papa embarked cheerfully on the long climb to the top, but it was a slow business and several students from the art school passed them on the way. They'll all sit round John, thought Anna, for gallery seats were not numbered and you sat where you liked.

Sure enough, when she and Papa emerged from the stairs into the sloping space below the roof of the theatre, she discovered John Cotmore surrounded. A whiskered man whom she recognized as another art teacher was on one side of him, Barbara was on the other, and there were students all round. She stood looking at them glumly while Papa sniffed the air beside her.

'Marvellous!' he said. 'The smell! It's years since I've been in a theatre, but it never changes.'

He suddenly darted forward.

'Shall we sit here?' he said, indicating an empty space near the gangway. 'Or perhaps,' he added, 'you would rather sit with your friends?'

Anna looked gloomily at the crowd round John Cotmore.

'This will do perfectly well,' she said.

She heard only little of the concert.

It began with some over-symmetrical early Mozart which left her mind free for other thoughts. Perhaps I'll talk to him in the interval, she thought. But when the lights brightened John Cotmore did not move from his seat and the crowd of students remained. Only Barbara came over to greet her and to be introduced to Papa. They had quite a long conversation and Anna felt better when Barbara said in her usual warm way, 'Anna, I love your father – I do hope you'll let me meet him again.'

Perhaps she would tell John Cotmore, and then he, too, would want to meet Papa – perhaps when the concert was over . . .

'Charming,' said Papa, watching Barbara go, 'absolutely charming.'

Seeing his clever, responsive face, Anna felt suddenly ashamed at having thought of him only in terms of usefulness. She moved closer to him on the hard seat.

All the same, she thought, why shouldn't she introduce him to John Cotmore? It would be a perfectly reasonable thing to do, and Papa would probably be pleased. She could seek him out after the concert . . .

The orchestra had finally reached Beethoven's Seventh Symphony and for a while she was swept along by the grandeur of the noise it made. Marvellous! she thought as it thundered through the funeral march in the slow movement. But the next movement was less compelling and gradually it lost her.

She would have to intercept John Cotmore before he left the gallery, she thought, otherwise he might have gone before she and Papa reached the bottom of the stairs. She would say, 'John, I'd like you to meet my father.' But she would have to be quick, so as to catch him before he passed them in the gangway. Instinctively, she moved in her seat, and as she did so she caught sight of Papa.

He was sitting quite still, his face a little raised and his hands folded over his coat. His eyes were half-closed, and then Anna saw that they were full of tears and that there were more tears running silently down his cheeks.

'Papa!' she said, all other thoughts stripped away.

He tried to speak but couldn't, shook his head to reassure her and finally whispered something about 'the music'.

Anxiously, she put her hand over his and sat close to him while the music roared about them, until at last it came to an end. All round them people clapped and stood up and put on their coats.

'Are you all right?' she whispered.

He nodded. 'In a moment.'

They stayed in their seats while the gallery began to empty.

'I'm sorry if I alarmed you,' he said at last. 'It's just —' He spread his hands. 'I hadn't heard it for years.'

He got to his feet and they moved out slowly in the wake of the others. Once in the fresh air he seemed to feel more himself. It was almost dark. As they picked their way through the crowd he looked back towards the shadowy theatre and murmured, 'Wonderful!' Out of the corner of her eye Anna could see John Cotmore with Harry and Barbara in a group, and for a moment she wondered — but it was no good. She took Papa's arm and they set off towards the tube. They were buying the tickets when he stopped in his tracks.

'Such emotion,' he said, making her laugh, 'and I've forgotten my hat!'

'I'll get it!'

She raced back to the theatre through the dusk, and at once the wild hope sprang up again inside her that she might yet meet John Cotmore, that the evening might yet turn out quite different.

The gallery entrance was closed and as she went round to the foyer she suddenly saw him. He was only a few feet away, a dim shape in a doorway, and his back was towards her. There was someone with him, so close as to be almost hidden behind him. They were clinging together and even before Anna heard them speak she knew who it must be.

'What will we do now?' asked John Cotmore, and Barbara's voice answered him in the darkness, 'Let's go home.'

CHAPTER 22

Anna never quite knew, afterwards, how she got home. Somehow she walked past the two shapes in the doorway, retrieved Papa's hat and rode home with him on the tube. The fact that he needed her was a help and at the sight of his face, still not quite re-set in its usual ironic composure, her own tumultuous feelings receded into some kind of proportion.

But Barbara! she thought. She could have understood if it had been his wife. How long had it been going on? Since the holidays? Or even last term? And did Barbara know about her? Had she and John Cotmore perhaps talked about her and laughed at her and her idiotic devotion to him? Showing him all her drawings, buying him saccharine in her lunch-hour . . . Each thought was more painful than the last and part of her wanted only to burst into tears and blurt it all out to Papa, while another knew that she couldn't possibly bear to talk about it.

'Are you quite well?' asked Papa. 'You look pale.'

She nodded. 'How about you?'

He was sitting next to her in the tube, nervously massaging one hand with the other.

'I've got pins and needles,' he said, and it was such an anticlimax after all her emotion that she laughed, and at the same time tears came into her eyes and she leaned against him and cried, 'Oh Papa! Oh, dear Papa . . . !'

'There,' he said, putting his arm round her shoulders, 'I'm sorry I frightened you.'

She shook her head. 'It wasn't that.'

For a moment she was afraid he would ask her what was the matter, but he only said, 'There,' again and then, very tenderly, 'Whatever it was, it will pass.'

The next day was dreadful. There was nothing to do at the office. Mrs Hammond didn't come in and even Miss Clinton-Brown and Miss Potter were away on holiday. Anna spent the morning alone with thoughts of John Cotmore while she pretended to busy herself with index cards and skeins of wool.

There's nothing left, she thought. Nothing I want to do, no one I want to see. She searched for phrases to comfort herself. Jilted? Abandoned? Crossed in love? They were corny, but they did not make her laugh. They could not keep out the humiliating memories of how she had smiled at him and hung on his lips, how she had been ready to take his arm that evening at the restaurant – and all the time he and Barbara . . . he and Barbara . . .

After lunch Mrs Riley arrived with a large scrap-book.

'My life on the boards,' she said. 'I've brought it to show you.'

There was nothing better to do, so Anna spent the afternoon with Mrs Riley by her side and Mrs Riley's miasma wafting over her. She looked at Mrs Riley in spangles in 1891, Mrs Riley in fishnet tights in 1902, Mrs Riley with a shepherd's crook and a stuffed sheep, Mrs Riley in bathing drawers. And all the time something inside her cried out for John Cotmore, for last night not to have happened, for everything to be as it had been before.

She got back late, for there was no more point in going home than going anywhere else, and was completely unprepared for the desperate figure which rushed out to meet her.

'Anna!' cried Mama, all tears and clutching fingers. 'Oh, Anna!'

'Dear God,' said Anna, since the worst seemed determined to happen. 'Is it Max?'

It was not Max. It was Papa.

Mama drew her into the house and then stopped and clutched her again in the hall.

'I found him when I came home,' she said. 'He was on the floor in his room. He'd been there for hours. His voice is all strange and there's something wrong with one of his hands.'

They stared at each other.

'Sam is coming to see him – thank heavens he's in town.' Mama let go of Anna's hand. 'He'll know what to do.'

'Can I go up to him?'

They went up to his room together.

Papa was on the bed – Frau Gruber had helped Mama to lift him. His face looked heavy and half-asleep, but when he saw Anna his lips moved as though he were trying to smile.

'Papa!' she said.

The lips moved again. 'I'm sor-ry . . .' His voice sounded thick and he could not find the words he wanted. One hand gestured helplessly while the other lay limp on the cover.

'Papa,' said Anna again and sat on the edge of the bed. She put her hand over his unmoving one and smiled. She did not say anything, so that he wouldn't have to answer.

'Sam will be here soon,' said Mama from the foot of the bed.

Papa seemed to nod and closed his eyes. After a while Mama made a sign to Anna and went.

She stayed where she was and looked at him. Was he asleep? His eyes had remained closed and his face looked calm. The curly grey hair at the sides of his head (there had been none on top as long as Anna could remember) straggled a little on the pillow. She suddenly remembered how, when she was quite small in Berlin, she had played some form of Happy Families with Max. She had usually lost because she had sacrificed everything to getting hold of one particular card in the pack – the baker, who had a thin face and a balding head. 'He looks so pretty,' she had explained to Max, 'just like Papa.'

Now Papa was lying there with his shirt collar undone and breathing slowly. Of course he was quite old. Seventy-one? Seventy-two? Anna had always known this, but it had meant nothing. He had not seemed old. He was different from other people's fathers, but not because of his age – because of the sort of person he was. Suddenly, while she was looking at him, he opened his eyes and looked straight back at her.

'An-na,' he said very slowly.

She tightened her hand over his and said, 'Don't talk,' but there was something he wanted to say.

'An-na,' he said again and then, with great difficulty, 'The con-cert . . .'

She nodded and smiled, and in spite of terrible obstacles his face moved, his lips stretched and he smiled back. 'It was . . .' The word eluded him, but he pursued it and tracked it down.

'Beau-ti-ful!' said Papa triumphantly.

The Professor confirmed what Mama and Anna had already guessed. It was a stroke.

'How bad?' said Mama.

He shrugged his shoulders. 'We'll know better in a few days.'

Papa could not be left, so Mama stayed with him always, sleeping on a makeshift bed in his room. Anna relieved her for a few hours when she came home from work. Papa clearly knew exactly what was happening to him, but did not seem afraid. On the third day, when his speech had become easier, he suddenly said, 'Strange.'

'What?' said Anna.

Papa gestured towards himself, the bed, the shabby sick-room. 'This,' he said. He added, almost admiringly, 'An amazing experience!'

When the Professor came to see him again he seemed pleased with his progress.

'We've been lucky this time,' he told Mama. 'He should recover quite quickly.'

'Completely?'

He nodded.

'Thank God.'

'But whatever possessed him?' said the Professor. 'A man in his condition – to climb up to the gallery of a theatre?'

Mama was laughing with relief. 'You know what he's like,' she said. 'And of course he didn't know – he had no idea –'

Something suddenly struck her.

'Did he?' she asked.

He looked at her with his sad black eyes.

'Three weeks ago,' he said. 'He came to me with all the classic symptoms. Headaches, pins and needles, very high blood pressure. I warned him then to be careful. And straightaway, what does he do? Drags himself up about a thousand steps to listen to Beethoven!'

Mama stared at him. 'He knew,' she said.

Anna remembered Papa during the Seventh Symphony. 'I suppose,' she said, 'that was why.'

They were sitting in the garden. For once it was a warm evening. The Woodpigeon was mowing the lawn, the Poznanskis were arguing with each other in Polish, and Frau Gruber was shelling peas into a basin.

'You said earlier,' said Mama, ' "we've been lucky this time." What did you mean?'

'Just that,' said the Professor.

'But – "this time"?'

The Professor seemed put out. 'My dear,' he said, 'your husband has had a stroke which could have been fatal. Instead, I think he'll make a complete recovery. So be grateful!'

'I am,' said Mama, 'but what did you mean?'

'For heaven's sake –' the Professor glanced uneasily at Anna – 'you must know how these things are. Once there's been a stroke there may be another. Perhaps not for years, but your husband is not a young man. And next time –' He spread his hands. 'Next time,' he said sadly, 'we may not be so lucky.'

Papa recovered quite quickly. Even after a week, his speech was back to normal. His hand still troubled him, but by the time Max came on leave he was up, and Max was surprised to find so few signs of his recent illness.

'He just looks a bit tired,' he said.

But they all knew that from now on Papa was living on borrowed time.

Anna found it almost impossible to grasp.

'Don't worry,' said Papa, glancing towards the ceiling. 'The old rabbi up there is on my side.'

Anna looked at him across the breakfast table, at the eyes now studying the newspaper, at the hands (one still a little clumsy) manipulating the knife and fork on the chipped plate, and tried to imagine that one day they would not be there. It seemed impossible.

She spent as much time with him as she could, always haunted by the thought that one day he would no longer exist. When she saw his spiky handwriting, so proliferous on his desk, in his room, everywhere they had ever lived, she thought that suddenly, one day, there would be no more of it. She even had the mad idea of asking him to write something, a whole lot, so that it would somehow not matter so much when he stopped.

She tried to paint his portrait. He sat for her patiently in the room above the garage, but it was no use. There was so much that she wanted to put in. Every time she had got anything down she wanted to scrap it and start again.

And all the time the best news of the war was coming in, like a film unrolling irrelevantly in the background.

Paris was liberated, then most of France. Letters arrived from French friends who had, miraculously it seemed to Anna, survived the German occupation. If only Papa didn't have another stroke, if only Max didn't get killed, if only a buzz-bomb didn't fall on one …

One day Papa asked her, 'Why don't you ever go to art school now?'

'Oh,' she said. It all seemed so long ago. 'I fell out with my drawing teacher.'

'And that's all?'

'No.' They were sitting in his room after supper – Mama was playing bridge. 'I don't know,' she said. 'Perhaps he was all I was ever interested in, really. I don't seem to be able to draw any more. I don't even want to.'

'A phase,' he said.

She shook her head.

'Has the term started?'

She smiled at his vagueness. 'About six weeks ago.'

'Then you must go back. You can't give up your work just because you've had a tiff with someone.'

'It wasn't just a tiff!' she cried, but he raised his hand.

'Please,' he said. 'I wish you to go back. Please go tomorrow.'

She found the school much changed. The class had grown, and the whiskery man who had been with John Cotmore at the concert now shared the teaching with him. John and Barbara were openly devoted to each other and it was common knowledge among the students that she had moved into his house, and that it had taken her three days to clean up his kitchen.

'Where have you been?' he asked Anna, and she answered carefully, 'My father has been ill.'

She had drawn almost nothing for weeks, and waited tensely for the class to start. Perhaps at the sight of the model something inside her would revive. The model was fat and sat well back in the chair, with one hand on her knee. It was not a bad pose, but when Anna looked at it there seemed no reason why she should draw it. She felt quite dead. What am I doing here? she thought. How am I going to get through the evening?

In the end, rather than sit there doing nothing, she made some pencil marks that vaguely resembled what was before her, but there was no purpose in them and they bored even herself. When John Cotmore came round to see her she turned her drawing-board round to hide it, but he did not seem to notice.

'I'm glad you're back,' he said. 'I've been wanting to talk to you.'

Her spirits rose violently. He was going to explain. Barbara was really his sister . . . his cousin . . . his aunt . . . !

'How would you like,' said John Cotmore, 'to have a scholarship?'

'A scholarship?' She was confused.

'Yes – full-time art school attendance for three years, no fees and a grant to live on.'

She stared at him.

'How? When?'

'By showing your work to a selection committee, on your teacher's recommendation. With luck, beginning next September.'

She could not think what to say.

'It won't arise until the spring,' he said. 'But the war looks like ending fairly soon and people are beginning to think about the peace. There are only going to be a few of these scholarships available, and I'd like to recommend you for one.'

'But –' She still couldn't take it in. 'I can't draw,' she said.

'What do you mean?' He was becoming irritated with her lack of enthusiasm.

'Just that. I haven't done a decent drawing for months.'

'Oh.' He laughed briefly. 'A bad patch. Happens to everyone.'

'I doubt it.'

'For heaven's sake,' he cried. 'You've thought of nothing but this for years – what's the matter?'

She looked round the room for guidance – at the model, the students bent over their work, Barbara frowning at a piece of charcoal. While she looked at her Barbara glanced up and caught her eye. The frown disappeared and she smiled. Anna smiled back uncertainly. Then Barbara nodded, with a side-long glance at John Cotmore, and did the thumbs-up sign. What did she mean? Did she know what they were talking about? Then, suddenly, it hit her. Of course she and John Cotmore had discussed it. It was all arranged – a consolation prize. Poor little Anna, she'll be so upset, let's at least get her a scholarship.

She turned back to John Cotmore.

'I don't want it,' she said.

'You don't want a scholarship?'

'Oh, leave me alone!' she said. 'I don't know what I want!'

She continued to go to the classes, partly to please Papa, but nothing much came of them. Some of her drawings turned out better than others, but they all had a pedestrian quality which infinitely depressed her.

She dreaded the journey home on the tube, with nothing to think about except the failures of the evening, and carried a book with her wherever she went. As long as she was reading she couldn't think. It didn't seem to matter what she read – Tolstoy, Jack London, Agatha Christie – just as long as it was print. If she had finished a book, or forgotten it, she flew into a panic only to be assuaged by buying a newspaper. She wore her oldest clothes and forgot to wash her hair, because nothing mattered any more and there was no particular reason why she should exist.

And then, on top of everything else, Mama got 'flu. Anna found her red-faced and feverish one day when she came home, with Papa sitting on the edge of her bed. Mama had the huge thermometer from Paris tucked into her armpit, and they were having a ridiculous argument about Papa's work. Papa was saying that his prose was the best thing he had written, but Mama insisted that the poems were better.

'Ach, lyrical poems,' said Papa. 'They're easy.'

'Nonsense!' cried Mama, causing the thermometer to quiver.

Papa shook his head. 'The prose will last longer. After all, I wrote it. I ought to know.'

'But you don't!' Mama half sat up in bed. 'Just because you find the poems so easy, you underrate them. No one else can write poems like you.'

Papa got quite angry.

'I prefer the prose,' he said. 'If ever there's a chance of reprinting I should like it to be the prose rather than the poems. I shan't be here, so you'll have to see to it.'

It was like a door closing.

Mama extracted the thermometer and found that it was 102.

'Oh, for heaven's sake,' she cried. 'Get off my bed, or you'll only catch it too!'

She was quite ill for a week.

It was bitterly cold, and there was a fuel shortage. To keep even a meagre fire in the lounge in the evenings, Frau Gruber and the Woodpigeon had to go each day to a distribution centre and collect some coal in a makeshift handcart. It was as they returned from one of these expeditions that Aunt Louise met them. She had come to commiserate with Mama, now sitting up in her dressing-gown, and she was horrified by the cold in the hotel.

'You've got to get out of here,' she said. 'You'll never get well in this icy place.'

Mama demurred, but Aunt Louise would not be denied, and the following day she arrived in her car to wrap Mama in a large rug and carry her off to the country.

'Anna can look after her father, can't you, dear?' she said.

'There's nothing to do, anyway,' said Anna ungraciously, and she and Papa waved from the freezing lounge as the car drove away.

CHAPTER 23

'It's fearfully cold,' said Papa, the following week. 'Do you really think you should drag all round Golders Green in this weather?'

'I'd better, I think,' said Anna.

Aunt Dainty had rung up two days before to say that Victor, who had been getting steadily worse for months, had finally died. Since Mama was away, Anna had promised to go to the funeral.

'You hardly knew your great-uncle,' said Papa. 'I'm sure Aunt Dainty would understand.'

'No, I'll go,' said Anna.

It was not just that she felt sorry for Aunt Dainty, it was also the hope that – what? Something might happen to make her understand, she thought, to fight down the terrible vision of emptiness whenever she thought of the world without Papa.

'I'll come straight back,' she promised, and saw him installed by his gas fire before she left.

She had put on her warmest clothes but even so, as she came out of the tube at Golders Green, the wind blew right through them. It was as though the weather, knowing that the war was coming to an end, was determined to do its worst while it could.

She had miscalculated the time it would take her to get there, and when she reached the cemetery the service had already begun. She could see it from the gate – a few shabby people standing forlornly in the cold. Aunt Dainty was wearing a large knitted black shawl and looked pale but composed. She saw Anna and nodded, and then Anna stood next to a woman with a feathery hat, wondering what to do.

Uncle Victor's coffin was already in the open grave – was he really in there? she wondered with a kind of horror – and a man with a book in his hand was making a speech over him, but the wind carried the words away and she could not understand them. She watched the mourners' frozen faces and tried not to stamp her frozen feet and thought of nothing. There was a buzzing sound in her ears, her hands were cold and she wondered whether it was disrespectful to keep them in her pockets, and then she realized that the buzzing sound had increased and that it was not only in her ears. The woman in the hat had heard it too, and her eyes met Anna's in embarrassment and alarm.

As the sound grew louder it became impossible not to look up and even the man making the speech glanced away from his book, to see the buzz-bomb puttering across the sky. It seemed to be coming directly towards them and Anna, calculating that there was no shelter she could possibly reach in time, decided to stay where she was. The other mourners must have come to the same conclusion, for nobody moved. Only the inaudible stream of words from the preacher gathered momentum. His mouth movements became faster, his arms gestured above the grave, there seemed to be some kind of quick blessing and at last he stopped.

As he did so, the puttering sound stopped also and the bomb tore down from the sky. For a split second Anna considered sheltering in the grave with the coffin but decided against it, everybody ducked or flung themselves on the ground, and then the bomb exploded – after all, some distance away.

There was a silence as the mourners picked themselves up and stared at each other, and then Aunt Dainty shook her fist at the sky.

'Even at his funeral!' she shouted. 'Even at his funeral they couldn't leave him in peace!'

The reception afterwards in Aunt Dainty's basement almost had an air of celebration. It was warm by the paraffin stoves, and Aunt Dainty served hot chocolate sweetened with real sugar which Otto had sent from America.

'He's in the States now,' she said proudly. 'His work is so important that even President Roosevelt knows about it.'

There were several hand-made rugs on the floor – rug-making was Aunt Dainty's latest enthusiasm – and two women who turned out to be fellow evening-class students were inspecting them with interest. The rest of the mourners seemed to be either lodgers or neighbours and they sat on Aunt Dainty's home-made cushions, sipping chocolate and admiring the furnishings. Aunt Dainty bustled about with cups and seemed quite excited to have so many people to talk to at once. She introduced Anna to one of her lodgers, a little old man with bright eyes who threw up his hands when he heard who she was.

'But I know your father!' he cried. 'I knew him in Berlin! Once we spent the most wonderful evening together.'

'Really?' said Anna.

Next to her Aunt Dainty was telling someone about Otto.

'Even Einstein,' she was saying. 'Otto discusses things with him all the time.'

'An unforgettable evening,' said the old man. 'I met him at a friend's – the poet Meyer in the Trompetenstrasse – do you remember?'

Anna shook her head. 'I was quite small,' she said.

The old man nodded regretfully.

'Your father had read a book I had written – he was quite complimentary about it. I remember it was a beautiful summer evening, and your father – he was supposed to go to a performance at the theatre and then to a party, something quite important, but suddenly, do you know what he said?'

'What?' said Anna.

'He said, "Let's take the steamer to the Pfaueninsel." You must know the Pfaueninsel,' said the old man anxiously. 'An island in a lake near Berlin, with peacocks?'

Anna dimly remembered a school outing. Had that been the Pfaueninsel?

Aunt Dainty was saying, 'And they've given him a house, and a car . . .'

The old man was waiting for her answer, so she nodded. He seemed relieved.

'Also a very good restaurant,' he said with satisfaction. 'So we went there, just your father and I and two others, and we ate, and we drank a very good wine, and we talked, and your father, he was so very amusing and witty. And when we came out we saw the peacocks asleep all together in the branches of a tall tree – your father had not known that they did this, he was very surprised. And then we took the steamer back to Berlin in the moonlight. Wonderful,' said the old man. 'Wonderful!'

Anna smiled. All she remembered of Berlin was the house and the garden and her school.

'It must have been lovely,' she said.

The rug enthusiasts had seen their fill and prepared, reluctantly, to leave.

'Such a lovely party,' said one, momentarily forgetting the occasion, and the other corrected her, 'In the circumstances.'

One of the neighbours said she must get back to her little boy and Anna, too, excused herself. As she put on her coat she thought that there had been, after all, no point in coming. She had felt nothing, learned nothing, received neither comfort nor enlightenment. Aunt Dainty saw her to the door.

'Give my love to your parents,' she said.

It was the first time Anna had been alone with her and she suddenly realized that she had not offered her any condolences.

'I'm so sorry,' she said awkwardly, 'about Uncle Victor.'

Aunt Dainty took her hand.

'Not to be sorry,' she said in her warm, thick voice. 'For me you can be sorry, because I loved him. But for him –' She shook her head above the large shoulders as though to ward something off. 'For him, better it should have happened years ago.'

Then she kissed her and Anna went out into the icy street.

Aunt Dainty was right, she thought as she hunched her shoulders against the wind. It would have been better for Uncle Victor if he had died before. There had been no point in those last years in England. She trudged along the frozen pavement and it struck her that this thought was even more depressing than the fact of his death. To have to go on living when you no longer wanted to, when it no longer made sense . . .

Like me, she thought, momentarily overwhelmed by self-pity, and was shocked by her own lack of courage. Rubbish, she thought, not like me at all. But like Papa? In her mind she saw him in his poky room with his typewriter that kept going wrong and his writings that no one wanted to publish, in a country whose language he did not speak. How did it feel to be Papa?

A few specks of snow were beginning to fall, dotting the walls, the bushes and the pavement with white.

Did Papa's life still make sense to him? When he remembered Berlin, did this shabby, frustrated existence among strangers still have any point? Or would he have preferred it if it had never happened? Would death, perhaps, come as a relief? She tried to find some comfort in the thought, but only felt worse. There's nothing, she thought, as the snow blew and whirled about her. Nothing . . .

She had to wait a long time for a train and by the time she got home she felt chilled to the bone. She went straight up to see Papa, but there was no reply to her knock and she found that he had nodded off in his chair. The gas fire was spluttering – it needed another shilling in the meter – and some of Papa's papers had fallen off the table. The room was cold and gloomy.

She stared at it dispassionately in the fading light. Why should anyone want to live here? Especially someone like Papa who had travelled and been acclaimed and whose life, until Hitler disrupted it, had been a series of choices between different kinds of fulfilment?

She must have moved inadvertently, for Papa woke up.

'Anna!' he said, and then, 'How was it?'

'Awful,' said Anna. 'A buzz-bomb nearly fell on us and Aunt Dainty shouted at it.'

'You look frozen,' said Papa. He took a shilling from a tin box marked 'shillings' and after a moment the gas flared yellow and the part of the room closest to it became a little warmer. 'Would you like something to eat?'

She shook her head.

'Then come and get thawed.'

He gave her a folded rug to sit on – there was only one chair – and she crouched at his feet by the fire. In spite of the shilling, it did not seem to give out much heat.

'I had a letter from Mama,' said Papa. 'She's quite recovered from her 'flu and she says she'll be home by the weekend.' He looked at her anxiously. 'I hope you're not catching it now.'

'No,' said Anna, though it was strange how the cold in her bones persisted.

She stared up at his face. What was he thinking? How could one ever tell how people really felt?

'Papa,' she said, 'do you ever regret – ?'

'What?' he asked.

She gestured vaguely at the room. 'These last years. Here and at the Hotel Continental. I mean – after the way you used to live in Berlin?'

He looked at her attentively. 'If you mean, would I rather have gone on living as before, well of course I would. There were so many more opportunities – so much to choose from. Also,' he added simply, 'I would have preferred to be more help to Mama, and to you and Max.'

But that was not what she wanted to know.

'What I meant,' she said, 'is – did you ever feel . . . I mean, you must sometimes have wondered – if there was really any point . . . ?'

'In these last years?'

She nodded. Her head was throbbing and she had the strangest conviction that if Papa could reassure her she would get warm.

'Well, of course there was.' Papa had got up from his chair and was looking at her in surprise.

'But it must have been so awful!' said Anna. 'With losing your language, and never having any money, and Mama always so wretched, and all your work . . . all your work . . . !' She found to her horror that she was crying. A fat lot of good I am to him, she thought, and Papa bent down and touched her face.

'Your head is very hot,' he said. 'I'm sure you're not well.'

'But I want to know!' she cried.

He searched among his things and produced the thermometer from a box marked 'thermometer'.

'In a moment,' he said.

When she had tucked it under her arm he sat down again in the chair.

'The chief point about these last, admittedly wretched years,' he said, 'is that it is infinitely better to be alive than dead. Another is that if I had not lived through them I would never have known what it felt like.'

'What it felt like?'

He nodded. 'To be poor, even desperate, in a cold, foggy country where the natives, though friendly, gargle some kind of Anglo-Saxon dialect . . .'

She laughed uncertainly.

'I'm a writer,' he said. 'A writer has to know. Haven't you found that?'

'I'm not a writer,' said Anna.

'You may be one day. But even an aspiring painter –' He hesitated, only for a moment. 'There is a piece of me,' he said carefully, 'quite separate from the rest, like a little man sitting in my forehead. And whatever happens, he just watches. Even if it's something terrible. He notices how I feel, what I say, whether I want to shout, whether my hands are trembling – and he says, how interesting! How interesting to know that this is what it feels like.'

'Yes,' said Anna. She knew that she, too, had a little man like Papa's, but her head was spinning and she imagined him, confusedly, turning round and round.

'It's a great safeguard against despair,' said Papa. He plucked the thermometer from under her arm and looked at it. 'You've got 'flu,' he said. 'Go to bed.'

She went along the freezing passage to her room and got between the cold sheets, but after a moment Papa appeared, awkwardly carrying a stone hot-water bottle.

'Is this all right?' he said, and she hugged it gratefully.

He lit the gas and drew the blackout curtains, and then he stood uncertainly at the foot of her bed.

'Are you sure you wouldn't like something to eat?' he said. 'I've got some bread and fish-paste.'

'No!' she said.

He insisted, slightly hurt, 'You've got to keep your strength up,' and the thought of keeping her strength up with fish-paste when the room was whirling round and her head was splitting seemed so funny that she laughed.

'Oh, Papa!' she cried.

'What?' he said, sitting on the edge of the bed.

'I love you very much.'

'And I you.' He took her hand and said, 'The last years haven't been all unhappy, you know. You and Max have given us great joy. And I've always had Mama.' There was a pause and then he said, 'I have written about these years. A sort of diary. When you read it I hope you'll think, as I do, that it's the best thing I've done. And one day, perhaps, my works will be reprinted and this will be among them.'

'In Germany?'

He nodded. 'Mama will see to it.'

He stroked her hot face.

'So you see, as long as I can think and write I am grateful to the old rabbi up there for every day that he keeps me on this extraordinary planet.'

She felt better, but there was still something wrong. It was hiding from her, but it was there – a kind of horror, she imagined it crouching at the foot of the bed. It was to do with Uncle Victor and it was terribly important.

'Papa?' she said.

'What?'

She couldn't think. Think and write – he had said think and write. But Uncle Victor hadn't been able to think and write. He had just lain there – brain damage, Aunt Dainty had said, doesn't remember, better he should have died years ago. But didn't a stroke have the same effect – wouldn't Papa . . . ?

'Papa!' cried Anna, clutching his hand, 'But if you couldn't think . . . ?'

His face was blurred as she tried to focus on it, but his voice was clear and calm.

'Then of course I should not want to go on living. Mama and I have talked about it.'

'But how?' she cried. 'How – how could you . . . ?'

She made a great effort and his face suddenly reassembled, so that she could see his eyes and the extraordinary, confident smile with which he spoke.

'Mama,' he said, 'will think of something.'

CHAPTER 24

The cold spell had ended by the time Mama came back from the country. Anna recovered from her 'flu in thin sunshine and the world suddenly looked more hopeful. The Professor announced that Papa's health had improved. His blood pressure was lower, and the effects of the stroke had almost disappeared.

'I told you,' said Papa. 'The old rabbi up there is on my side.'

Gradually the war began to run down.

There were still buzz-bombs, so you could still get killed, but they were fewer. The news on the radio was always good, and for the first time since 1939 small glimmers of light were allowed in the streets at night. One day Max appeared to announce that his squadron was being disbanded.

'No more flying,' he said quite regretfully, to Mama's rage. 'I suppose it really will all be over quite soon.'

As the armies advanced, pictures appeared in the papers and on newsreels of devastated German cities. Hamburg, Essen, Cologne – they were not places Anna had ever seen, and they meant nothing to her. Only once, when she heard on the news that the Grunewald had been set on fire, something stirred inside her.

The Grunewald was a wood near their old home. Long ago, when she and Max were small in the past which she never thought about, they had tobogganed there in the winter. Their sledges had made tracks in the snow and it had smelled of cold air and pine needles. In the summer they had played in the patchy light under the trees, their feet had sunk deep into the sand at the edge of the lake – and hadn't there once been a picnic . . . ? She couldn't remember.

But that was all before.

The Grunewald that was burned was not the one she had played in. It was a place where Jewish children were not allowed, where Nazis clicked heels and saluted and probably hid behind trees, ready to club people down. They had guns and fierce dogs and swastikas and if anyone got in their way they beat them up and set the dogs on them and sent them to concentration camps where they'd be starved and tortured and killed . . .

But that's nothing to do with me now, thought Anna. I belong here, in England.

When Max said to her, later, 'Did you hear about the fire in the Grunewald?' she nodded and said, dead-pan, 'It's just as well we left.'

As the spring grew warmer, she started to draw again. It began one day in her lunch-hour. She was walking aimlessly through some little streets at the back of Vauxhall Bridge Road when she saw a child. He was the fourth she had seen since she had come out and she thought, the war really must be ending if the children are coming back! This one was about ten and was sitting on a heap of rubble, staring up at the sky with a pleased expression. I suppose he's glad to be home, thought Anna.

There was something about him – the way he was clasping his skinny knees, the way his over-large sweater hung loosely on his shoulders, the way he squinnied up at the light – that was very expressive. Suddenly she had a great desire to draw him. She did not have a sketch-book with her, but found an old letter in her handbag. Feverishly, she started to draw on the back. She was so anxious to get the boy down on paper before he moved or stood up and walked away that she didn't have time to worry about how best to do it. She just thought, that goes like that and that goes like that, and there's light on his face and on his knees and a dark patch of shade under his chin . . . and suddenly there was the drawing, she'd done it and it looked just right!

She walked back to the office in a daze. It's come back, she thought. I can do it again! That evening at art school she made two good drawings and when she rode home on the tube, for the first time in months she chose not to read, but drew an old man asleep in his seat. That came out well, too.

Suddenly she couldn't stop. She bought a new sketch-book and filled it in a few days. At weekends, in her room above the garage, she worked on a painting of shelterers. This time she planned it more carefully and it had at least something of the feeling she had wanted to put into it. She also painted a portrait of Mama. Mama posed for it, crouched over Anna's paraffin stove and looking, as always, both crushed and ebullient at once, and Papa said it was one of the best things Anna had done.

Finally she gathered all her work together in a portfolio and put it down in front of John Cotmore.

'You were talking about a scholarship,' she said.

He looked pleased. 'I hoped you'd do that,' he said.

Anna glanced at the whiskery man, not far away. 'Do you think he'd like to see my work as well?' She did not want the scholarship on John Cotmore's recommendation alone.

'All right,' he said after a moment.

The whiskery man came over and he and John Cotmore looked through the portfolio together. John Cotmore said 'Good' and 'I like that' several times, but the whiskery man said nothing.

Damn, thought Anna, suddenly wanting nothing in the world so much as three years at art school, why couldn't I have left well alone?

John Cotmore had finished.

'Well,' he said, 'what do you think?'

The whiskery man ignored him. There were still two drawings which he hadn't seen and he looked at each one in turn, slowly and methodically. He was north-country and did not like to be hurried. At last he turned to Anna and she saw to her dismay that he looked quite annoyed.

'Don't act so daft, girl,' he said. 'You must know you've got enough here to get you anything you want.'

After he had moved away, John Cotmore smiled at her.

'Well,' he said, 'that's that. Now the world lies before you.'

She smiled back, carefully.

'You'll get your scholarship,' he said, 'and there'll be peace and all the young men will be coming home.'

She shrugged her shoulders. 'Oh,' she said, 'the young men . . .'

'Who will be much better for you than I ever was. Except for your drawing.'

She was packing her work back into the portfolio and one of the drawings caught her eye. It *was* good.

Suddenly, on an impulse, she said, 'Thank you for teaching me to draw.'

She could feel how pleased he was. The air all round them was filled with his pleasure.

'You always were my favourite student,' he said and, almost absent-mindedly, he let his hand rest on her shoulder. She was conscious of a sudden warmth, a curious fluttering sensation (extraordinary! noted the little man in her forehead) and then Barbara was upon them. Her placid mouth was set in a firm line and she was carrying his briefcase and his duffel coat.

'Come on, John,' she said. 'We're having the rabbit.'

He withdrew his hand quickly.

'It's been stewing for hours,' she said. 'And then you've got to look out those drawings for your exhibition.'

He sighed and stood up.

'There, you see, Anna,' he said, 'all the world lies before you, while middle-aged people like us have to go home and eat rabbit.'

'Speak for yourself,' said Barbara. She peered at the drawings which Anna was putting away. 'Are you going to try for that scholarship?'

Anna nodded.

'I should think so, too,' said Barbara.

In April the British and American armies overran the first concentration camps, and the first horrifying descriptions appeared in the press and on the radio. Anna was astonished at the reaction. Why was everyone so surprised? She had known about concentration camps since she was nine years old. At least now the English will understand what it was like, she thought.

She watched the newsreels, repelled but not shocked. The gas-chambers, the piles of dead bodies, the pitiful, skeleton-like survivors – it was all terrible, she thought, terrible. But no more terrible than what she had tried for years not to imagine. As the appalling stories poured out, as the indignation burst forth all round her, she could think of only one thing – that at last it was over. At long, long last it had stopped.

Berlin fell at the beginning of May. Had there been fighting round their house, in their garden? She pushed the thought aside. It didn't matter. It's finished, she thought.

I need never think about it again.

For a few days there were rumours and unconfirmed reports. Hitler was dead, he had been captured, he was holding out, he had surrendered – and then at last an official statement. The war in Europe was over.

On the day set aside for official rejoicing, Anna, Mama and Papa went to have lunch with the Rosenbergs. The flat in Harley Street was back in use, and Aunt Louise was already worrying about the peace.

'Whatever you do,' she said to Mama, 'don't tell Fraulein Pimke that the war is over!'

'Why not?' said Mama, surprised.

'Because she'll use up all the rations and we'll have nothing left to eat. She thinks that food will automatically become plentiful the moment the war stops.'

'But surely –' began Mama.

Aunt Louise waved her down.

'After all, it doesn't really matter to her,' she said. 'And she's old and quite deaf and she doesn't speak a word of English, so she wouldn't hear from anyone else. In fact, if we're careful –' Aunt Louise suddenly became quite happy – 'there's really no reason at all why she should ever find out about the peace!'

Max arrived in time for lunch, and the Professor proposed a toast.

'To us!' he said. 'Who would have thought, five years ago, that we would outlive Adolf Hitler?'

'And to the English,' said Papa. 'They won the war.'

Aunt Louise made everyone stand up to drink to the English and worried whether she wasn't supposed to fling her glass on to the floor afterwards ('Only we have so few left,' she said) until Max reassured her.

'A wonderful wine,' said Papa.

The Professor showed him the bottle.

'Johannisberger-Schloss,' he said, 'from the Rheingau. I've kept it specially for this.'

They looked at each other.

'Perhaps one day . . .'

'Perhaps,' said Papa.

Fraulein Pimke, though unaware of what was being celebrated, had cooked a delicious meal.

'Well, and what now?' asked Aunt Louise afterwards.

'Will you be going back to Cambridge, Max?'

'When I'm demobilized,' said Max. 'I hope by next term.'

'And then you'll become a lawyer,' said the Professor. 'Perhaps you'll become such a judge, with a wig like a poodle and a long coat with fur on. You could never have done that if it hadn't been for Hitler.'

Max grinned. 'I have a lot to thank him for.'

'Anna has won a scholarship at her art school,' said Papa, and she was warmed by the pride in his voice. 'She too will be starting next term.'

'Really?' said the Professor.

Anna looked at him. He was sitting with his back to the window, his arms folded across his chest. The colours of his face, his clothes and the chair he sat in glowed dark and rich in the shadows of the room. They made a curious, complicated shape against the rectangle of light behind him. I'd like to paint that, she thought as the conversation flowed round her, and began to work out how she would do it.

'. . . isn't that true?' asked Max.

'What?' she said, startled, and he laughed.

'I was explaining,' he said, 'that you're the only one of us to whom the emigration has made no difference. I mean, if Hitler had never happened you wouldn't have learned three languages and you might have avoided a certain amount of worry, but you'd have ended up exactly the same as you are now, wandering about with a vague expression on your face and looking for things to draw. It really wouldn't matter whether you were in Germany or in France or in England.'

'I suppose not,' said Anna.

She thought of her scholarship, and John Cotmore, and Mrs Hammond with her old ladies, and a policeman who had once lent her a shilling, and firewatching in Putney, and Trafalgar Square in the dusk, and the view of the river from the 93 bus.

'But I like it here,' she said.

A little later, Max got up to go.

'Walk to the tube with me, Anna,' he said.

Papa stood up too and embraced him.

'Goodbye, my son,' he said. 'May you be as successful in peace as you have been in war.'

'And ring up as soon as you hear anything,' said Mama. 'About Cambridge and being demobilized. And don't forget to tell them about your scholarship.'

Anna and Max rode down in the lift in silence. The commissionaire opened the door for them, and they could hear singing in the street outside. He glanced at Max's uniform.

'Quite a day,' he said. 'Young Englishmen like yourself have a right to be proud of themselves.'

They grinned at each other.

The street was full of Union Jacks. A few girls in paper hats were dancing to the music of an accordion, and a soldier was sitting on the pavement with a bottle by his side. They picked their way among them.

'Well,' said Max, as so many times before, 'and how is everything?'

'All right,' said Anna. 'Papa seems quite well, doesn't he, and they're both very pleased about my scholarship. But Mama is going to lose her job again.'

'Why?' asked Max.

'It seems her boss has promised it to his niece when she comes out of the Women's Land Army. Mama doesn't mind too much at the moment – she says it was just a stop-gap and she'd rather work for English people, anyway. But I don't know – once everyone comes out of the Forces it'll be even more difficult for her to find a job than before.'

Max nodded. 'It doesn't sound as though the peace would be much help to them.'

They reached Oxford Circus, but Max showed no sign of catching the tube and they walked on down Regent Street.

'Perhaps one day,' said Anna, 'Papa's work will be published again in Germany.'

'It will be a long time,' said Max.

'And I suppose now the war is over we'll all be naturalized.'

They both smiled at the thought of Papa as an Englishman.

'Mama can't wait,' said Anna. 'She's going to drink tea

with milk and love animals and go to cricket matches. There's no end to the things she's going to do.'

Max laughed. 'But it won't make any difference,' he said. 'Won't it?'

He shook his head.

'You and I will be all right, but they'll never belong. Not here.' He made a face. 'Not anywhere, I suppose.'

The crowd had thickened and they stopped for a moment to let a man with a child on his shoulder pass them. Someone saluted Max and he had to salute back.

'You remember,' he said, 'what you used to say in Paris? That as long as you were with Mama and Papa you wouldn't feel like a refugee?'

She nodded.

'Well, now I suppose it's the other way round.'

'How, the other way round?'

Max sighed. 'Nowadays,' he said, 'I think that the only times *they* don't feel like refugees is when they're with us.'

Anna stared at the scene around her – the flags, the noise, the relaxed contented faces – and thought of Mama and Papa travelling back to Putney on the tube.

'We'll just have to do the best we can,' she said.

At Piccadilly Circus Max left her, and she walked into the crowd. The square was swarming with people, they were all around her, old men, people in uniform, couples holding hands, women and children. Some danced or sang, some were drinking, but most of them, like herself, were just walking about. No processions, she thought. No waving of banners. A sailor had climbed to the top of a lamp-post. A small boy shouted, 'Wheeee . . .' and then made a crunching noise like an explosion. 'No,' said the woman with him. 'No more bombs.'

As she reached the centre of the square, the sun came out and everything suddenly leapt into colour. Water flashed in the fountain. An airman, his uniform changed from grey to blue, splashed some on a laughing girl in a pink dress. A bottle blazed momentarily, passed from hand to hand. Two women singing 'Roll Out The Barrel' in printed blouses seemed to burst into flower. Pigeons wheeled. The sky shone.

At the foot of the fountain a soldier leaned, fast asleep. He was half-sitting, half-lying, his head supported by the stone. The sun lit up the top of his face, one hand clutched a kit-bag, the other trailed, open, on the pavement. The legs sprawled exhausted. There was something triumphant about the way he slept. If only he doesn't wake up, thought Anna.

She got out her sketch-book and began to draw.

When Hitler Stole Pink Rabbit

Judith Kerr

Anna was only nine in 1933, too busy with her school work and her friends to take much notice of the posters of Adolf Hitler and the menacing swastikas plastered over Berlin. Being Jewish, she thought, was just something you were because your parents and grandparents were Jewish.

Suddenly, Anna's father was unaccountably missing. Shortly after, she and her brother were hurried out of Germany by their mother with alarming secrecy. Then began their rootless, wandering existence as refugees. Their life was often difficult and sad, but Anna soon discovered that all that really mattered was that the family was together.

An outstanding book for readers of ten upwards.

Private, Keep Out!
GWEN GRANT

I have written a book. It's all about the street we live on – me and our Mam and Dad, and our Pete and Tone, and Lucy, Rose and Joe. They're my brothers and sisters. worst luck.

I don't see why I should be nice to that stuck-up dancing teacher Miss Brown just because Pete's going to marry her, and how *can* you tell if angels are really men or women?

Growing up in a north-east Midlands colliery town just after the War, the narrator, youngest in a family of six, is never out of trouble. She is high-spirited, impulsive, stubborn and often exasperated by her parents and older brothers and sisters, but she will win the heart of every reader in her determined efforts to keep her end up.

Harriet the Spy

Louise Fitzhugh

Harriet the Spy has a secret notebook, which she fills with utterly honest jottings about her parents, her friends and her neighbours. This, she feels sure, will prepare her for her career as a famous writer. Every day on her spy route, she scrutinizes, observes and notes down anything of interest to her:

> Laura Peters is thinner and uglier. I think she could do with some braces on her teeth.

> Once I thought I wanted to be Franca. But she's so dull, if I was her I couldn't stand myself, I guess it's not money that makes people dull. I better find out because I might be it.

> If Marion Hawthorne doesn't watch out she's going to grow up into a lady Hitler.

But Harriet commits the unforgivable for a spy – she is unmasked. When her notebook is found by her school friends, their anger and retaliation and Harriet's unexpected responses explode in an hilarious and often touching way.

'Harriet M. Welsch is one of the meatiest heroines in modern juvenile literature. This novel is a *tour de force*.'

Library Journal

'MAROON BOY
Robert Leeson

When Matthew Morten went to sea in 1568, he was a Bible-reading merchant's apprentice and the youngest hand aboard *The Golden Way*. He returned four years later with a reputation that included mutiny, raiding, and the nickname "'Maroon Boy".

'Maroon is short for Cimaroon, a name given to escaped slaves who fought the Spanish in Panama and the English in Jamaica. It is known that Drake joined forces with the Cimaroons at one time, to harass the Spaniards: but where he was seeking gold, the Cimaroons wanted revenge on the white man.

Matthew Morten's motivations were even more complicated – though he didn't realise consciously what they were. Why he did what he did adds a fascinating moral dimension to this tale of swashbuckling adventure.